Our Southern Breeze

Jim and Terry what a blessing you have been in my life. Thank you for believing in me and time. I am praying for Andrea and friends. May God's Southern bless over and more.

God bless,
Daphene

Our *Southern* Breeze

*"We once were lost . . . but
now we're found . . ."*

Daphene Jones
With Andrea Taylor, Ph.D.

3rd CHAPTER PRESS
3411 Preston Rd., Ste. C13-182
Frisco, TX 75034

ISBN-13: 978-0-9830129-6-2
ISBN-10: 0983012962

Library of Congress Control Number: 2011940827

Printed in the United States of America

Cover Designer & Typesetter: Michelle Kenny, Fort Collins, CO

Consulting Editor: Tim Boswell, Lewisville, TX

3rd CHAPTER PRESS
3411 Preston Rd., Ste. C13-182
Frisco, TX 75034

Dedication

To my husband, John Angelo, who stands firmly beside me in all things, even patiently listening to me read the manuscript aloud to him. Amazing man, my husband.

For my children, Denise and John Kevin, who showed me such extraordinary forgiveness.

In memory of my sisters, Deborah Hall and Gretchen Molmen.

Table of Contents

Foreword

by Ron Hall, *New York Times* bestselling author of
Same Kind of Different As Me,
as a letter to his late wife, Deborah Hall

Dear Debbie,

Daphene asked me recently how you would feel about something she is very excited about. After days of contemplation, I woke up this morning and decided to write you a letter, hoping for an answer to her question. She's persistent like you. I would expect that of your twin. She always desired your approval. She still does.

Shortly before you departed this earth, Denver (the man in your dream) said he believed you were an angel. I looked up a definition, which said angels deliver messages from God and carry out His desires on earth. I believe Denver was right, so Daphene and I need to hear from you. How is it that it took God using the poorest and most dangerous homeless man in our city to inform me I was married to an angel? Forgive me for not recognizing that sooner. I still marvel at how God used Denver as His messenger during our most desperate times. Do you remember him ever being wrong? I don't, though he was far from perfect.

It seems so silly to ask you if angels read. And I'm smiling as I write this with the same childlike faith I had when I would write to Santa expecting toys. Someone said angels just know because God tells them. If that's the case, you won't need to read this letter; but Daphene keeps asking what you would think.

Today is October 25, 2011, our forty-second wedding anniversary. Did you remember? Does an angel ever forget? What a dumb question. Of course you remembered. You always had the memory of an elephant, though you know I've never spent time with elephants; I take that reference to mean a long and perfect memory.

I'd be shocked if by now your Father in heaven hasn't told you about the popularity of *Same Kind of Different As Me*. It was Denver's idea to write it. He said, "Nobody will ever believe this story about you and me and Miss Debbie." So, it's your story that millions have read . . . hold on . . . what did you say? Yes, of course, Debbie, please forgive me; I meant to say God's story!

Sometimes I joke about your fifteen minutes of fame that Andy Warhol said everyone would have. Of course, you remember Andy. He is the one who painted that yellow and green self-portrait that hung in our Greenway Road "Beaver Cleaver" house in 1976. You hated it, and as a highfalutin art dealer, I hate to admit that I did too. Remember, I gave it to Julio, and you won't believe it, but I saw it in Basel, Switzerland last year for sale at $6 million. Since you never cared about money, that news probably doesn't hurt you like it did me. Please excuse this trivial chatter, but you know I chased after money while you chased God.

Unlike me, you never sought to draw attention to yourself—just to Jesus (proof of your angelic nature). In your heart you wanted your face to disappear so that "God's People" could see the face of Christ. Daphene and I talk a lot (are your ears burning?), and we both agree you were content to let us shine and, like the words of a song say, to be "the wind beneath our wings." But don't laugh since, unlike your wings that were earned, if you ever saw wings flapping on our backs they would have been purchased at a costume shop.

Do you remember one of our first dates in 1965, when you invited me to dinner at the Old Swiss House to meet Daphene? As we were driving there, you told me she was the "pretty" twin and always full of surprises. Then over the next thirty years we watched from the sidelines while she surprised us with amazing successes, and even a little tap dancing. And how can I forget all the mornings I saw you on your knees, praying her through her more painful surprises? Well, Honey, in case you haven't heard, Daphene is up to big surprises again. Are you sitting down? (Excuse me for not knowing, but do angels ever sit down?) Debbie, this is no joke. Remember "Daffney Snort from Sider," yes, the very one you let copy your homework and tests, the one you wrote term papers for? Now, here is the shocker: this same Daphene wrote a book—a really good one—about you. Well, not really just about you; about the two of you, the twins, and how God restored the "Ya-Ya" sisterhood bond that the devil tried to steal away.

That's what she keeps calling and calling me about, wanting to know what I think you would think about the book. Don't tell her, but sometimes I screen her calls. Like I said in the beginning, she has desperately wanted your approval her whole life. Nothing has changed.

Her heart is pure in wanting to honor God by telling your story—her story—okay, okay, yes, I mean God's story about your lives. Oh, there you go with that memory. You remember I'm a better talker than listener. Thanks for the gentle reminder.

Anyway, Daphene is worried that you might be upset about her spilling the beans on her twin. Is it crazy to think angels get bothered by anything?

Really, it's not our fault (well, maybe it *is*) that people hunger for more Debbie stories and now Daphene stories. *Same Kind of Different As Me* whetted appetites. *What Difference Do It Make* caused an itch that hopefully *Our Southern Breeze* will scratch.

You wanted people to know Jesus. *Our Southern Breeze* is about Jesus. All the things you believed (sometimes I doubted and you knew it) are real. The prophecies and words you were sure came from God became reality. *Our Southern Breeze* confirms them all.

Need I remind you that Daphene and I caused you to spend lots of time on bended knees? (Did I hear you chuckle?) No wonder your heart went AWOL and took resident alien status in an iceberg somewhere near the North Pole. *Our Southern Breeze* is a celebration of the melting of that iceberg, which was prophesied in Anaheim. Our lives are now afloat in the summer waters warmed by the breeze of your forgiveness and love.

Please indulge Daphene in telling these stories that hopefully will bless and heal others frozen in their own icebergs. We promise to give God all the glory.

After the southern breeze came, do you remember telling Daphene that God gave you a vision of her standing in front of thousands telling her story? Well, get ready; God was telling the truth (no, duh!). She has been invited to speak to thousands and, per your final instruction to her, she promised not to make a fool of herself. And, of course, she will tell funny stories. They are all in her book.

Now, changing the subject–this is not in her book–but I'm sure you already know that I recently got married, like you encouraged me to do in those final days we had together eleven years ago. Her name is Beth and she is from Charleston, South Carolina. She is quite different from you; like you, though, she is a woman with a daily allotment of words larger than most. Since you left, I got out of the habit of listening, so now I am having to really work on those old skills you taught me. It doesn't help that I'm getting hard of hearing. Daphene and Denver approved of her and she of them.

Oh, and BTW, Denver says to tell Miss Debbie "howdy," and that you are still the bossiest white lady he ever met! LOL!

OMG, I'll bet you don't recognize all these three-letter, all-cap abbreviations. It's something new called texting. King Solomon said there is nothing new under the sun, but he said that two thousand years ago, and texting is new here on earth. As smart as you are, I'll bet you've already figured it out.

FYI, according to your final words to me, I did not give up on Denver (no catch and release) and the good news is that he did not give up on me, either. He has taught me volumes about life, and he lived with me for eight and a half years. Now he has his own place, a smoking suite in a hotel near Beth and me.

He and I have carried your torch for "God's People" all across America and helped raise more than $70 million. What's that you said? Sounds like bragging? Sorry. I didn't mean us; I meant God, through us, raised the money. You angels don't like bragging, but since I'll never be one, please cut me a little slack.

When we were in Georgia raising money to build a new shelter for those you called "God's People," an elderly woman told me she heard I was famous. I told her I didn't think so, but she pointed her skinny little finger at me the way you used to when making a point and said, "Listen, Mister, I saw you on CNN," (I know you wish it had been Fox, LOL) "and I want to remind you that, apart from your friendship with Denver Moore, you would be a big fat nobody!" (Gulp. I've gained twenty pounds.)

"What about Debbie?" I asked her. "She's the one with the dream."

"Well, young man–" (That was the nicest thing she said and that gives you a clue as to how old she is, since she called me young and I now draw social security. Otherwise, I look pretty much the same–a little more gray–but I haven't gotten any tattoos like you know who!) "–thank God for her faithfulness. But, Denver rewrote your life story!"

Debbie, have you seen the new chapel at the Union Gospel Mission? I hope you can see it from heaven. I'm not sure how that works. It would be cool if God lets you see the cool stuff and skip the bad. It's named after you! I know, I know. You told me not to name anything after you, and I didn't; but your friends did!

Thanksgiving is just around the corner and, as always, we will celebrate at Rocky Top. I know it was your favorite holiday, and you continue to inspire Regan, Carson, and me to open it up to the multitudes. This year, thirty-two!

Speaking of Regan and Carson, you would be so proud of them as adults. They married well. Carson, of course, married Megan, and Regan married Matt. Foolishly, I tell you all this like you don't know. We are confident that from your perch in the heavens you prayed it all into existence. I remember fondly those last ten years we had together, kneeling beside our bed and praying for our kids' spouses long before they married. How your voice would sharpen as you petitioned God to protect our grandchildren, years before they were born.

Praise God for four little answered prayers: Griffin, almost 6 now; Sadie Jane is 4½; Kendall Deborah (your namesake) is almost 4; and the newest answer to prayer, Whitney, born August 2. They call me "Rocky Pop," and you, "Debbie" (since you never liked grandmother names). Like you, they love Rocky Top; they put wildflowers on your grave and speak about you as if you are still here. Why not? Of course, you are still here in our hearts. They love to feed Rocky, your old palomino, apple wedges just like you did, and he nickers with delight as they rub his velvet nose the way you used to. I've hung your saddle in the tack room in the big barn, waiting for your granddaughters to grow into it.

Eleven years ago today, I lay in bed beside you and penned these words as a line in the poem I wrote on our last anniversary on earth:

> "The years pass so quickly,
> it seems like just a few
> since you walked by me in the student center
> wearing your angel flight blue."

What do angels wear? I'll bet you're as beautiful as ever and the uniform still fits.

Enough of the rambling reminiscence—I sometimes get lost in the memories. But, back to the purpose of this letter. We are giving a launching party for Daphene and *Our Southern Breeze* in January. Do you see the humor in that? I hope God does. As always, we would cherish your prayers for a warm southern breeze that day. It is Texas. Remember those January ice storms? We have faith. Save the date—we expect to see you there.

A big "howdy" from earth to Jesus . . . and to Abraham, Isaac, and the rest of the gang.

Love,
Ronnie

Meet the Author

You are about to meet an amazing woman. She is the reason that I have Jesus in my heart today and a foundation for the rest of my life. She has been my friend and inspiration for over thirty-five years. More importantly, she has an amazing story to share that will speak to your heart–perhaps in ways that you don't expect.

It has been said that if God ever leads you to the proverbial edge of the cliff and you feel like He is speaking to you, listen to Him and obey His voice. My dear friend, Daphene, did just that. The Lord led her to the a precipice and she jumped off–totally and completely–and a *southern breeze* caught her and has brought her to today. If God leads you to the edge of the cliff, He will either catch you or teach you to fly.

It is with great pride and tremendous honor that I introduce to you, dear reader, my dear friend, author, and soar-er in life, Daphene Jones. I think you will love her story.

Sue Langston

Preface

The Lord stands beside me like a great warrior.

(Jeremiah 20:11 NLT)

When *Same Kind of Different As Me,* written by Ron Hall and Denver Moore, became a *New York Times* bestseller followed by the sale of big-screen film rights, I received numerous requests from readers who wanted to know more about my life as the twin sister of Deborah Hall. The story told in Ron's book was about my sister's love for Christ that led her and Ron to minister to the homeless and dispossessed in Fort Worth, Texas at the Union Gospel Mission, where they met an illiterate black man named Denver Moore. If you have read their story, you know how powerful and miraculous it is. If you haven't, I think you will want to.

But there is so much more to be told. Deborah's life, and even her death, touched so many people, especially me. As her fraternal twin, I knew her like no one else could. And, even though we each had our own personality, interests, and friends, and we didn't look that much alike, our voices and mannerisms were so identical that if you weren't looking right at us, you could not tell who was speaking. We were very close when we were little and didn't really reestablish that special bond that deeply connects twins until . . . well, that is part of the story I am about to share.

Because of the enormity of the physical and mental abuse we were subjected to in our family and the overwhelming influence this had on my self-identity, I ended up believing that I was worthless. This unhealthy view ultimately led me down the path of one destructive relationship after another. And, because I had spent a good part of my life living out the lie that I was "too dumb to be anything but a failure," I never thought of myself as someone who could actually write a book that anyone would be interested in reading.

But I started journaling in 1990 because I felt the hand of God upon me, and I didn't want to forget how He was restoring the life I had lost. Writing down my thoughts and feelings comforted me like a long hot shower on a cold winter night. Later, as I went back through my journals, I realized that I had been writing this book all along.

I hope that as you read our story—the Deborah-Daphene restoration—you will realize that you need to tell someone you love him or her before it's too late; that you need to forgive yourself and others for past mistakes; that no matter how awful your life is, there is hope; that you are never too old to find true love; and that God is always with you—through the valley and on the mountaintop.

The history of mankind is divided into two parts: the "before"—B.C.—and the "after"—A.D. People living at that time of division were more than likely unaware that they were actually living the events that marked the turning point of world history, but they were.

The same is true for me. I had no idea that my turning point had begun that mid-January morning in 1990. As I looked back over the years, though, I found myself referencing events of my life by my personal turning point: they were either "before Anaheim" or "after Anaheim."

My twin sister, Deborah, raised the banner of love (Jehovah Nissi) over me when my life was a mess, and she said things to God that I didn't yet know to say for myself. She showed me God's love and seemed to me to be Jesus with skin. At the Anaheim conference, when God promised to send a southern breeze over Deborah and me, little did I realize just how many people would also be touched by that gentle wind.

Part One of my story tells about my life *before* that fateful weekend that I shared with my estranged twin sister. Part Two of my story shares how everything changed *after* that weekend, as the southern breeze gently blew on the two of us, across our families, and beyond.

As I share my heart through this story, I pray that God will heal the deep hurts that many are carrying. What I kept hearing as I worked on this book is that *God is a God of Second Chances.*

Daphene (Short) Jones

PART ONE
The Lost Life

*For the Son of Man came to seek
and to save the lost.*

(Luke 19:10)

Chapter 1

Early Years

Fathers, do not embitter your children,
or they will become discouraged.

(Colossians 3:21)

Our mother, Virginia Annette Bulow, was born on June 7, 1910, in Poplar Bluff, Missouri. As a young woman, she was a tall and curvy brunette with a hint of aristocracy about her–she even won the title of Miss Poplar Bluff one year during high school. She played a banjo in a little band with some of her friends, and those who knew her well expected her to be a famous artist, writer, or film star one day. She had a warm smile, a caring heart, and was completely at ease moving among the business and financial elite of that city with her parents. But after she completed her education, earning both an English and an art degree, she moved with her best friend to Edinburg, Texas to be a school teacher. They chose Edinburg because it had experienced a building boom in the late 1920s and established itself as a leader in education reform. Both girls were ambitious and saw themselves as having something to offer. The town had built several new schools, including a junior college, and our mother had dreams of teaching there at some point. But our mom ended up teaching junior high school English for almost thirty years instead.

This move to Edinburg, Texas changed the course of our mother's life. That's where she met our daddy and married him in 1940 after having known him only a few months. They were both thirty years old, had jobs, and wanted a family. She called herself Ginny back then. That's what our daddy called her, too.

A tall, stern man who never talked to us much about his childhood or family, our daddy was born Rupert William Short on April 6, 1910, to Sercy and Mable Short. He was one of five children and grew up in Luling, Texas. Luling was located in the heart of the state—about an hour from both San Antonio and Austin—and was known for being one of the roughest towns in Texas in its early days. It was cattle country, an agricultural hub, and a railway shipping center. In 1922, when our daddy was twelve years old, one of many major oilfields in the Southwest was discovered, exploding the population of Luling from five hundred to over five thousand in a very short time. Within months, you could see a brand new hotel, general store, bar, or bank on every corner, and in the fields, those tell-tale pump jacks shaped like slick, black grasshoppers popped up everywhere like a swarm come to stay.

Daddy was over six feet tall and hard driving even as an adolescent, so it wasn't surprising that he received a basketball scholarship. But because the scholarship was not from the school he most wanted to attend, he chose to just

2

get a job and start his *real* life. So it was off to Edinburg, Texas to work in the oil fields for Sun Oil Company.

After five years in Edinburg, he met and married our mother. Everything in Daddy's life had an order about it and that order was followed to the letter–both at home and at work. I remember even his work clothes had to be ironed and his shoes lined up to face north. That need for order made him a much better "company man" than a family man. His fierce loyalty kept him at Sun Oil Company (now called Sunoco) for thirty-four years which allowed him to retire with a nice pension and a gold watch that he took tremendous pride in.

Probably because our mother was an only child from a well-to-do family, she never learned how to do household chores. She didn't know how to plan, shop for, or cook the kind of hearty meals that a hungry and tired oil-field worker wanted and needed after a long hard day. I remember hearing the story that on one occasion–early on in their marriage– Daddy came home expecting a substantial dinner and found a neatly arranged platter of chicken-salad finger sandwiches waiting for him. He sat down heavily at the kitchen table and stared at the platter.

"Ginny. For heaven's sake, I'm starving. You call this supper?"

She turned to face him from the kitchen sink where she stood cleaning up. "Didn't you have a big lunch today? I thought you said–"

"Just get me something decent to eat," he hissed at her through clenched teeth.

She turned back to the running water and watched it drain, trying not to cry.

As hard as she tried, though, she never really mastered the art of cooking. My two sisters and I struggled, along with our daddy, to learn how to choke down our meals without too much complaining. At some point, she did figure out how to cook the traditional roast beef dinner and the accompanying salad of the day—the very essence of gourmet delights—iceberg lettuce topped with a pineapple ring, a dollop of Miracle Whip, and a cherry. We devoured it almost every Sunday after church. Over the years she added the German version of apple dumplings with that delicious warm vanilla sauce we had all come to know and love. Her own mother, a lady we called Mama Grace, helped her to perfect it.

Our daddy was working his way up the company ladder, and with each promotion came another move. From Edinburg, they went to Brenham, Texas, where their first daughter, Gretchen, was born. That was January of 1942. The difference between the society scene our mother left behind in Poplar Bluff, Missouri and the oil camps where she now lived must have seemed just about as far apart as the east is from the west. The oil holding tanks became the new skyline; roughnecks and their families became the new social circle.

The camps I remember living in were small, and we relied on the local towns for supplies and entertainment. But some of them were more self-contained. The company built row houses for the oil field workers with families in one section and set up bunkhouses for the single workers in another section, providing them free of charge for all the help. They usually built a school, a post office, and a small store near the big company building where all the meetings were held. This area served as a kind of hub for the community.

When they moved again, it was to Beaumont—another oil-rich area—where our daddy became the "on-site boss." His good looks and outgoing personality on the job made him an excellent candidate for continual promotion. The only obstacle he faced was the lack of a college degree. But being the on-site boss had its benefits. One of those benefits was that they had the nicest house and the highest social position possible in the camp for our mother.

Our house sat up a little ways on a hill overlooking the rest of the camp. It was larger than the "shotgun houses" that the workers lived in. They were called that because you could look in the front door and see out the back door. Most of those houses had a living room, one or two bedrooms, a tiny bathroom, and a kitchen—each directly behind the other. Our house was not only set apart but was arranged differently, too. Our living room and kitchen were separated by a hallway from the three bedrooms and the bathroom. Our back door to the yard was off the kitchen, which allowed a much-needed breeze once in a while. All the houses had corrugated tin roofs, no attics, and no insulation other than the sheetrock. In the summer it got very toasty. Eventually we got large window fans, which helped. Until then, though, we just endured the hot, dry Texas summers.

Living in the camps wasn't like living in town, for sure, but being at the top of the ladder made life a bit easier and more pleasant for our mother. She liked that our house was always set off separately from the others, while the rest of the houses crouched together like pop-up toys on a shelf. That made her feel important again, at least until she went into Beaumont to shop; then she would be reminded that "camp" people and "city" people were two different species.

Mother had three aunts she adored—Annette, Louise, and Marie—who were my grandfather's sisters and lived out in California. Our oldest sister, Gretchen Annette, was named after the first aunt. I'm not sure where the name Gretchen came from, but in German it means "pearl." Maybe it was because she was their first child, or maybe it was because of the arrival of twins three and a half years later, but it always seemed to Deborah and me that Gretchen was Mother and Daddy's favorite—their chosen child. Everything about her seemed to make Mother and Daddy happy.

Daddy had wanted a boy next . . . but got twin girls, instead. Deborah and I arrived by C-section in a San Antonio hospital on July 14, 1945, one month before the end of World War II. We caused quite a flurry because not only were twins being born, but both of us had to undergo a complete blood transfusion immediately after birth because our mother was RH negative and our daddy was RH positive.

We were named after our mother's other two aunts: Deborah Louise and Daphene Marie. Having three girls in a family is a pattern scattered throughout our genealogy like ducks on a pond. My name means "laurel" in Greek mythology, but Deborah's name is from the Bible. Since neither Gretchen's name nor mine appeared in the Bible, I always thought that God named Deborah, not Mother and Daddy.

As toddlers, Deborah and I were inseparable—often pictured holding hands and smiling wildly while trying to do toddler things. Because she was born five minutes before me, Deborah took it to mean that she had the right to take charge of my life, like some kind of drill sergeant, even back then. Although I was bigger, she advanced much faster than I did. Mother said that when we were still in baby beds, Deborah would climb into mine and try to change my diapers, even powdering me. She led me by the hand around the house for the first three or four years of my life.

Growing up in the Short family wasn't easy. We moved often, from oil camp to oil camp, throughout those early years. Times were difficult and our parents weren't prepared for twins. Daddy was busy being the boss at work, and when he came home he wanted peace and quiet. Our house was anything but that. And since we were sickly babies, Mother stayed home and kept busy tending to us because she didn't have anyone to help her. As we got older, we grew more active and needed new outlets for our energy.

"When you learn to tie a bow," Mother told us girls one day, "I'll let you take dancing lessons."

We worked at tying bows every chance we got, and before we were four years old we were signed up for ballet lessons at the Sprolls Dance Studio in Beaumont, a square room filled with mirrors, rails along the walls, and a dozen little girls skipping around in tutus.

"Those two are mine," Mother said, pointing us out to the other parents. She was beaming. There we were—two darling little ballerinas, hand in hand, our pink slippers tip-toeing across the floor and our matching bows bobbing in our hair.

Without being instructed to do so, Deborah kept a tight hold of my hand during the class. To everyone's surprise, though, I eventually became the better dancer.

* * *

As we grew up, we found that keeping secrets was a requirement in the Short family. And then the secrets faded until many of our childhood memories were just gone. Years later when Deborah and I talked, we discovered extensive gaps and disturbing feelings that just couldn't be explained away. So Deborah, brave as always, went into counseling to find out why. Then she called me and told me several stories about our childhood that had surfaced. I was stunned but not totally surprised. I had no memory of any of them but the one that follows sure answered a lot of questions for both of us. We figured out that we must have been between three and four years old when this particular experience happened. Gretchen would have been six or seven by then.

It was a hot and windy Saturday morning. Mother and Gretchen had gone into town to buy groceries and we were left alone with Daddy. When mother opened the front door upon returning and took one step into the living room, she dropped the bag of groceries she was carrying and stepped in front of Gretchen, who was trying to push past her and enter the house first. "Rupert. Oh, Rupert," she gasped as she scanned the room. "How could you do this to our baby girls?" Deborah sat propped against the wall by the kitchen, curled up in a ball with her head buried in her hands. She was not making a sound or moving a muscle. I was on the floor by Daddy's chair, whimpering and rocking back and forth, grasping Juicy Fruit gum wrappers in both hands. When I saw my mother step through the door, I reached out both hands to her, letting the wrappers fall to the floor. She didn't miss a thing: medical help was needed; time and distance were required for her sanity; and the drive to protect her daughters was stronger than the fear of her husband.

In the next instant, she ordered Gretchen to take Deborah to the car as she scooped me up into her arms, pushing the bag of groceries out of the way with her foot. Daddy was sitting in his chair smoking his Camel cigarettes when

Mother burst into the house that morning. But he didn't move a muscle or say a word. He just watched with eyes of emptiness as she got all three of us out of the house as quickly as she could. We were in the car and winding our way out of the camp before any of us could think. And we didn't return home until almost dawn the next morning. The hospital was far away from our house.

No one outside those four walls would ever know what unspeakable loss of innocence had taken place that Saturday morning. Mother vowed to make sure of that. *It did not happen. It did not happen. It did not happen.* She kept repeating this as she drove home in the early light of dawn.

Despite Mother's best efforts, things were never really the same for any of us after that, especially between Deborah and me. We were fraternal twins, sharing a special bond that connected us more deeply than normal siblings. Even as toddlers we seemed to feel each other's emotional and physical pain. But the abuse—both witnessed and experienced—broke that bond we had shared and replaced it with a barrier. We stopped talking. And we stopped holding hands. Without my hand in hers, I was forced to find my own way. I went on after that, feeling lost and alone. And I wasn't the only one.

Gretchen retreated further into her own world, too. But it was different from ours because it was obvious that Mother and Daddy continued to favor her. Even at an early age we understood that to them, Gretchen was special. Not only was she smart and obedient, but she was also cute as a button with her long, pretty hair. But she wasn't a happy child. She distanced herself from Deborah and me in every way she could, wanting no part of anything we did. Neither of us ever saw her get a spanking. In fact, she rarely was disciplined for anything. I think that she wanted to be an only child, have her own room, and live in a kind of make believe world of her own. During the time we were growing up, we referred to her (always behind her back, of course) as "The Queen" and her room as "The Queen's Room." We were never allowed in unless we were invited. And we never were.

Deborah retreated into her own world, as well, but she couldn't get too far away by herself because we shared a bedroom together, which was referred to as "The Twins' Room" until long after we left home. The differences between Deborah and me became apparent early on: She was small physically and advanced developmentally; I was big for our age but lagged behind emotionally. She led the way, and I followed her. She liked order, and I was comfortable in clutter.

I didn't really care if my side of the room was a mess. I just cleared a space on my bed big enough for me to sit and draw pictures from a stack of comic books I had collected. It was a wonderful way to hide my increasing pain and forget that I was alone—even when everyone was home. And my drawings got better and better.

I retreated into my own world, too, but I never stopped longing for that connection with Deborah. I wanted her to pay attention to me, to need me, and to love me. I wanted to be more than just a way to satisfy her need to control. One day, feeling especially desperate for attention and angry at Deborah's aloofness, I stuffed her little Siamese kitten named Sammy—a treasured gift from a friend—into a bobby sock and hid him in the hall closet. She could hear his pitiful cries, but she couldn't find him. She was helpless and frantic, and I was glad. I liked it that she felt for a little while what I felt most of the time.

This incident mirrored how I was living my life—stuffing my anxieties, hiding my sleeplessness, disguising my inability to focus or concentrate at school. No one seemed to see the abuse that was going on in our home or respond to our silent cries for help.

From all outward appearances, life went on after that Saturday morning incident. Mother carried on as if nothing had happened. She went back to teaching school during the week and keeping the house on the weekends. When she went shopping, though, she took us three girls with her. We went back to staying out of our Daddy's way as much as possible for a while, keeping busy with our school activities and friends. But Deborah and I never held hands again as children.

* * *

While we were still living in Beaumont, Daddy and Mother left us with a babysitter one afternoon and evening to visit friends in another nearby oil camp. It didn't take long before we ran out of things to do outside.

"I have an idea." Deborah pointed her finger straight at me with that mischievous grin I knew so well.

"I want to help," I said, following her to the shed in the far backyard. We both grabbed a bag of the chicken feed that Daddy had purchased for his latest project of raising chickens and dragged them up the back steps and into the house.

"Shhhhhhhh." Deborah tossed the command over her left shoulder like she was flipping her hair out of her eyes. I wasn't making a sound but whispered "Okay" anyway. We pulled the bags down the hallway and into the bathroom and then shut the door. We both took a deep breath and looked at each other with matching grins.

"What are we doing?" I whispered to her, still grinning.

"We're making a big batch of oatmeal, silly." She began pouring her bag into the bathtub. She then took mine and poured it in too. "Now turn on the water—just a little so it doesn't make too much noise." I did it and we stood there watching the chicken feed rise to the surface and then sink back down to the bottom of the tub as it took on water. We filled the bathtub to the very top before turning the water off.

Needless to say, when Mother and Daddy returned home they were not happy. Mother stood in the doorway of the kitchen while Daddy made us explain what we had done. Then Daddy explained to us what was going to happen next and why. We understood. Mother then turned and walked out the back door, slamming it shut as she left. We watched her until she disappeared around the corner of the yard. Daddy marched us into the small bathroom, made us take down our panties, and spanked us with his belt until our bottoms were red and shiny. I cried long and hard after that spanking, but Deborah didn't shed a tear, which infuriated Daddy. We were sent directly to bed. I fell asleep and didn't hear Mother come back.

During our early school years, we didn't have television so we spent a lot of time outside playing Cowboys and Indians. And, of course, Deborah was always in charge and got to be either Roy Rogers or Dale Evans, her heroes. By the time all of the characters were chosen by our friends in the camp, I got to be whoever was left over and never considered asking for anything else. Gretchen never played those outside games with us, though. She had friends of her own and wasn't interested at all in such childish activities.

If we weren't playing those games, we were building a tent using old blankets flung over the clothesline behind our house. These clotheslines were strung across the backyard of every house in the camp, so if ours was otherwise occupied with laundry, we would just find a friend's that wasn't. We discovered that the shade from those tents provided some relief from the heat and a perfect place to play house without the peering eyes of grownups.

When we were in the first grade, Deborah decided that she needed to form a "Fire Club" with her group of friends in the oil camp where we lived at the time, outside Premont, Texas. I had been sick in bed for several days, but when I was well enough to play outside, I went looking for them. They were playing several rows of houses away from ours and back behind one of many holding tanks that looked like huge unwrapped soup cans with ladders attached to them. They were strictly off limits to us kids. That's why the location was chosen. I asked Deborah what she was doing and she said they were playing "Fire Club." I asked if I could join.

"Maybe," she said without looking at me.

"What do I have to do?" I asked.

"Well, you have to steal some matches—just like everyone else did."

To get in, each member had to steal matches and present them to Deborah in order to become official. Trust me—I was not the only one who did everything she wanted done. So I slipped back into the house, found Daddy's cigarettes by his chair, and searched for his matches. I found a little box with several matchsticks inside and, clutching them inside my shirt so no one would see them, happily pranced back to join the club.

Once Deborah had in her hand the matches I had stolen, she ordered everyone to circle closer around her while she built a fire. She, of course, was the only one allowed to actually strike a match and light a fire, being the President and all. Before I had joined them, everyone had gathered paper and twigs and anything else that they thought might burn. The bigger that fire grew, the wider our eyes got, and once it got going it reached nearly five feet high.

While our little club was enjoying the growing fire, a man that worked in the camp happened to drive by and see it; he immediately reported it to his boss—our daddy—to keep us from burning the camp down. Boy, were we surprised and horrified when he slipped up behind us.

"Hey, what do you kids think you are doing out here? Now get home—all of you." The community life in the camps was such that no one could do much of anything without the busy-bodies making it known. Parents were everywhere. He had some of his men extinguish the fire, and we were transported back to our own house in his car.

True to his usual form, though, he made us wait for our punishment. Mother made dinner and then we all had to sit down with him at the table and eat, knowing what was coming. When we were done, Mother disappeared out the back door, as was her custom, and he marched us off to the bathroom. Deborah went in first and Daddy shut the door hard. I leaned my head against the bathroom door and heard Daddy order her to bend over and pull her panties down. He then began administering the life-altering, belt-

14

snapping whipping. When she refused to cry, he gave her a few extra whacks, but he never did bring her to tears with his beatings. Never. Not Deborah.

While this was going on with Deborah, I began sobbing with fear and sorrow for her. Then it was my turn. "Daddy, please," I whimpered. "Please don't whip me. I didn't do anything." I begged him until the first blow took my breath away. I tried to protect myself with my hands, but he spoke in a whisper, "Don't you dare," and slapped them hard with his belt. Many times we had welts on our bottoms, on the backs of our legs, and sometimes across our hands long after the offense. It seemed to Deborah and me that Daddy derived some degree of pleasure from inflicting pain on us, which only added to our miseries. We knew all the kids involved got well-deserved spankings that day. None of the others, however, had welts and bruises a week later. We never did get to have another meeting of our almost famous "Fire Club."

Another time, we had a friend come over to visit while our mothers played bridge at our house. The kitchen table had been moved into the living room to give the ladies more room and better access to any breeze that might blow in. This time, however, it was the friend who had the great idea. She said we should gather some bullfrogs from the pond nearby. It sounded like fun, so we took an old pillowcase and headed out. When we had bagged seven or eight of the big slimy things, we slipped into the living room and let the frogs loose right onto the bridge table where the women were playing. All four women jumped away yelling, overturning the table and sending everything on it flying, which brought their card game to an abrupt halt. After the mess was cleaned up and everyone was gone, we waited for the family ritual to begin—like inmates waiting on death row.

That same year, we had what we later referred to as our wonderful "watermelon adventure." Summertime in the Texas oil fields was brutally hot, and we were so excited when a couple of Mexican workers pulled up in an old green flatbed truck one day with a load of cold watermelons to sell. Several of the kids nearby, including Deborah and me, jumped up into the back of the truck where they were slicing them up, and every time the truck stopped, they would hand us another piece to eat. So we stayed in the truck as they made their way around our oil camp.

The camp houses were all painted white with red trim—the company colors—and arranged in neat rows. The blacktop streets in front and dirt alleys behind made getting around the whole area easy enough, and they seemed to know where to go to attract a crowd to purchase their produce.

At each stop, we would get more. We ended up riding around the camp for hours eating and laughing and having a great time. When they finished selling watermelon in our camp, the strangers in their broken-down truck invited us to go with them to the next camp to do the same thing. Like fleas off a dog just powdered, most of the kids jumped out of the truck. Deborah, however, piped up with a confident "Yes" for a few of us who wanted to remain . . . and off we went. None of us gave a thought to anything but riding in the truck, eating cold watermelon, and having the time of our lives.

Back at our camp, however, things were not going so well. At dusk, our parents went out looking for us; not long after, the whole camp was out searching. And then the police from town got involved. I don't know how Daddy knew where to go, but out of nowhere, he pulled up beside the truck in a camp quite a ways from ours. Not much was spoken on the ride back to our place, but it was dark outside, dinner was cold, and we were scared. Mother sat in silence and nervously adjusted her glasses while she pushed bits of tuna casserole around on her plate. Then she left the table. We ate in fear and trembling and then endured our punishment. Those blows left more than physical marks on our bodies.

One night when we were about eleven years old—in 1956—we were in the kitchen cleaning up after dinner. Deborah was doing her job, washing the dishes, and I was doing mine, drying and putting them away. Gretchen had retreated to her room to study—or do whatever she did in there. Mother was more and more absent in our daily lives. She was taking lots of pills, all prescribed to her by the doctor, and was spending most of her time in the bedroom with the blinds pulled and the fan blowing on her.

This particular evening, we were arguing about *always* having to do *all* the work and Daddy called us into the living room where he was sitting in his chair. He was irritated and quipped, "If you girls like to argue so much, let's see what you can *really* do. I want you to fight—right here in the living room where I can watch you. And the one that gives up first gets the spanking."

Even though I was much bigger than Deborah, I had never won a fight of any kind. But this battle was different. A spanking was at stake. I fought hard and won but only because Deborah had burned her leg with the iron a couple of days before, and to win, I scraped her wound on the carpet. She gave up because the pain was too severe to keep fighting. After she got the spanking, she went stomping off to our bedroom and I followed sobbing after her. I closed the door and opened my mouth to tell her how sorry I was for what happened, but nothing came out. We didn't speak to each other the rest of the night and never spoke about the incident at all. For a very long time after that, I hated Daddy.

* * *

I have some good memories of the Christmas visits from our grandparents, Daddy Carl and Mamma Grace, Mother's parents from Poplar Bluff. We came to know our maternal grandparents better than any of the rest of the extended family. It was probably because our mom shared so much with us about how proud she was of her German heritage and, because she was an only child, her parents spent almost every Christmas holiday with us. Their presence and presents changed everything about Christmas.

We could tell that our mother dearly loved her daddy and I could see why. He was a large man with thinning hair and kind eyes. His voice was as booming as his hug was gentle. When I whispered in his ear, his face lit up and his chuckles rolled out easily. We understood each other somehow. I came to love him dearly, too.

Daddy Carl was born in Leavenworth, Kansas, graduated college, and became a very successful businessman. He joined his father, Paul Bulow, in the Bulow & Son Plumbing, Heating, and Sheet Metal Company and helped preserve the spirit of their company motto–"Service and Quality." It became one of the most successful businesses of its type in Southern Missouri. Paul Bulow is credited for having invented the percolating coffee pot, so the story goes in our family. Mother always kept a framed copy of the newspaper article about him, which was proudly hung for visitors to see. Daddy Carl was so much fun to be with and so full of life— so very different from our daddy. I can easily understand how our grandmother, Grace Pilquist, fell in love with him. As well as being financially well off, they were both active and respected members of the community of Poplar Bluff, Missouri.

Mama Grace had a tight, sweet smile that matched her tight gray curls and rubbed herself down with BENGAY every night. I don't know what she suffered from . . . but oh, the smell of BENGAY. Gretchen even joined in with us when we snickered about Mama Grace behind her back, ridiculing her for the strange things she said, the way she always smelled, and the funny way she carried herself— tripping once in a while and stooping more and more as the years went by. Sometimes we secretly followed her around our house and watched as she picked things up in one room and placed them in another—over and over again. Mother was not happy with us when she caught us doing this.

Mama Grace doted on our mother when they were together, much to the annoyance of her husband. Daddy Carl showed great patience with everyone else but her. We always looked forward to their visits to our house, and we three girls always enjoyed the obligatory pat on the head Mama Grace gave us each time they departed. Of course, Deborah and I had to give up *our* room for the two weeks that they stayed with us. Each time they left, Deborah and I created a new game to play as we tried to find our stuff and return it to the original place. Mama Grace was very creative in her "reorganization."

No one even considered how much easier it would have been for Gretchen to give up her room. There would have been one person sleeping on the living room couch instead of two. And Gretchen would have had to deal with the after-effects of the "BENGAY factory" and go through the great reorganization that we had to each time. Mama Grace's advancing senility made life interesting for everyone around her.

On one Christmas that was extra special we were surprised by gifts from our grandparents. Each of us received a doll that not only walked, but also was chosen specifically because, supposedly, it resembled us. My doll was special because I was the only one of the three girls with blond curls. Oh, how I adored my doll. Deborah and I loaded our dolls into our wagon and paraded them up and down the narrow sidewalk in front of our house and then down the hill and across the pavement to our friends' sidewalks to show them off.

Daddy Carl and Mama Grace brought unconditional love and security to our early years and gave some periodic relief to the silence, fear, and isolation we were immersed in.

The few Christmas holidays without our grandparents were stressful and unhappy for us. Daddy managed to take the excitement out of the celebrations because nothing could be spontaneous. Before opening presents on Christmas Eve, we *had* to have dinner first, and then the kitchen *had* to be cleaned completely. And he always invited a friend of his over to play Santa Claus for us. Even though all three of us girls knew that he was not Santa—we were way past believing in that stuff—we were expected to go through with the charade of being excited. Once "Santa" left, we finally were allowed to open our gifts. Mother always took us shopping before Christmas to let us pick out our own outfits, then she would wrap them up and put them under the tree. She did her best to make those shopping trips fun for us, but she made it perfectly clear that our part was to act surprised when we opened them. And Daddy always tucked an envelope with our names on it in the branches of the Christmas tree and inside there would be a check for $25. My sadness was never about opening up presents that we had already seen, and it wasn't about the size of the check; it was that we were always just going through the motions of having fun, our lives filled with artificial happiness.

* * *

After we got a television set in 1956, Daddy spent Saturdays watching any kind of sports that he could. That year the New York Yankees baseball team beat the Brooklyn Dodgers in the World Series. He was thrilled. But when the TV was on, we weren't allowed to make any noise whatsoever. He would turn the volume down some on the television and turn on the radio to a completely different game so he could listen to both. It was maddening to the rest of us who lived in the house, so most of the time we all retreated to our respective bedrooms: Mother to nurse her migraines, Deborah to read her books, and I to draw pictures. When he wanted something to drink or eat or the volume turned up or down on the TV or radio, he would whistle for someone to come. I was always the one to respond. I was still trying to please him . . . still striving to earn his love. But he loved his work, and he loved his sports, instead. In fact, Daddy was such a baseball fan that whenever we were in the car, the only thing we could listen to was baseball games, which seemed to last forever. And when they were on, we weren't allowed to even speak. Not a word.

Vacations were another time of stress for Deborah and me. One summer we went on a trip in an old station wagon to California to visit Mother's aunts—the ones we were named after. Deborah and I were in the very back of the car. Not knowing Daddy could see us, we made faces and stuck out our tongues at him. All of a sudden the car began to slow. Deborah and I caught a glimpse of Mother's fallen face as she turned slightly around. He pulled the car over on the side of the road and stopped. We knew we were in trouble.

"Out," he ordered, breaking the silence that had fallen on all of us. He stepped out of the station wagon and unbuckled his belt. "Stand right here beside the car."

"Rupert. Not here. Not like–" our mother protested.

Daddy completely ignored her, not taking his eyes off us. "Bend over," he growled. So we did. There we were– humiliated and dreading the blows–watching the passing cars and gawking people as each blow was delivered. The rest of the time in the car was torment. Mother was silent. Daddy was content to listen to sports on the radio as he drove along. Gretchen stared out the side window. And Deborah and I suffered with our wounded hearts and bruised bottoms. Some of our trips seemed to last forever.

Daddy's parents, Sercy and Mable Short, hosted Thanksgiving holidays at their house in San Antonio during our growing up years. We always looked forward to seeing our many cousins there. And we were amazed at how happy and funny our daddy became when he was with his siblings. Even his voice sounded different when we were there. They all seemed to idolize him.

Although their house was small and very full when we all got together, we kids somehow found places to sleep, most of the time on pallets that spanned the living room floor from wall to wall. That fullness was often more than Sercy was able to bear. That little silent man with a scruffy face–

who we lovingly called Bampaw—was so thin that he wore suspenders to hold his pants up. He stayed in his chair in the corner of the room observing the chaos until it reached a certain level. Then he would disappear out the back door, down the stone sidewalk leading to the detached garage, and into a small apartment he had created for himself, not to reappear until breakfast. All of his spare time was spent tending to his garden . . . his pride and joy. Bampaw was more of a mystery to all of us kids than anything. None of us really ever got to know him.

We were all happy to be there with our daddy's family because Mamaw—that's what we called our grandmother Mable—was a wonderful cook. Boy, did she bring smiles to our faces at the kitchen table. I especially loved her biscuits, which were so light it seemed you had to hold them down to keep them from floating off the plate. I watched in amazement as she made them because she just put in a pinch of this and a scoop of that, never once referring to a recipe. Along with the traditional Thanksgiving meal, Mamaw cooked almost nonstop for the long weekend. She nearly always made the pinto beans and cornbread that our daddy so loved because Mother never mastered making either dish. Then she packed up a bunch of each and sent it home with us for Daddy to enjoy later. We helped him enjoy it, too. I always felt comforted when I was near Mamaw—she made me think that everything was going to be okay. She seemed to be the glue that held all the pieces together at her house, and I liked the way that felt.

On these trips to and from San Antonio, though, I never understood how we got our assigned sleeping arrangements in the car, even if Daddy and Mother seemed to think they were fine. Because Gretchen was the favored one, she took the whole back seat; Deborah took the place above the back seat where the window was—looking like a sleeping mannequin in a store window. The only place left for me . . . was the floorboard. The time for sleep always followed shortly after we got into the car, so we found our assigned "places." While the other girls slept, I sweated on the floorboard of that old car, experiencing all the bumps in the road and the heat of the pavement, and felt like a slab of well-done barbeque.

After a while, Gretchen and Deborah would wake up and I could finally crawl back up onto the seat, taking the place in the middle. I was dripping with sweat and exhausted. Every time I began to doze off and lean against either of them, they would squeal with horror, not wanting my sweaty body to touch theirs. The pecking order was obvious and remained intact over the years.

* * *

When we were in the fifth grade, Daddy Carl, thinking we could perform like the Lennon Sisters, sent Mother some money to buy a piano and find someone to give us lessons. She found a teacher in town. Since we were twins, the teacher thought we should play a duet for the first recital. I don't remember that we ever practiced together, but I can still remember the new taffeta dresses Mother made for us. She was an accomplished seamstress by then. They were dark green with pink satin ribbon for ties. When our turn came, we sat side by side at the piano, looked at each other, smiled, and began playing the tune. It seemed like another adventure for us because the audience was fairly large and there was an air of excitement in the room. Unfortunately, though, neither of us could remember how to end the piece. After playing the same song for the fourth time, we looked at each other again and then at the piano teacher in

24

desperation. With no help forthcoming, we both stopped suddenly in the middle of things, burst into tears, and ran off the stage. That was the beginning and the end of the Short girls' musical career. Thankfully.

Daddy loved to go hunting on the weekends during dove season. So, one Friday evening, sitting at the dinner table, I asked if I could go along with him.

"Sure," he said. "I think that would be fine." I looked across the table at Mother. She had stopped eating and was looking at our daddy but didn't say what she looked like she wanted to. I remember looking down at my plate of meatloaf and lima beans, wondering if she would say something to keep me from going . . . and how I was going to get my supper down. The meatloaf was rough to look at and even tougher to chew; if I tilted my head just a little, and squinted my eyes just right, the lima beans turned into macaroni and cheese—like the kind I had eaten at my friend's house. I could choke them down then. And Mother said nothing.

I was pretty excited about going hunting with him, so after eating dinner and doing the dishes, I ran to my room to lay out my clothes. Early the next morning, Mother packed us a little picnic lunch, and off we went. We drove a ways outside the oil camp where we lived, parked the car on the side of the road, and walked through some brush down to the bank of a stock pond I had never seen before.

"Now just be quiet, Daphene," was all he said to me. For what seemed like the longest time, I sat there swatting mosquitoes, holding my breath, and listening to the cooing of the doves in the distance. Then a thunderous shot rang out, breaking the hot silence that had settled all around me. I jumped up to see the results. "Go get that bird. Now, run and bring it here," he shouted, waving his arm at me and pointing the way.

I didn't know whether to be honored to have a part to play or horrified that I had to pick up those dead or dying birds. After that, every time he shot one, he made me find it and then, if it wasn't dead, I had to twist and twist its poor little head until it came off in my hands. It seemed that no matter how hard I tried to make my daddy love me, things always happened that just made life worse. I sat beside him in the car on the way home–hot, tired, bloody, and sad.

In 1957, the summer before our sixth grade year, Daddy got his final transfer to an oil camp just west of Snyder, Texas. I heard Deborah's future husband, Ron Hall, describe Snyder many times over the years, calling it "a tumbleweed-tossed West Texas town so flat you could stand on a cow chip and see New Mexico." Snyder's claim to fame back then was black gold. In late November, 1948, Standard of Texas struck oil in Scurry County and changed everything and everyone in the area. Snyder, the county seat, boomed almost overnight, transforming itself from a quiet little agricultural community to an up-and-coming oil town with a population of over ten thousand people.

Later, by the time we were in junior high, we were required to do most of the cooking and had full responsibility for cleaning the kitchen because Mother came home from teaching exhausted most days and then spent weekends in bed nursing her migraines. I don't remember Gretchen helping out with any of the chores–ever. One night it came to a head for Deborah.

"I don't want to do the dishes tonight. I have too much homework. Can't Gretchen help Daphene tonight?"

Deborah had followed our daddy to his normal place after eating and stood right beside his chair. Confrontation was in the air.

"You're kidding, right?" was his reply. And the look on his face ended their conversation.

When Deborah returned to the kitchen, I was the only one there. Mother and Gretchen had gone to their rooms.

"This stinks," Deborah hissed so close to my ear that I felt it. "It gripes me, it really does." She dropped the load of plates in her hands so hard into the sink full of dishwater that water and bubbles went everywhere. We both groaned. "This stinks," she repeated as I hurried to clean up the mess before Daddy could see it. "She's an imbecile . . . and so darn lazy . . . that I really can't stand her at all. The Queen on her throne makes me sick."

"She thinks she is *so* smart," I added, trying to come up with words worse than Deborah's. "No wonder she only has friends for a week and then they dump her."

"And she studies but doesn't get straight A's like I do," Deborah added. I didn't say another word at that.

Even though Gretchen didn't do much around the house and she never seemed to get into trouble, she did not escape the effects of our troubled family. When she started her periods, Mother insisted that she take medication to help ease the pain of her cramps. Mother took a lot of prescribed narcotics for her pain and didn't think twice about giving Gretchen diet pills to control her weight during her run for the Miss Snyder beauty pageant. Being introduced to such strong narcotics at such a young age did tremendous damage to her and created an addiction she struggled with for the rest of her life.

As we got older, my side of the room became a clearer picture of me like Deborah's became of her, and the room as a whole was an image of the kind of twins we were. At this stage of my life, it was a stroke of luck if any of my clothes made it onto a hanger. And my shoes were piled up much like a game of "Pick-up Sticks." But Deborah vacuumed her half of the carpet, cleaned her half of the mirror, and dusted her half of the dresser—often. Her clothes were hung by grouping colors and styles together, and her shoes were lined up like soldiers on parade.

During junior high, Deborah had developed into a many-sided perfectionist and loved being regarded as one of *the* outstanding students at our school. The minute we got home from school she wanted to hurry up and start studying. But that was the last thing I wanted to do. I wanted to retreat into my "studio"—that quickly cleared corner of my bed—to work on my pen and ink sketches of trees. Of course, if she was studying, I was expected to study, too.

Because Daddy expected me to do well in school like Deborah, I resorted to cheating to try to please him. Somewhere along the line, I came to understand that everyone in the family believed what I believed about myself—that I was stupid and incapable of making it on my own. Mother would read the books I was assigned and then stay up late writing the required reports. All I had to do was turn them in. How nice. How convenient. Deborah felt sorry for me, too, and helped me get through my classes. Since Mother was a teacher, surely she must have known that I was becoming a compulsive cheater. But in our family we did not talk about things like this.

I do remember one time Mother told me I had scored high on an aptitude test I had taken in the sixth grade. Because it didn't seem possible that I could really have done it, I just dismissed it and went on believing I was dumb. I cheated on every academic assignment I could. Then on test days, I would walk into class sweating–my heart pounding and my hands shaking–knowing that I had to find someone smart to sit next to. Many times I could hardly hold onto my pen as I took the test. What drove me on was the fact that I had discovered how to avoid being berated for grades that didn't equal Deborah's. I had finally discovered how to please Daddy.

Living in the company-owned oil camps made our world small. Living on the heat-scorched plains of West Texas made our lives uncomfortable. But living in the well-hidden and cruel abuse in the Short family made our lives almost unbearable. Each of us found a way to survive . . . at least for a time.

Chapter 2

Separate Lives

They exchanged the truth about God for a lie.

(Romans 1:25)

The summer before our freshman year in high school signaled many changes to come in our lives. The company sold all of the camp houses, so we had to move into town. We were thrilled. Daddy bought our first house that had a real yard. We were doubly thrilled.

Our new house sat on the corner of 33rd Street and Denison Avenue. It was the biggest house we had ever lived in and the nicest, too. We loved that it was red brick and in a new housing development where our best friends, Susie and Helen, lived. We had a big front yard and two large peach trees in our fenced backyard. There was an alleyway behind a concrete block fence in the back. It seemed like heaven to us.

One Saturday, shortly after getting settled in our new house, I plopped down on the front step to watch my daddy as he mowed meticulously back and forth across our new lawn, creating a kind of graph paper pattern. I searched his face and longed for a smile or kind word from him. He had never repeated the worst offense and had finally stopped spanking both Deborah and me, but he had developed over the last year such a profound way of just ignoring us—as if we didn't exist. I couldn't bring myself to give up, though. So the next week I asked if I could help, and the week after that I got permission to do it all by myself. When he saw what I had done, he didn't say a word; he just mowed over my work, creating the graph paper again. I didn't bother to try to mow the lawn after that. And I never watched him do it again, either. I tried to ignore him like he ignored me.

Being the oldest, Gretchen was the first to leave the nest. She had been accepted at Texas Christian University in Fort Worth and left for college in late August, when we were freshmen. She had pledged Tri Delta and, following in Mother's footsteps, wanted to become a teacher. Our parents were so proud of her. Her room remained intact, though— ever The Queen's Room—until our parents retired and moved from Snyder years later. Deborah and I continued to share a room until we left home. We had settled into a kind of working relationship, hanging around together with our friends at school but keeping our distance once inside the house. I desperately wanted Gretchen's room for myself because by that time I was painting with watercolors and oil and needed more space. I loved painting trees and flowers of all kinds and colors. I taped them up on my wall for a time and then tucked them away under my bed. Once in a while, Mother would pop in and give me some tips on composition and color combining. I loved the way her face lit up when she took my paintbrush and demonstrated how to do the next thing. When I was painting, I was in another time and place . . . confident, accomplished, and happy. It was a respite from the anxiety, sadness, and fear I walked around with.

* * *

That summer before ninth grade was so fun for me. One of my best friends lived across the street from the football field. One early morning a group of us soon-to-be freshman girls gathered on her lawn to watch the football team practice and spent a couple of hours picking out who would be our boyfriend when school started. I chose a good-looking junior with thick, dark hair named John Weaver.

I can still remember the first time he spoke to me at school. I had just walked out of my second period English class and was talking nonstop to my friend about the outfit she was wearing. She was not looking where she was going because she was looking at me, looking at her outfit, and she ran right into John Weaver in the hall.

Everyone was a little flustered, but in the few seconds that followed that embarrassing scene, he looked right at me with amazing hazel eyes and said, "Hi, Daphene. My name's John Weaver."

My heart started racing and I thought I would faint. When I referred to him after that, it was always as John Weaver—just the way he first said it to me—never just John. In the weeks that followed, we would chat once in a while in the halls, but I never thought he would ask me for a date.

When he finally did, I was as nervous as a novice on stage. He said he would pick me up at 7:00 the next Friday night and we would go to the Dairy Queen for a hamburger and

Our Southern Breeze

then do what everyone did in Snyder . . . hang out there for a while and then cruise the square.

All of us kids loved riding around from the Scurry County Courthouse to the Dairy Queen about a mile and a half away, making the loop as many times as we could, depending on time and money for gas, to see who all was "out." If we didn't find anyone interesting to stop and talk to, we headed out for the baseball fields to see if there was a Pony League game being played. We girls took to heart the words of a popular song at the time and longed to be . . . "where the boys are."

I kept a journal of every time John Weaver called me, what we talked about, and what we did when we were together. Whenever we had a date I always found something to keep in "My John Weaver Box." What looked like a stash of trash—a used straw, a dried-up lemon, movie ticket stubs, a Doublemint gum wrapper—became my most treasured possessions.

My mother loved John Weaver. When he came over to see me, she always found a way to come into the living room and visit for a minute. I think she must have thought I hit the boyfriend jackpot. He was handsome, athletic, and from the right social class. I put him on a pedestal and she helped me keep him there.

His mother wasn't thrilled about our relationship, though. I was a couple of years younger than he was, and his mother and grandmother, who lived with them, already had a special girl his age picked out to be his future wife. I remember one time when he told me he thought it would be better if we didn't date anymore because his mother didn't want him to date for a while. But I knew in my heart that she was talking

34

about me. Unfortunately, I didn't have the confidence to convince him otherwise. That night I cried myself to sleep.

When I woke with my eyes swollen shut, Mother drew me in and hugged me close to her. She decided to let me skip school. That afternoon when she got home, we went on a shopping spree to buy a new outfit to lift my spirits. She didn't mention any of this to Daddy because he would not have been happy about it. I think she loved John Weaver as much as I did because she suffered right along with me.

It wasn't long until he decided to go against his mother's wishes and we started dating again. There were times when he would come over in the evening to listen to our favorite songs on the stereo. Wisely, he chose nights when Daddy had meetings. Often Deborah was off studying with one of her friends and Mother would retreat to her room with a headache. We both liked to be outside, so we would sit on our front step where we could still hear the music and just talk.

All I have to do now is hear "The Theme from a Summer Place" to be transported right back to those times. We both dated other people during high school but John Weaver was my first love. I will always treasure my memories of our early time together.

* * *

During my freshman year, Nan, one of our dear friends, lost her mother. It was a shock to Deborah and me to face the idea of death because we had never known anyone who died, much less a parent. The funeral was at the Methodist church we attended. It was an old church and the sanctuary was in the shape of a half circle. Nan had asked all of her friends to sit next to her family, so I plopped down at the end of a pew on the aisle near the front. I sat cross-legged during the entire service, which caused my left leg to go to sleep. I could see Nan from where I sat. She was physically shaking all over and sobbing into a wad of tissue in her hands.

When it was my turn to step into the aisle to view the body, my left leg buckled and I fell flat—just a couple of yards from the casket. My ankle had snapped, shooting a terrible pain up my entire leg. I closed my eyes and let the tears flow down my face, expecting help to arrive any second. *Oh, I am so thankful that John Weaver isn't here to see this,* I thought, as the seconds ticked by.

But instead of my sister or my friends coming to help me up, they stepped over me as if I wasn't there. *Am I invisible? Is this a bad dream? Where's my mother?* One after the other, I watched them approach, step over me, and continue on to the casket. They then proceeded around the outer edge of the sanctuary and out the front door to form the procession line. I laid my head back down on the aisle carpet and wept silently.

One of the adults must have called for help because before long I could hear a siren blaring in the distance. As it grew louder, I grew more horrified. The church was empty by this time except for the casket and the pallbearers. They were standing around waiting for me to be removed when two men with a stretcher hurried down the aisle to load me up and carry me off. Unfortunately, I was carried out between the two long lines and was humiliated as people gawked at me. I tried to hide my face with my hands. Then, with sirens blaring, the ambulance rushed me right past the Dairy Queen and on to the hospital.

My parents had left the funeral early and were sitting at the Dairy Queen when they saw the ambulance speed by. When they got to the hospital, Mother told me that Daddy had commented when he saw the ambulance that one of the family members must have fainted or something. No such luck. It was just me. And I bore the brunt of many jokes at school as I struggled to keep my composure and drag myself around for the next month on crutches.

It was about this time that depression became an issue for me. I remember the first episode like it was yesterday. It was the Christmas of our freshman year in high school and the last holiday our grandparents spent with us in Snyder. The winter had been unseasonably warm, storms were blowing through every two or three days, and the wind howled through many of the nights Deborah and I slept on the living room couch.

Gretchen got home from TCU about the same time they arrived. It was mid-afternoon and the house was in a flurry with everyone trying to find a place and get settled in. I stood at the door of Gretchen's room while she unpacked the beautiful clothes she had collected while at college. I really wanted to borrow something for the date I had that night with John Weaver.

"Can I borrow at least that blue outfit? Just for tonight?" I asked her.

"You're kidding, right?" she snapped. "Absolutely not. No."

"Why not, for heaven sakes? I'll be careful with it."

She walked over to me and shut her bedroom door in my face.

I waited about an hour and went back to her room. No one else was home at the time, so I carefully opened the door a crack and peeked in. She was asleep on her bed and her closet door was ajar. I slipped in, tip-toed to her closet, and eased myself inside enough to close the closet door. I rummaged through her clothes and quickly found what I really wanted to wear, but when I attempted to open the sliding closet door, it was stuck. I tried everything I could think of but without success. I was sweating and breathing hard, and I couldn't believe that I was trapped in my sister's closet. *Oh, brother! How am I going to get out of this fix?*

"Gretchen," I finally yelled from inside the closet. "Help me! I can't get out."

Of course, she was furious. The whole house heard about my misdeed. Daddy didn't say a word to me, but I heard him complaining about my behavior to Daddy Carl and Mamma Grace. That hurt worse than a tongue-lashing from him.

When Christmas Eve finally arrived, we had to wait to open presents until after the meal and the dishes were done, like always. We had gathered in the living room to await the ritual of unwrapping gifts we already knew about and finding the checks that were hung in the tree. All of a sudden, everything went silent for me and I found myself floating somewhere up on the ceiling, watching myself and everyone else below me. They were talking and laughing and carrying on, but I couldn't hear a thing. It was as if I had been transported to the balcony of a silent movie theater and was watching a film I had seen over and over.

No one ever knew what happened because I didn't tell anyone–it sounded way too bizarre to share. And we didn't share anything with anyone in our family, anyway. Just like I had found a way to survive at school by directly cheating on tests and by indirectly receiving help at home, maybe I had found a way to survive at home too. Maybe I could just disappear.

My growing depression made studying difficult, if not impossible, even if I had wanted to do it, and my concentration eventually became nonexistent. But while I suffered with anxiety and the fear of being discovered as a cheater in school, Deborah flourished there.

As a teenager, Deborah was tall, slender, and graceful–like a model. She wore her thin brown hair at shoulder length with bangs and dressed with perfect style. It became increasingly obvious that the teachers loved her. One time she and I took a homemaking class together. Of course, it was silly for us to make two batches of everything, so each time there was an assignment, like making biscuits and banana bread, we would make both recipes together at home, split them, and then turn them in. The teacher would inevitably give her an A and me a C–the story of my life.

When Deborah decided to join Future Teachers of America because she wanted to be a teacher, like Mother, I decided to join, too, in order to get out of class. The first meeting we went to was out of town. We gathered in a large room filled with future teachers from all over Scurry County. There were about ten of us from our school but we were mixed together and arranged alphabetically as a combined group. When the leader announced that each one of us had to stand up and share our name, grade level, and home town, I gasped. *Is my hair okay? Am I sweating too much?*

Because our last name was "Short," Deborah and I were seated at the back of the room together. *Maybe if I practice I won't be nervous and forget what to say.* I must have repeated this statement a hundred times to myself: *"My name is Daphene Short and I'm a senior from Snyder."* Deborah was sitting next to me, and being the poised young woman that she was, when her turn came to stand and speak she said, "My name is Deborah Short, and I am a senior from Snyder."

When she sat down, I stood up, stretched to my full five foot eight, and ran my fingers nervously through my hair. "My name is Daffney Snort, and I'm a Snior from Sider."

Deborah's head whipped around to look at me in shock and horror. The room started to spin so I sat down quickly, completely humiliated. I could feel my ears burning with embarrassment. In years to come, whenever Deborah and her family called my house they would always say they were looking for "Daffney Snort from Sider." While it was anything but funny at the time, she and I had many good chuckles about it over the years.

Our senior year, we took almost every class together. Deborah was fiercely proud of her academic performance and didn't want her reputation tainted by her twin's failure. So she made sure I did well, one way or the other. Once, after taking a big test, we spent several days in agony because neither of us felt we had done very well. When we got the test results back, however, we discovered that she had made an A+ . . . and I had failed. She had been worried that she'd missed a few questions; I had hoped to have answered a few of them correctly. We had studied together because we had assigned seats in that class—and our seats were not together. I became so accomplished at cheating by choosing to sit by my smartest classmates that by the end of the year, both Deborah and I were doing so well that neither of us had to take finals. What seemed like a great setup early on actually started me on a very destructive path that I remained on for many years to come.

* * *

Gretchen got married in September of 1962 to Jimmy Richardson, a rebound relationship after her high school sweetheart found someone else. I remember that she came home the weekend before the wedding to talk with Mother and Daddy. She looked more stressed than we had ever seen her. She must have been scared to death to tell them what was on her mind. Her thin brown hair fell around her face haphazardly and she seemed even shorter than her five-foot frame usually looked. She sat down and plopped her purse on the table in front of her as she began presenting her case to Daddy.

Deborah and I cracked our bedroom door just enough that we could see and hear the rather heated conversation taking place at the kitchen table.

"No, that's not right, Daddy. Just listen for a minute, would you? I don't love him. I never have. We just don't click." Gretchen coughed and rummaged around in her purse for something to suck on.

"What's not right about it? I am fed up to here with the money I have spent on you girls lately and I'm done. Jimmy can take it from here . . . at least with you." He gestured with his hand like he was cutting his own throat. "The wedding is paid for and the plans are set. And *you* are getting married, young lady."

"But . . . Daddy . . . Jimmy doesn't love me, either. He doesn't want to have a wife."

"Do I need to call and talk to Jimmy about all this?"

"You wouldn't," she gasped at him.

"It's paid for and it's happening. Everyone will be here for it. You are not going to embarrass me, Gretchen. I won't have it."

From our room we could smell her perfume, even over the cigarette smoke that lingered on her clothes. She sat tapping her fake fingernails on the table, a habit that had irritated the whole family for years. It was the first time we had ever heard our daddy raising his voice to her or denying her anything.

"Well, I'm going to bed, then," she said. "See you in the morning before I leave to go back to school." And that was that. Mother never said a word.

Gretchen and Mother had worked hard on wedding plans and everything went smoothly. Several of Gretchen's Tri Delta sorority sisters were in the wedding along with Deborah and me. We all wore knee-length gold taffeta bridesmaid dresses with matching hats, which Deborah and I thought looked like some kind of prairie sunflower that hadn't fully bloomed. After they had been pronounced man and wife and were partway down the aisle of the church, Gretchen turned and looked over her shoulder past me. I followed her eyes to see what she was looking at. It only lasted a split second, but she exchanged glances with her high school sweetheart and the love of her life, and as she did, tears welled up in her eyes. I didn't see them fall because she turned back around and continued on out the door to the waiting car, but I knew. She loved him. And despite everything, my heart hurt for her. After the wedding, they moved to Columbus, Georgia where her new husband was stationed in the army, to begin their life together.

* * *

When we graduated high school in May 1963, we went on another of our famous family vacations–this time to Ruidoso, New Mexico. A few hours into the trip, Deborah took her turn at driving. Daddy was sitting in the front seat with her, and Mother and I were in the back. He glanced at me and then said to her, "I know you both smoke, so go ahead and stop at the next town and buy some cigarettes." The summer before our senior year, we had begun smoking regularly with two of our girlfriends, Helen and Susie. Of course, when Daddy smelled cigarette smoke on our clothes we always denied it, blaming the smell on our friends who smoked instead.

But when he made that statement, I was horrified. And even more horrified when Deborah actually stopped at the next town and came back to the car with a pack of cigarettes. Daddy got out of the front seat and told me to take his place. He climbed into the back seat, and he and Mother watched us as we smoked nonstop for the rest of the trip. I never did really understand how all of that happened–it was so unlike any of us. Deborah wasn't scared of Daddy. I envied that about her and longed to be like her. I didn't understand why I was still so afraid of him.

When it was time for us to head off to college that fall, Deborah chose Texas Christian University where Gretchen had gone. Both girls had been awarded academic scholarships. Both pledged Tri Delta, which was the same sorority that Mother pledged. Deborah excelled in chemistry and had dreams of becoming a doctor. But Daddy's dream for her was to become a teacher so that if she married a coach, she would always have a job. He had her life all figured out.

There was no way I could get into TCU, and even if I did have the grades, trying to keep up with Deborah would have been impossible. After much discussion, Mother selected West Texas State in Canyon, Texas. She knew that they had a good art department and thought it would be a good place for me. And, besides, it was easier to get accepted and the tuition was much cheaper because it was a state college, not a private one like TCU. Canyon was also a much smaller town than Fort Worth, and they both felt like I would do just fine there. We made the 188-mile trip from Snyder to Canyon mostly in silence.

The same day Mother and Daddy dropped me off at college I headed to the nearest store, bought a carton of cigarettes, and then went shopping for a purse—something that would become a passion of mine. I spent my entire month's allowance that first day.

The second day at WTS, I went to my English class. Walking into the classroom made me start to sweat. I hadn't bought my books (because I had already spent all my money), and I felt completely lost during the whole explanation of the syllabus and discussion of the upcoming assignments. I walked out of there in a daze. *Where is Deborah? Who is going to help me?*

I went back to that English class a week or so later and was handed the first quiz. I froze. I had not been back to class since that first day. I had not done any of the reading. I had not heard any of the lectures. I did not know a single soul in the class. My heart was beating a hundred miles an hour and sweat was popping out all over my face. I took the copy of the quiz, wrote my name on the upper right as directed, and sat staring at it, a pen shaking in my hand. I began to respond to the multiple-choice questions just hoping that I could somehow bluff my way through. *They grade on a curve, right? Surely there are others who will do worse than me, right?* But it didn't turn out well for me there. So I didn't go back.

Not long after that, I came down with a severe case of tonsillitis. I had a high enough fever that I was admitted to the infirmary for a week, where the doctor in charge recommended that I drop out of school and go home to recover. The timing was perfect because, just before I got sick, I had sold my meal ticket in order to buy much needed makeup.

I could tell that having me at home was the last thing Mother and Daddy wanted, and they pushed me to go back to school. I refused but tried to find a job to placate them. I didn't have much luck, though, because I had neither training nor experience doing anything. Daddy wouldn't even let me work at Sun Oil Company where Deborah had worked the summer before.

When summer rolled around, they insisted that I enroll in WTS's summer school. I ended up on probation during that summer session and dropped out again. I couldn't quite figure out why on earth my parents were willing to waste their money just to get me out of their way.

In the fall, they sent me to Sam Houston State in Huntsville, Texas to live near Gretchen. When it was decided that I should move close to her, everyone hoped that she could help me enough to keep me in school. And I liked the dorm and thought that with Gretchen's help, I might just make it, too.

They had moved to Huntsville after Jimmy got out of the army so Gretchen could graduate from college. They had presented our parents with their first grandchild–a girl named Dee Dee—about nine months after their wedding, and she was pregnant again before she even went to the doctor for the regular six-week checkup. She had decided to stop taking her birth control pills because they made her gain weight. Their second child's name was Kyle.

After being in Huntsville for less than a month, I found out I was pregnant. The father of my baby was my high school sweetheart, John Weaver, who was currently a junior at University of Texas in Austin. I had been crazy about him since my freshman year in high school, but we had only started dating seriously that summer when he came home from college and I was back and forth from my summer classes.

After I phoned him, he drove from Austin to Huntsville to take me to a doctor in Houston so that we could confirm our fear. Once we got over the shock, we went to tell Gretchen the news.

John Weaver and I walked slowly up the sidewalk to her front door, not saying a word to each other. I knocked twice and then opened it. "Gretch, it's me. You home?"

"Yeah, come on in. I'll be right there," she yelled from somewhere deep in the house. "What are you guys doing here today?" she asked a moment later, walking into the room with her arms full of clothes and her little dog following close at her heels.

John and I looked at each other and then at her. "We have some news."

She put the clothes down on the couch and then sat down by them. "Okay. Sit. What's going on?" Her little dog never left her side and quickly hid behind her leg.

Neither John nor I moved to sit down. We just stood there in her living room, feeling awkward and out of place. "Gretchen, I'm pregnant."

The look on her face said it all. Then she stood up quickly, took two steps toward me, and slapped me hard across the face. I was speechless and so was John. I couldn't even hear what she was yelling at me for a minute or two. Then John took control of the conversation and things quieted down a bit.

We ended up sitting around her kitchen table, drinking coffee and devising our big lie. We would tell everyone that we were already married in order to save them all the embarrassment of the gossip and scandal.

Chapter 3

Many Struggles

*Every wise woman builds her house, but the foolish one
tears it down with her own hands.*

(Proverbs 14:1 AMP)

We started our future with a lie. After leaving Gretchen and
Jimmy's house and feeling confident in our made-up story
about our fake marriage, we went to my dorm to pack up all
of my belongings and then drove all night to Snyder. When
we finally arrived in Snyder before the sun came up, we
stopped at a nearby all-night restaurant to wait until John's
parents would be awake. He wanted to call them before
arriving at their home to break the news. Then we would be
off to see my parents. Plan A was underway.

John called and told his mother we were in Snyder and had
something to tell them. When we arrived at the Weavers'
house my heart was beating so fast I was afraid I would have
a heart attack. I knew how his family felt about me.

We sat at the kitchen table and told them we had eloped
and had been married for several months. I could see by the

look on his mother's face that she was devastated—all of the plans she had for her "perfect" son had just gone down the drain. She opened her mouth to say something and then closed it again.

"Well, Son," his dad began. "This is sure a life-changer for you both. Welcome to the family, Daphene." He got up and came over to me with outstretched arms. I got about halfway up from my chair as his arms wrapped around me.

"Thank you, Mr. Weaver," I whispered, hoping that no one saw how conflicted I felt at his response to our lie. Mrs. Weaver remained seated and silent at this scene. Then she spoke up.

"You two look exhausted. Why not rest up a bit in John's room before you go over to see the Shorts?" It was an awkward scene for a couple of reasons: we weren't married, and we had never been alone in John's bedroom before. I was watching her face as she made the recommendation, while she was watching mine to see my reaction. I think we both realized what was transpiring and tried hard to hide it. John's face, however, was an open book. And his mother had read it easily and often. He was an only child . . . and well attended to.

Neither of us could really rest, so we decided to go ahead and do the next thing on our list. Telling my parents was much different and turned out to be quite easy. Mother had created such a fantasy family that instead of questioning our story, she immediately began planning a wedding shower.

"I want to have enough time, though, Daphene, for both your sisters to be here for it." She had risen from her place on the couch and was pacing in circles around the living room like a caged lion at the circus. "And I want to invite

the ladies from our church . . . and your friends from school
. . . and some of my teacher friends, too." I let her rattle
on about all the plans while I watched Daddy to see his
reaction. He sat in his chair not saying much at all. It was
embarrassing and uncomfortable and John and I were eager
to get out of there, so we rose to leave at the first break in
the conversation. Mother had finally run out of words and
was out of breath when she wandered off to her bedroom.

Now that Plan A was complete, we moved on to the next
thing. Since John was living in an apartment with several
of his fraternity brothers, he called when we left Snyder to
tell them that we had told our parents the news and that he
was bringing me back to Austin. By the time we got there,
they had moved their things into the fraternity house. Our
next task was to actually get married. We needed to plan the
wedding.

I didn't quite know how to go about finding what we needed,
but after some searching, John finally located a church and
pastor who would marry us. It was a large Baptist church
near the campus. The pastor was willing to perform the
ceremony but wanted to meet us as soon as possible. We
got the marriage license and found two of his fraternity
brothers who agreed to go with us to get married, but the
only nice thing I had to wear was a black dress that looked
just like poodle hair. Thank heavens the groom had a suit.
There was no music, but John Weaver had slipped off and
bought me a ring and a small bouquet of flowers to carry.
My "bridesmaid" ended up being Dalton, one of John's
fraternity brothers and our best friend from Snyder. John's
best man was another one of the brothers in the fraternity.
When we all four arrived at the church, we were directed to
a small chapel on the side of the building. John and I were

hardly a picture of joy, but we tried to hide our stress from our friends and the pastor. *Am I really marrying the love of my life? Is this all a dream? Where are my bridesmaids . . . and our beautiful dresses . . . and all the flowers . . . the music . . . and the guests?*

The whole thing took about twelve minutes and when it was over none of us knew what to say or what to do. We didn't even know we were expected to pay the pastor and walked out leaving him empty handed. It was just the beginning of our not knowing what we didn't know.

There we were, four college kids on a hot but beautiful September afternoon in the great college town of Austin, Texas. We should have been planning a tailgate party or something fun with our friends before the biggest thing happening that day—the University of Texas football game. Instead we stood outside the pastor's office at the church trying to figure out what we should do to celebrate our "wedding." John and I decided that we should grab some barbeque (all we could afford), and his fraternity brothers were off to the big game. We went "home" to the apartment to start our real marriage off with no jobs and no money. John Weaver's grandmother was not only paying for his college but also for all of our living expenses.

When we finally told both sets of parents that we were expecting a baby, they all seemed pleased and surprised . . . at least on the outside. And we were relieved that our Plan A had worked so well. This baby was going to be the first grandchild for the Weavers and they were very happy about it.

John desperately wanted to continue to be a "fraternity man," so we attended the fun parties they had at the frat house for a while. But when I began looking pregnant, I felt out of place there.

"Why do you care if I go without you, Daphene? If you don't want to go, fine." This was his irritated response to my hesitations.

"Why would you want to go without your wife?" was my more irritated reply. His resentment grew as the months went by. He began to realize just how much being married was changing his life and ruining his dreams for the future.

We ended up living in Austin for the next ten years. That first year, we traveled to Dallas once a month because John was in the Marine reserves and had to go there for training. I was so thankful that Deborah agreed to let me stay with her at the sorority house during John Weaver's time at the base, because I was miserable at home by myself. John was either in class, with his buddies, or doing his "Marine thing." I was left alone to clean the house, do the laundry, shop for groceries, cook the meals, and throw up in between each one. When I was with Deborah, I pretended that her life was mine. It was a weekend-a-month kind of fantasy. But in reality, they were dressed in their sorority finest and I wore my maternity clothes, which were cheap and never very cute. I always felt that Deborah was embarrassed about my condition even though she never said a word about it. She was preoccupied with this guy she had met.

Deborah met Ron Hall on the campus at TCU. She was attracted to his good looks and happy-go-lucky approach to life, and she was awed at his courage–he rode bulls. He said that her looks caught his eye, but it was her voice that captured his heart. He tried to imitate her sweet southern twang over the years and gave everyone a good laugh with his attempts. After being "just friends" for a while, Ron was drafted and went off to boot camp in Fort Polk, Louisiana, and then to a permanent duty station in Fort Carson, Colorado. They wrote to each other over the next couple of years to stay in touch.

* * *

By the time our baby arrived, we had moved from that first apartment to a cute little one-bedroom house. Deborah Denise Weaver was born on May 25, 1965. I never considered naming our baby girl after anyone but Deborah. John didn't resist and offered the name "Denise" as a middle name because it was a name he liked even though it had no family connection. Because she was two weeks late, the timing of our wedding and the birth didn't seem off by too much, if anyone was counting.

John Weaver bonded with Denise from the very beginning. He adored her and couldn't keep her close enough during those early months. Because he was an only child, I suspected that he had received as much attention as a child could withstand. He talked to Denise in the sweetest voice I had ever heard, which made me long for him to talk to me that same way. And I wondered why my daddy hadn't talked to me like that. No one had ever talked to me like that.

When John bathed her or changed her clothes, he seemed to be in a completely different world. He kissed her little face and giggled at her yawns and stretches until I thought I would scream. I wanted to have what they had . . . but I didn't feel it. I was numb.

I struggled with the duties required to care for a baby–so many more things to do in my already overwhelming life. I began to sleep more, and binge eat, and cry secretly at odd times during the day. I had no idea that I could be suffering from what is now called postpartum depression. I felt ill-equipped to be a mother, I was depressed most of the time, and eventually I just gave up and let John do the parenting.

When John Weaver's grandmother bought us a mobile home to live in shortly after Denise was born, I was overwhelmed again with the task of moving all our stuff. But somehow it all got done. We settled in to get John through school and to care for little Denise.

It was about this time that Mother sent me a check for $10,000. I was so excited that I could hardly hold the check—my hands were shaking so badly. Mother had convinced Daddy Carl and Mama Grace to disperse some of the money she would inherit early and to share it with us girls. Her note stated that this was the first installment they had set up in order to lessen the inheritance tax burden. It was like rain in the desert to us.

One day, out of the blue, Deborah called. We didn't talk regularly and hadn't seen each other for quite a while.

"Daphene, I just got off the phone with Daddy. They are forcing Mother to retire. Can you believe that? I mean, after all she has done for those kids and the other teachers . . ."

"What?" I asked, surprised.

"Daddy said that they weren't going to fire her but force her to retire."

"Are you sure? That seems so odd."

"The principal told Daddy that the kids were out of control in her classes and that she was just getting stranger and stranger."

"But Mother isn't retirement age, is she?" I pressed Deborah. "How old is Mother?" I couldn't imagine my mother without a school to go to and kids to teach.

"The kids in her class are putting tacks in her chair and she sits on them every time, like it's the first time. Can you imagine?"

I couldn't. And I could. Mother had not been right for a while but I just didn't have the energy to think too much about it. I was using up my complete supply of fuel to get through each day of motherhood, with none left over for anything else.

"I'm going to Snyder to help Daddy figure out what to do. Can you come?"

"Are you kidding? What is Daddy going to do? Fight the principal for her job?"

Deborah drove to Snyder and she and Daddy took Mother to Scott & White Hospital in Temple, Texas for a complete checkup. The doctors diagnosed her with advanced senility, although now her condition would be called Alzheimer's. Deborah called me from the hospital when Daddy was in Mother's room with her.

"She's not doing well at all. In fact, she reminds me of Mama Grace the more I am around her."

"Oh, no," was all I could say. The memories came flooding back. For as long as I could remember, Mama Grace hadn't been right. *It must run in the family. I shouldn't be surprised. Will it happen to us, too?*

Daddy was horrified at the news. We both knew how hard it was going to be on Daddy because we had experienced the life he was facing when Mama Grace and Daddy Carl visited. Daddy Carl did his best but it was not easy. What both women had needed was a loving caregiver. I think Daddy Carl tried.

But instead of being helpful to Mother, Daddy began to resent her for being sick and ruining his dreams for retirement. Their lives began to change rapidly as Mother deteriorated. She began to gain weight, and every time we visited them, her symptoms were worse. She spent her days lying on the couch in the den watching TV and eating. She went from the beautiful and confident young woman from Poplar Bluff to a pitiful, overweight, confused, and frustrated old woman—not even sixty years old. She had lost all of her grace over the years, and it broke my heart to see her like that. We took turns visiting them to help out, but none of us knew how it was when we weren't there and assumed that Daddy was making it worse for her.

* * *

For three years we lived in our two-bedroom mobile home, which I grew to hate. Life was a struggle, partly because we had no money and partly because John and I blamed each other for what was happening to us. He constantly pressured me to try to find a job. I stubbornly resisted because I had never had a job before and didn't feel qualified to do anything. I finally started filling out applications and landed my first job interview at a department store in downtown Austin. It was one of those "process" interviews—I had to meet with several people over a couple of days. I did pretty well talking with the people, but when the last person I talked with told me that I would have to take a "simple" aptitude test, I thought I was going to pass out on the spot. Instead of following her directions to the testing room, I started crying, got up from the chair, gathered up my stuff, and headed for the nearest door without saying a word. I came home empty handed from that ordeal and John Weaver was not happy. I tried to explain that I couldn't do it.

"Well, why not?" he asked.

"Denise needs me," I said, trying to sound convincing. I didn't want to leave her—that was the truth—but I also didn't want to tell John how I panicked and fled from the interview.

"We need the money, Daphene. Don't you get that?"

"Denise needs me . . ."

"Just find a job. Period."

I went out looking again every day for the next week or so and did finally find a job at a truck stop taking orders for vehicles that needed repair. It wasn't far from the mobile home park, so I wouldn't have to drive far to work. Because John wasn't passing any of his classes and we desperately needed more money, he finally just dropped out of school. His mother was furious and felt his problems were because of me. And when John had trouble holding down job after job, she blamed me for that, too. Somehow everything was my fault. I could feel her vibes across the miles: *John married the wrong woman.*

Many of the problems John and I had resulted from my depression and his inability to take responsibility for our family. It was obvious to anyone watching that neither of us was equipped to be a spouse or a parent. The decisions we had made were certainly taking their toll on both of us and on baby Denise.

* * *

In February of 1966, when Denise was about nine months old, I got a call from my mother.

"Daphene." That was all she could say. I gripped the phone in my hand and waited for her sobbing to subside. "Oh, Daphene," she tried to go on. "It's Daddy Carl. He's gone. He died this morning. Oh, Daphene."

I was stunned. *Daddy Carl . . . dead? Could Mother be wrong . . . just confused?* I couldn't hear a thing or move a muscle. It was as if I had turned to stone. And that stone was heavy, pulling me down into a place I had come to know. It was a dark and lonely place; it was a quiet place where I could cry without restraint, or scream, or sleep the sleep of death, or die myself.

I could feel myself going there, but I could not stop it. It always started first with heaviness in my chest and numbness on my face–like an x-ray blanket being placed over me, smothering me internally, making me claustrophobic. Then dullness would creep up from my feet, filling my whole body with dread and despair. I would go into a kind of deep sleep for days at a time–sometimes lasting a week or more. Those who knew about these times referred disdainfully to them as my "spells"–as if I had chosen them over facing life.

When I got off the phone with Mother, I called Deborah. She told me that Daddy Carl had been driving in his car heading to a meeting that morning when he had a brain hemorrhage. The wreck was not a pretty scene. I tried not to imagine it.

I was still in my "spell" the next day when Mother wired money so that I could go to the funeral. She wanted us there. She wanted the *three* of us there–all of her daughters. Mother somehow managed to rise to the occasion and flew ahead of us to help make arrangements for the funeral. She wanted us to meet Daddy in Snyder and drive with him to Poplar Bluff. So Gretchen drove from Sam Houston State College at Huntsville to Snyder, leaving her husband behind to take care of Dee Dee and Kyle; Deborah drove from TCU in Fort Worth; and I drove back home to Snyder from Austin, leaving John Weaver to care for Denise.

Seeing Daddy's condition was a shock. He had always been so tall, so strong, so forceful. When I opened the screen door and stepped into the house, he rose from his chair and met me in the middle of the living room.

"I'm so glad you came home, Daphene." He put his hand gently on my shoulder and stood there for a moment, looking at me. He seemed reduced, vulnerable, and timid in a strange kind of way.

"Daddy," was all I could say as I stood there so close to him. I finally asked if Deborah or Gretchen had arrived yet. They had, but they were out together filling the car with gas and picking up some snacks for the road trip. We girls took turns driving but other than that the 650-mile trip went by in a blur.

Seeing Mama Grace without Daddy Carl was like seeing the beach without the ocean. Something about the emptiness of the house, the quietness of the neighborhood, and the stillness of the whole town that week created in me a gnawing desire to choose my own casket, crawl in, and shut the lid, to sleep away the remaining years of my life. At the cemetery, I looked around for a spot near Daddy Carl.

Driving up to the house after the funeral was startling. I hadn't noticed it earlier but the beautiful house that Mother had grown up in had really deteriorated. The grass was overgrown, the gate of the wrought iron fence was broken in a couple of places, and the paint was chipping around the front windows.

After the funeral service, burial, and reception were over and all the friends and family members were gone, Deborah and I slipped off to tour the house with new eyes. Daddy had gone to get some sleep in one of the guest rooms in the basement where it was cool, and Gretchen wandered outside to the backyard's overgrown garden to smoke. It was obvious to Deborah and me that things had not been right around their place for some time. What we found proved us right.

We discovered dozens of gallons of milk frozen in the freezer. When they stopped drinking so much, instead of stopping the delivery service or cutting back on their weekly order, they just stacked the glass bottles in their chest freezer in the garage. We also found a chicken that had been baked at some point and just left in the oven. It was long past the smelling stage and looked more like it had been worked over by a taxidermist to preserve it for posterity.

We left Mama Grace lying on the brocade sofa in their living room with Mother sitting next to her in the chair by the fireplace—both asleep—so we felt comfortable exploring the bedrooms on the second floor. We had been in our mother's childhood room before, but it had been years ago when we were younger. Her parents had kept it for her, just the way she left it when she moved to Edinburg to teach school. The cleaning lady had been instructed to keep it usable, with clean sheets and dusted furniture, at all times. We smelled the Old English furniture polish when we opened the door and entered.

Her room was filled with beautiful pieces of furniture, some purchased before she was born and others handed down through the family. Several chests contained glass-enclosed shelves holding engraved silver dishes that Mama Grace had moved from the dining room into Mother's room for some reason. A thick dark rug covered the hardwood floor. The mauve bedding and drapes matched perfectly with the flower pattern in the rug. A huge wooden bookcase that held old books and the china doll collection that Mother had so cherished covered one whole wall. Deborah and I both stopped just inside the door, trying to take it all in.

"Do you remember how to open the *other* door?" I asked Deborah. I felt like we were characters in a Nancy Drew mystery novel.

"Of course I do." We both moved toward the closet together and went in. Hanging clothes had been replaced by stacks of boxes—all labeled—and a pile of extra bedding, which was not even folded, just wadded up and dumped. Deborah moved a couple of things and found the handle. The little door opened into the secret room and we stooped to enter. At some point in the house's history, a small section of the attic had been turned into a secret room for Mother, and she had moved in all her special treasures. Most of them were still in the trunk. We had seen them before, but we wanted to see them again—her paintings, her diaries, and her jewelry collection. We were lost in our memories when we heard Mother call for us from downstairs. We closed things up and went downstairs quickly.

Daddy Carl's death and funeral were hard on both women: Mother had not been doing well even before, but Mama Grace was doing worse. And now she was even more distraught, confused, and almost unmanageable. It was obvious that she could no longer remain in the house without someone to help her, and the cleaning lady was not the level of help she would require. Deborah and Daddy decided that Mama Grace had to be moved to a nursing home in Snyder so that Mother and Daddy could help care for her. Mother and I agreed. It took the rest of the week to make all of the arrangements.

* * *

I returned home with such great emptiness that I feared I would implode. Thoughts of suicide were just below the surface of the slow boiling stew that was my mind. Sometimes I blanked out completely and came to awareness screaming in front of the mirror in our entryway. When I stopped, I would hear in the background the screaming of another. It was Denise. Hours would have passed since I checked on her. I needed help.

I finally found a psychiatrist who offered some relief. After hearing my complaints, he explained to me that I was suffering from depression. The word depression had never been uttered to me by anyone, so I thought that I was the only one in the whole world who had these spells.

"Your grandfather—you called him Daddy Carl?—was the anchor in your life, Daphene. When he died it altered your psyche to the point that, if I understand your description of things, you feel like you are being sucked into a deep hole that you can't get out of. Is that right?"

I nodded.

"I can prescribe a pharmaceutical to help you sleep at night, another one to keep you awake during the day, and, best of all, one to help you with symptoms of what you call your spells."

I nodded again.

I left his office, filled the three prescriptions, and went home. My heart remained heavy from disappointments and fear and worry until the effects of the pills began to take hold. I was desperate for relief and hoped that they would make me "normal," somehow. But what I found was that they became a kind of relief *from* my life and the source of great guilt *for* my life. I began to feel like all that was left of me on the outside was a shell. And the inside was all darkness and trembling. Even with the pills I became less and less able to function as a wife or a mother. We were a house of miserable ones.

I remember picking up little Denise from the babysitter's one day, dragging myself home from my job at the truck stop, sticking an infant feeder in her mouth to stop her crying, and then putting her to bed—without changing her diaper or her clothes. There were days when she would stand up in her baby bed and cry to be picked up. But all I could do was stand in the doorway of her room and scream and sink lower and lower into that dark place that was my life.

But things were not always like that. We had spans of time—several months here, another couple there—that John Weaver and I tried to create around us the semblance of order and normalcy.

John Weaver had finally landed a good job at a large insurance company and started working hard at it. He seemed to enjoy it for a while and managed to keep that job and do well for several years. So well, in fact, that we were able to sell the mobile home and build a home in a nice neighborhood in Austin. I loved the name of our street: Tulsa Cove. It sounded so . . . family, so . . . middle class, so

. . . normal. We planted shrubs under the windows in the front yard of the one-story brick house and a big tree by the sidewalk leading to our front door. It was a little more than we could afford, but with his steady job and me working we thought we could make it. We even joined a small Baptist church and eventually made some friends there: Barbara and Milton Holloway. Barbara seemed different from anyone else I had ever met and I was immediately drawn to her. Our hearts connected and she seemed to love me for who she thought I was—not who I thought I was or pretended to be. She somehow made me feel good inside, even hopeful, about something yet beyond me.

The Holloway family became a model for me because I had never experienced anything like what they had. The husband loved his wife, and she loved him back. Both parents loved dearly and cared tenderly for their two daughters. They talked. They laughed. They hugged and went shopping and to the movies together. I was awed. And I wanted what they had. I didn't know how to show them what they meant to me, so I baked the cinnamon rolls that they all had come to love and spent some Saturday mornings with them, eating and talking and laughing.

John managed to stay with this company for several years and did well. Unfortunately, he finally lost that job, and for nearly a year he didn't do anything but stay in bed and sleep. He didn't want anyone to know that we didn't have money, so we continued spending as if we did. From the very beginning of our marriage, either his parents or mine rescued us with "loans" and gifts of cash, thousands of dollars at a time. We always had nice things and lived beyond our means at their expense. Instead of trying to find a way to pay our bills, he would just throw them in the trash with the comment, "No money—no can do." That seemed to work for him . . . but I was the one getting all the calls at work from our angry creditors. It didn't work so well for me. So what money came in went out just as fast. The $10,000 from Mother was gone, and John's wages were gone, and his job had fallen apart, and we were right back where we were before. John was growing increasingly unhappy. There was no way we could manage on my small salary.

"John, you need to find *another* job—and stay there," I insisted. But whenever this conversation began, he would just get up and walk out the front door, slamming it shut before all the words were out of my mouth. And on and on it went.

Until 1967. That's when I finally got my first real job. It was at Southwestern Bell in Austin, Texas. I think the only reason they hired me was because they liked me, not because I did well on their testing; I know I didn't, but I had forced myself to take it anyway. I was so happy to finally have a good job, a *real* job, as John always called it.

I was surprised one day by a phone call from Daddy.

"Daphene, how are you?"

"Fine, Daddy. How are you and Mother doing?" I tried to hide the shock in my voice. He had never called me before.

"I heard about your job at Southwestern Bell. I knew you would turn out to be a company woman. It's a good job and I expect you to stay there and make a go of it. I want to have at least one child that follows in my footsteps and retires with a gold watch." He laughed at his own statement and I tried to, too.

"Did Deborah tell you about it?" We chatted for a few minutes longer and hung up. *Daddy proud of me after all these years? Can it be?*

* * *

Ron Hall had returned to Fort Worth in 1968, and he and Deborah began dating seriously. Then in July 1969, they got engaged and set an October wedding date. Deborah had already graduated from TCU, and they decided to get married in Fort Worth because all of their friends were there. Deborah did a wonderful job planning the wedding and reception. I was delighted that she wanted me to be in the wedding, even though we weren't that close. Gretchen, however, pulled her normal stunt and refused to be in it–still separating herself from anything Deborah or Daphene. Mother and Daddy attended, of course, but were more like guests than family. Daddy had just retired from his career at Sun Oil Company and was trying to figure out how to take care of Mother and have the kind of retirement he had always dreamed of. He spent his time at the wedding trying to make sure that she didn't wander off or do or say something strange.

I had just learned that we were expecting another baby, but I wasn't sick and I wasn't showing yet. Deborah looked beautiful and so happy and I was excited for her, but I couldn't help feeling a little envious that I hadn't had a "real" wedding like hers. She had already begun teaching elementary school in Fort Worth. Ron was finishing up his degree by going to school at night and learning the business of investment banking during the day. They were going to live a normal life, the kind I could only dream of: she went off to school each day and taught beautiful little children how to read; he went off to work every day and helped rich men spend their money.

When Ron finished his MBA and began selling expensive paintings to even richer people, they bought their first home and moved in high society. When I talked to her on the phone every few months, she filled the space between us with the social news in Fort Worth and the fun things she was involved in. But it wasn't long before they moved to Dallas, where Ron's art business was booming. While it flourished there, Deborah didn't. She and Ron had become Christians and had developed close ties with a group of like-minded friends in Fort Worth. She was determined to make a home for her family in Dallas, but her heart never quite made the move from Fort Worth.

* * *

My pregnancy went smoothly and John Kevin was born on April 6, 1970, right before Denise turned five. He was an easy baby to care for and I was managing my depression much better during that time. Denise wasn't all that crazy about sharing her space with a little brother but that seemed reasonable to me—I had experience with that. She wanted her own room and her own stuff, and she didn't want anyone bothering her.

Denise began to withdraw and keep to herself much of the time. On the other hand, baby John Kevin had come out smiling and made us both smile right back at him. John Weaver continued to blossom as a father. I both admired and resented him for that. I really did.

After being in a nursing home for four years, Mama Grace died in Snyder on June 26, 1970. She always told Mother that she wanted to be buried near Daddy Carl in Poplar Bluff, so arrangements needed to be made. Mother was distraught and unable to make any decisions so we were thankful when John Weaver's uncle, who owned a small plane, offered to fly her to Poplar Bluff if one of us would agree to fly with the body. Of course, I was chosen for the trip.

When I got to the small airport outside of Snyder to meet the hearse, I was shocked to see Mama Grace's body on a stretcher covered only by a white sheet. My seat on the plane was right beside her. I was scared to death that if I fell asleep my arm would fall over on her, so I made myself stay awake the whole time. I never once looked under the sheet; I just couldn't.

When we arrived at the airport, someone from the mortuary was there to meet me and take the body. I rented a car at the airport and drove to the cemetery because I needed to wait until Mother arrived before we could figure out what clothes Mama Grace would be buried in. I walked right to Daddy Carl's grave without any trouble and sat down on the grass nearby. I missed him terribly and longed to have him hold me in his arms and tell me how much he loved me. No one had done that since he died. No one. He had been my rock and no one had taken his place.

With Mama Grace's death, things began to change for Mother and Daddy. Mother had inherited a lot of money and even got brave enough to buy a mink stole for herself that Daddy hated. Daddy eventually did talk her into buying an Airstream trailer with some of it so they could travel. That had been his dream for retirement—the two of them driving around the countryside. And they did for a while. A couple of times they went to Arizona to stay for a month or two in a campground during the winter, but those trips were a nightmare for Mother. She did not fit in with the campground crew and was so confused about everything. Daddy pressured her to act normal and made it miserable for them both. Deborah and I both could see that she was much worse after each trip.

The summer after John Kevin was born, Barbara Holloway, the woman in our neighborhood I had become friends with and who attended our little church, invited me to go with her to some special meetings at church. I was attending service on Sunday mornings but hadn't really gotten involved and hadn't joined the church. I usually sat next to Barbara in the second row of pews on the left if John wasn't with me.

That first night, after the pastor introduced the special speaker and I heard his voice, something inside me awakened. I sat spellbound, wanting to catch every single word he said. Even though the language he used was not familiar to me, something in my heart resonated with it. As little girls, we had been in church every Sunday at the Methodist church with our parents. We were expected to pray before meals . . . *Thank you for the food we eat* . . . but that was about it.

But when the speaker asked the congregation to be in prayer for those who were there without a Savior, I knew I had become the object of their prayers. So in those quiet minutes that followed, I silently prayed to accept the Savior, Jesus Christ, as my own—not really even knowing what all of it meant. I knew there was an emptiness in me that needed to be filled. I wept that night in a way I had never wept before. Since John had been raised in a Baptist church, we joined the little church as a family and continued attending until we moved to Houston.

While we were still in Austin, I got a call from Deborah one day that shocked me.

"Daphene, do you know what I just found out that Daddy did? He sold our house in Snyder. Did you know anything about that? I mean, how could he do that so quickly and without any of us knowing about it? Did you know about it, Daphene? Did you?" She seemed frantic.

"No. I didn't. Why did he do that?" A vision of our house passed before me, and I wasn't sad that I might not ever have to go there again.

"They are moving to Kerrville, for heaven sakes. I asked Daddy why there and he told me that he saw a sign that read 'Lose your heart to the hills' one day and thought that sounded nice."

"Oh, good grief. What in the heck is happening to Daddy?" I said.

"He told me that Kerrville was considered truly a Hill Country paradise because it was located in the heart of the Texas Hill Country. Can you believe that?"

"Who does he know there?" I asked Deborah, trying hard to comprehend all she was saying. "What about all of Mother's things? The furniture and paintings and dishes she got from Mama Grace? I'm gonna call Daddy and see what he says."

Before I could get him on the phone, though, he called me. I didn't get a chance to ask him all my questions because he had called to tell me how proud he was of me that I had been promoted.

"I ran into a couple of my men from Sonoco and told them about you being promoted to the Assistant Manager at Southwestern Bell, and they sure were happy for me." His voice had softened. His heart was changed. He told me he loved me before he hung up the phone. I had gotten no answers to all the questions that were rolling around in my head. But my heart felt so good.

* * *

When Denise started kindergarten, a friend of mine agreed to pick her up on the first day of school so I didn't have to pack John Kevin up just to take her. The first day of this arrangement didn't go so well. My friend honked her horn—like we had arranged—as the signal for Denise to go out to her car. But Denise didn't want to go. The scene was not a pretty one: I was holding John Kevin and Denise was holding me around my leg and wouldn't let go. I had to drag her along to the front door where my friend finally came and picked her up, still screaming.

This happened day after day, but I never thought for a minute that this was harming her in any way. I tried to comfort her by telling her, "Yes, you have to go to school, but everything will be okay and you will come home soon." And it was still happening when John's parents came to Austin to visit us before we moved to Houston.

I always liked his father but his mother and I had never really gotten along, and our time together was tense under the surface. This daily scene with Denise was upsetting to her. The morning before they left, John's mother sat me down at the kitchen table and proceeded to tell me that because of the way I treated Denise, my daughter didn't think I loved her. She knew that was why Denise was so withdrawn most of the time and having trouble going to school.

"Daphene, can't you see that Denise feels left out? She doesn't feel loved by you. Don't you see that, Daphene? Surely, you do."

I sat stunned and embarrassed but said nothing.

"I've talked to John about this, too, and he agrees," she went on. "I just think you had better make some changes in this house or you are going to have a very troubled teenager to deal with one of these days."

Make some changes, yes, right. Changes. Easy for you to say.

After she left, I sat and thought about what she had said. It broke my heart to think that Denise didn't know how much I really loved her. She didn't know how many times, after a very miserable day, I had knelt beside her bed while she was sleeping and wept because I wasn't able to show her how I felt. I didn't know what else to do, so I got up and went into her bedroom. She was sitting cross-legged on her bed playing with her Barbie dolls. "Sweetheart, do you know how much I love you?" She looked up at me and big tears immediately filled her eyes and ran down her cheeks. I sat down beside her and put my arm around her shoulder. "I need you to forgive me for not being the kind of mother that you need," I whispered through my tears. She crawled into my lap and we hugged and cried together for a long time.

* * *

Gretchen and I both had children and Deborah wanted her own. After no success in getting pregnant, Deborah and Ron finally decided to adopt. When they were notified that a young girl who was pregnant was considering giving her baby up for adoption, they were thrilled. Because there were no guarantees that the mother would actually go through with the adoption process, Ron and Deborah delayed doing any serious decorating in the room that would become the nursery. They didn't want to be disappointed.

But on May 8, 1973, they got the call they had been waiting for: a baby girl had just been born and the young mother had signed all the papers. Ron and Deborah were beside themselves with joy and wanted John Weaver and me to help them get things ready for her arrival to their home. Deborah had bought a new outfit for herself—a "new mother" outfit—and they left the house like a couple of kids off on a trip to Disneyland, with their new camera ready to capture as many memories as they could. We drove to Fort Worth, and while they went to the hospital, we put the baby bed together.

As they approached the house upon returning from the hospital, Ron began honking the horn—he wanted everyone in the neighborhood to know that something spectacular had just happened at the Halls' house. Seeing them as parents was amazing. They both looked so calm and at ease, and I had never seen Deborah so happy. She had longed to be a mom and now their prayers had been answered.

Regan Elizabeth Hall was a healthy and adorable baby with a head full of unruly black hair. Deborah tried everything to tame it, but without success; she finally gave up and bought lots of very cute baby hats to match her outfits until it grew out enough to deal with.

After getting Regan, they set in motion the necessary paperwork to adopt another baby. A few years later they adopted Carson David Hall. He was born on August 11, 1976 and was the cutest baby ever. He spent his first year with his little head buried deep into Deborah's embrace. We thought he must have been born shy, but he could have just needed the love that his new mother was eager to give him. Now the Hall family was complete. And Deborah had replicated the pattern that Gretchen and I established: a daughter born first and then a son.

* * *

We were thrilled when John finally got a big job with a dental company in 1977, though it meant that we had to move to Houston. It did not take long to find a great house to rent, but we ended up buying a house right down the street from it a year later. Our new house had a big backyard and we had our first microwave oven. I would cook all of our meals on Saturday and Sunday, and then the rest of the week we ate ready-to-serve meals that I could warm up in the microwave every day. The schools were close by, the kids quickly made friends, and we all fell in love with the house. Those first several years in Houston were the best of our marriage because we were both working and spending only what we made.

I was so thankful that I was able to transfer with Southwestern Bell. It was there that I met Sue Langston. Although Sue was small, only five foot two, she had a strong will and robust personality. I admired her tremendously because she had the organizational skills that I longed for. With Sue's constant encouragement, I grew professionally and eventually became a supervisor after just a couple of years. But there was lots of competition in our office for "best in sales" and "best in service." I began to work longer and longer hours. The pressure was building for me to produce more and more results. Even with Sue's encouragement, I suffered from grave insecurity and struggled to keep up.

One morning as I walked into my office, I became so overwhelmed by everything that I began to cry. And I cried and cried and cried until I was totally out of control, nearing hysteria. Sue found me in the bathroom sitting on the floor.

"Daphene! What in the world . . . ?" She sat down beside me on the floor and asked again. "What's the matter, honey? Did something happen?"

"I . . . uh . . . oh, she . . ." I offered, but nothing I said made any sense. It was like babble coming out of my mouth. She struggled to get me to our supervisor's office and then they both had to help me into her car. "It's going to be okay, soon. Just hang in there, Daphene." My hysteria was nearing convulsions.

The emergency room doctor contacted my personal physician, and together they got me settled down enough to go home. I spent the next six months at home trying to recover from what they termed a "nervous breakdown." My doctor diagnosed me as suffering from manic depression and put me on lithium. It was somewhat of a relief to finally have a name for the kind of unhappiness I had been suffering from for most of my life.

After a week or so at home, I called Deborah to fill her in on what was happening in my life. And I wanted to know how she was getting along with her two children. By that time, Regan was four years old and Carson was not quite one. When I got off the phone that day, I had the picture in my head of the perfect Dallas family: Father went off to work; Mother stayed home with the children; the bills were all paid . . . and all was right in the world.

I was off work for six months with disability leave. Oddly enough, it turned out to be the happiest time in our whole marriage. The lithium evened me out, John's job was going well, and the kids were flourishing under the calm roof of sanity that covered us then.

I purposefully planned menus, shopped, and cooked for us during this time, and the kids and I folded clothes together and planted flowers in the yard. I wanted so badly to have the storybook family that I thought everyone had but me.

We did some very fun things together, too, as soon as I started feeling stronger. We purchased running clothes and on Saturdays were off laughing as the kids and I trotted behind John, trying to keep up with him. John loved to make miniature airplanes, and we would venture out to the country and watch in much anticipation to see how high they would fly. Because of John's success with his company, we even won a couple of trips, which were so much fun for a couple who hadn't taken vacations. I was thankful that John's parents were available to care for the kids while we were gone. After six months, I returned to work and was welcomed back with open arms. All seemed right in my world now, too—at least for the moment.

But not so with Gretchen. Over the years she had become addicted to prescription drugs and her husband had become a full-blown alcoholic. Seeing how miserable they all were, I supported Gretchen in her decision to finally divorce him. She had stopped teaching, so when she left him, she needed a job. I was concerned that her problems with prescription drugs might be so bad that she couldn't get a job with Southwestern Bell, but she scored high on the entrance test and they hired her on the spot. I was so happy for her. Unfortunately, her instability kept her from ever being promoted.

Battles between Gretchen and her teenage kids grew fierce. It was obvious that they were all in pain, but I began to resent how they treated her. It was beyond the normal rebellion of late junior high or early high school behavior. I had my own life to try to navigate, so I tried to steer clear of theirs. Gretchen was just too much for me to deal with.

But then in 1979 everything changed again for us. John got a promotion and we moved to Atlanta, Georgia. I was fortunate that my boss in Houston had watched me become a strong supervisor for Southwestern Bell and I worked hard to make my transition to Southern Bell in Atlanta an easy one. The first person I met there was Gail Walker. Not only did she work for me, but she also became a very dear friend. Gail and her family welcomed me into their family with open arms. Her dad had been with Southern Bell for years and was always there for support when I needed it. And I did need it, both at work and at home, because for some reason John and I could not recapture the good times we had left behind in Houston. With each year, our relationship deteriorated a little more.

About a year after we moved to Atlanta, I found myself so lonely that one rainy Saturday afternoon I went to the mall. I found a chair off by itself, next to a large planter with tall overhanging leaves, and just sat for a couple of hours watching the people. John was gone again for the weekend—in Louisiana this time—for a special training class of some kind, Denise had spent the night with a friend and was going to the movies with her, and John Kevin was playing over at a neighbor's house for the afternoon. I felt like I had no one at all.

The mall was busy as people hurried by, most of them not even seeing me. I searched for friendly faces in the crowds but found none. I closed my eyes for a while and when I opened them again I saw a man and a woman walking toward me. For a minute I thought that maybe I knew them, or they knew me. They were holding hands and chatting easily with each other, smiling and swinging their arms—almost like they were dancing. They came so close to my chair that I could smell her perfume. But they walked right by without noticing me at all. My heart ached. I wanted what they had. I needed that . . . *John hardly touches me anymore.* She wasn't all that pretty, and she was even a little overweight. But I could see that he loved her anyway by the way he looked at her. *I wonder if I were prettier or thinner if my husband would love me that way.* I left the mall carrying a heavy heart and a preoccupation with my looks that would last well into the next decade.

* * *

I hadn't seen Mother and Daddy in a while but heard through Deborah that they had moved from Kerrville to Luling, Texas where Daddy had grown up. According to her, he was getting more and more forgetful and losing a lot of weight. She said she was as worried about him as she was about Mother.

Then one evening Deborah called me. "Daphene, I just got off the phone with Mother. She is totally beside herself and I'm afraid that she's going to injure her shoulder again if she isn't careful."

"Is she still in the rehab place?" I asked.

"She told me that Daddy had come to visit her, and they had a fight over something and he hit her. Can you imagine that? Right there in the rehab center?

"With his fist?"

"No, with his walking cane! The nurses had to come and help settle her down and then called me for her."

"Is Daddy still there?"

"No. I've gotta go. I'll keep you posted. Does this never end?"

I waited all night for another call, sleeping on and off on the couch. Deborah called me the next morning to let me know what was happening. The previous night, she had contacted a couple of the family members that still lived in Luling to see if our father had made it home yet. There had been no sign of him. So she decided to call the police to see if he had been in an accident or something. In the morning, she finally discovered that he was in jail. He had been stopped because his car was weaving in and out of traffic and he had been drinking a beer. Deborah told me she was leaving immediately to drive to Luling.

The next time she phoned me, she said that he looked absolutely pitiful and had no idea what was going on. She bailed him out of jail and took him straight to a doctor, who advised Deborah to admit him into the same hospital in Temple where they had originally taken our mother, because they specialized in treating advanced senility. After a couple of days and numerous tests, the doctor told Deborah and Daddy that he was already suffering from an advanced case of Alzheimer's.

Then she called again. "Daphene, this should not be a surprise . . . but it is. Now they both have it."

"You're kidding, right? Is it contagious? I can understand Mother getting it because of Mama Grace–but Daddy?"

We discussed how we should have known long before this. I guess because Mother was so bad, we didn't notice how bad Daddy had gotten. Deborah said she had a plan and would keep me posted but wanted me to come and help if I could get away. I couldn't.

So Deborah went back to Luling, had Mother released from the rehab center, and then went to their new place to pack up as many of their clothes as she could. I knew she needed me with her, but I just couldn't get off work at the time. I was sorry that she was the one having to make all of the decisions and do all the work. It made sense, though, because Gretchen was way too fragile emotionally to be of any help, and I was still suffering from depression and trying to hold down my job.

Because Mother and Daddy were both incapable of taking care of themselves any longer, the doctor recommended that they go directly into a nursing home. Unfortunately, Deborah needed time to get everything arranged for them. She called and said she needed to have them fly to Atlanta so that I could keep them until she found a nursing home for both of them. I agreed because she needed me to. No matter how depressed I was, she needed me.

When John Weaver and I went to the airport to pick them up, we were both shocked to see how much they had changed. It broke my heart to see my strong Daddy shuffling as he walked and needing help carrying his bag. The minute he saw me, we both started crying and he hugged me like he never had before. I knew that something had changed in him—something that allowed him to love someone beyond himself. I think he was seeing me for who I was for the first time.

On the second day at my house, Daddy and I were having our morning cup of coffee at the kitchen table when he stood up suddenly, pushed his cup back, spilling what was left, and said, "I'm going home. Thanks for the coffee."

"Daddy, you're staying with me for a while," I shot back as I jumped for the dish towel to wipe up the coffee before it ran onto the floor. "Sit down and I'll get you some more."

"I said that I am going home!"

About that time, Mother came around the corner and into the kitchen asking for some breakfast. "Where's the eggs? I thought I smelled eggs."

Oh, good grief. "Mother, I'm not cooking eggs. Do you want something else? What do you like for breakfast?"

"Well, Virginia, I'm going home," he shouted, louder than he needed to and using a name he never had before. Mother wasn't deaf and she looked at him in double surprise.

"Home? Aren't we home?"

"Daddy, why do you think you need to go home so soon? You just got here yesterday, so please sit back down and let's get Mother some breakfast and be together this morning. Can't we do that?"

No matter how hard I tried, I could not get him to listen to me. Mother wandered back into the living room and turned on the television without eating anything. Daddy went to the guest room where he was sleeping to pack his few things back into the suitcase he had brought with him.

I picked up the phone and dialed Deborah's number.

"I can't do a thing with him! I mean it. He is bound and determined that he is going home. What do you want me to do?" I was trying to speak softly so that neither Mother nor Daddy could hear me, but the tension was building and coming out in my volume.

"What do you want *me* to do from *here* is the question, Daphene. I mean, *really*, can't you distract him or something–try to change the subject–get him interested in something else and maybe he'll forget. He forgets everything else, for heaven's sake!"

"Do you want to try to talk to him, Deborah? Because I have tried and he is not listening to me."

"No, I don't. But I have found a place for both of them not far from our house. It's the nicest nursing home in the area, so go ahead and just buy him a plane ticket back to Dallas and I'll get him settled. Then we can deal with Mother next."

I felt relieved about Daddy going but was terribly worried about Mother. She was like a stranger to me. Her eyes were blank and her voice was tight, like she had just had her tonsils removed. Her hair was so thin that her scalp seemed to glow.

I was home by myself and trying to get them both ready for the trip to the airport so that Daddy could get "home." I told Mother to stay in the living room and watch television and not move until I came back for her. Then I grabbed Daddy's suitcase and followed him down the back stairs into the garage to get him settled into the front seat and the bag in the trunk. I had just loaded Daddy's luggage into my car when I heard Mother screaming.

Our house was a tri-level and the stairs from the main floor into the garage were steep. Mother had tried to follow me and had fallen halfway down those stairs. She was crying and in terrible pain. "Oh, Mother! Here, let me help you." I scooted her around and propped her against the nearest wall, then ran for the phone.

"Daphene! I don't want to be late for my flight!" was what I heard Daddy yelling as I dialed 911.

He was still yelling this at me when I called Deborah. "Good grief, Daphene. Was that too much to ask of you–to *just* get Daddy to the airport for me? I should have flown out to Atlanta myself and picked him up." I knew what she was thinking: *This would never have happened on my watch.*

I loaded Daddy into the car and followed the ambulance to the emergency room at the nearest hospital. The x-rays showed that Mother's leg was broken, and because she was already suffering from senility, the doctor told me that surgery would only make her worse. They checked Mother into the hospital and I took Daddy back to my house.

When I called Deborah back to update her, she said she would arrange for both of them to be transported by ambulance to Fort Worth to see what the doctors there said about surgery for Mother. She was anxious to get them checked into the nursing home she had found, too, and so was I. *So much for my help.* I ended up causing Deborah more trouble than anything. *Will it always be this way?* I didn't mean for it to happen, but now all of the responsibility for Daddy and Mother's care fell on Deborah's shoulders. She didn't complain, though, and I noticed it. She got them settled into a nice nursing home and did the best she could to run her own household while caring for Mother and Daddy. *You are one amazing woman, sister.*

* * *

By early 1982, John and I were barely speaking. Something seemed very wrong. And it was. The night before my scheduled hysterectomy, Denise, then sixteen, came to the hospital to see me.

"Hi, Mom. How are you doing?" I looked at her when she came in, but she didn't look at me. She was letting her hair grow out and her bangs covered part of her face. She seemed a little out of breath.

"Is your dad here, too?" I asked, not knowing if I wanted him to be or not.

"Mom . . . uh . . ."

"Pull that chair over here, Denise, and sit down by me. I'm nervous about the surgery."

When she had gotten settled, she started in again. "Mom, I have to tell you something. But I don't know if I really should or not." By this time tears were running down her face.

"What?"

"I think my dad is seeing someone else, Mom. I found . . ." She drifted into silence.

I opened my mouth to ask a thousand questions but nothing came out. I sat up in my hospital bed and made a move to get down. Panic was rising in my chest, but I didn't want Denise to see me in a full-blown meltdown.

"Mom, I found a letter in Daddy's briefcase. I was looking for something else for him and found this." She rummaged in her little purse and pulled out a wadded-up piece of paper. I took it from her and leaned back on my pillows while raising the head of the bed to a more upright position.

"Close the door, Denise," I ordered. My voice sounded like a stranger's to me. A calmness settled over me in that moment—the kind that lets you brace yourself for whatever is coming—the kind of dullness that keeps your mind from knowing too much too quickly.

I scanned it and then crumpled it up into a ball and threw it across the room. I knew our marriage was in trouble, but I had no idea that he had someone else in his life. Denise was never one to be nosy, and I could tell that what she had found devastated her. It devastated me, too. I couldn't look at Denise. I tried to breathe. I tried not to cry.

The surgery ended up being so complicated that I stayed in the hospital for ten days. John didn't come to the hospital to see me and I was glad he didn't. I don't know what I would have said to him. By the time I got home, everything and everyone had changed. I could see it in their faces that "it" had been discussed and was somehow "settled." I moved into the guest bedroom and stayed there longer than I should have, feeling paralyzed and trapped inside my life with no way out.

John was continually gone on business trips, but I no longer asked where he was going or what he was doing. And he never offered to tell me. I got up each morning and made the kids breakfast. I packed their lunches and took them to school. I came home and wandered around my own house, looking in all the rooms for signs that could tell me what was going on in their lives. I tried to eat, but nothing tasted good. I tried to sleep during the day, but just tossed and turned in a kind of in-between world where conversations were held among people I didn't know and couldn't see. I tried to walk in the neighborhood, but couldn't stand the obligatory "Hi, how are you?" from the nosy neighbors.

I fought hard to take one day at a time, but lost the battle. The pain was mounting. One day while John was out of town, I felt the pain so acutely that I knew it had to stop by any means. I took a handful of my lithium and climbed into the bedroom closet and locked the door. I was crying hysterically inside the closet when the kids came in from school. They both were terrified since they knew that was where John kept the gun he took hunting. It wasn't loaded, but they didn't know it. Denise ran to the neighbor's house for help. The neighbors called John to tell him what had happened, and he told them how to get in touch with my psychiatrist. The doctor told them I needed to be admitted to a psychiatric hospital immediately. They somehow coaxed me out of the closet and into the car.

After I was admitted into a psychiatric hospital, I lost all sense of time. The pain became a dull ache that I carried around inside me from room to room as I wandered the halls there. The counseling sessions with the doctor began after the first week and continued each day for the next two weeks. He was a nice man, and the sound of his voice soothed me. Just before leaving, he handed me a new prescription and said, "Daphene, this new medication should help your mood swings more than the last one did. And you need to remember that most married people go through hard times. These things have a way of working out."

"I know you are right. Other people do just fine . . . and so can I."

When I got out of the hospital and returned to work at Southern Bell, I decided I needed to file for divorce. John seemed relieved when I told him that I had taken the step because he would never have filed himself, even though living with a depressed wife for so many years had completely emptied him of any feelings for me. He refused to discuss the letter with me but, he agreed that I could continue to live in our home for several more months while we went through all the paperwork and the required waiting period in order for it to become final. And then I would leave.

He seldom talked to me unless we were exchanging harsh words. Then we would fall into prolonged periods of silence. Denise was in high school and John Kevin was in sixth grade, and neither of them was happy with how our family was functioning. I could see it in their faces and hear it in their voices. What would have been happy times for normal families were instead times of arguing, then silence, followed by separation and loneliness.

I had loved John Weaver since high school and lived with him as his wife for over seventeen years, and I just didn't see a life without him. A couple of weeks before the divorce was to become final, something snapped inside me. I was at work and out of nowhere I began to feel numb and detached—both inside and out—speaking without thought, moving without plans. I walked out of my office, telling my employees at the Phone Center, where I had been assigned, that I needed to go home for a few minutes and would be right back. I returned to my office and picked up the phone. I called my psychiatrist. And he answered—which had *never* happened before. I spoke to him briefly and he insisted adamantly that I come straight to his office. I hung up the phone and walked out the door and drove home.

Without thinking about what I was doing, I pulled my car into the garage and shut the garage door with my motor still running. I went into the house and up the stairs to my room. I found an old prescription of sleeping pills and took all that remained. Once I swallowed them, I felt a kind of

relief that the intolerable pain I carried around would soon
be stopped for good. And I was no longer afraid to die. In
fact, death looked good to me. I returned to the car without
asking God to forgive me; without writing the customary
"goodbye letter" that so many people do; without crying
over leaving my children. It was just me, and the pain, and
the longing for it to stop. I sat in the dark of my car, with my
eyes closed . . . breathing deeply . . . listening to the hum of
the engine . . . and then I drifted off to sleep.

By the grace of God, I woke up back in the psychiatric
hospital. My doctor had called John right after I hung up
and actually reached him. He almost *never* answered his
phone. But he did that day. The doctor told him that I was
in great danger and that he should find me immediately.
John came looking for me. And found me still in the garage
with the car running and the garage door closed. If the
doctor hadn't answered his phone, or if John had not been
in town and answered his, I know that I would have died.
I had not planned to do it. It had just unfolded before me.
And it *almost* happened.

Chapter 4

More Troubles

I am overwhelmed with troubles and
my life draws near to death.

(Psalm 88:3)

While recovering in the psychiatric ward from what was described as "profound depression with serious suicidal tendencies," my doctor, along with treating my emotional and psychological issues, decided to put me through extensive testing to see what was preventing me from learning. The day before my testing, he stopped by my room to talk to me about it.

"Daphene, we've talked about a lot of things, haven't we?"

"What do you mean?" I asked, not sure I wanted to have this conversation with him.

"Well, I think underneath a lot of your sadness and self-loathing there is an identity issue. I don't think you really know who you are or what you are capable of." He waited for a response. "I . . . I don't know," was all I could say.

"I have a question for you to consider before we do the testing tomorrow. What will you do if we discover that you're not stupid?"

When I left the hospital after a three-week stay, I met with my attorney again about the upcoming court date for the divorce hearing. He was furious that I had been in a psychiatric hospital and told me not to mention anything about it to the judge. So, on June 6, 1982, John Weaver and I signed the papers that ended our eighteen-year marriage. I remember being so nervous that all I could hear was ringing in my ears. Because we lacked the money to have separate attorneys, I signed the document without reading one word of it. I was given custody of both Denise and John Kevin and he was to pay child support.

The kids and I moved out of our home and into a little rented house. John stayed in our beautiful home and said that I could take anything I wanted, but once I left, I couldn't come back to get anything else. I did take a few things but couldn't think clearly enough to plan it out and then carry it through. He made sure he was not home when I came to get our things. I took an extra bed, several antique pieces of furniture that my mother had given to me, some of the dishes and cookware, the kid's furniture, a couch, a chair, and a table for us to have in the kitchen.

It was obvious to me that he didn't care what I took because he was planning to refurnish the house with his new wife-to-be. I hunted for a couple of things that I really wanted but couldn't find them: an antique pocket watch belonging to Daddy Carl and several things my mother wanted me to have.

It was a terrible time for me and the kids. I was working but broke and depressed. I had no energy to make the new house a home for us; instead, I began operating in a desperate kind of survival mode, not even caring that our windows had no blinds, our floors had no rugs, and our fridge had no food in it most of the time. The kids were seventeen and twelve and were often left to fend for themselves.

Several months later, a girlfriend called and asked if I wanted to go out for a while that evening. I jumped at the chance to escape my pain and said yes. John Weaver and his girlfriend were now officially engaged and planning to get married. I was suffering, so getting out of my empty house actually sounded wonderful to me–a time to leave my miserable life at home and be with people who didn't know me, people I could have fun with for a few hours.

But a few hours turned into all night. What caused me to do that without even calling home to check on the kids will forever be a mystery, even to me. They went from concern to fear to panic and ended up calling their dad, who came over immediately, packed up their stuff, and took them home with him.

The next morning when I walked in the door, my little house was completely empty of all their things. My devastation was complete. My dreams were shattered and my failure was final. I had lost my husband and my beautiful home; now I had even lost my precious children. For the first time in my life, I was utterly alone–the kind of aloneness that makes your heart race, your mouth dry. The kind that makes the world seem tilted, like everything is sliding sideways, out of control and into chaos. I needed something to hang onto so that I didn't slide right along with everything else even deeper into the hole I had come to know so well.

The kids now had their dad all to themselves. I heard from several mutual friends that Denise was managing the house just fine and had taken on the role of temporary mother to John Kevin. The three of them were close as a family and, from all accounts, doing great without me.

When John remarried, it rocked Denise's world. John Weaver's affection and attention were diverted to his new wife and she usurped Denise's position in the house. John Kevin had bonded with her, but the entrance of a new woman into the picture left Denise feeling unwanted and unneeded.

But John's parents welcomed his new wife into the family with open arms. She was a five foot bundle of energy with lots of things in common with their son, and they loved the happiness that their son and grandson just could not hide. I know it must have been hard for Denise to share her dad with his new wife, because she loved taking care of her brother and her daddy. I can only imagine how hard it was for that woman to be in the middle, trying to do her best to bring all the family members back together. Things were changing for all of us.

One night, sitting alone in the dark and watching TV, a commercial came on that listed the telephone number of a church hotline for people needing help. *Well, I sure fit that description.* I picked up the phone and dialed the number. As soon as the person answered, I started in about the terrible mess I had made of my life: I told her about the divorce, losing my children, my house, and almost my life. I was sobbing and talking all at the same time, barely taking a breath, desperate to get it all out in hopes that, once out, the pain would stop. When I did pause just for a minute near the end of this tirade, the nice lady on the other end of the line announced that she was only the answering service and asked if I would like one of the pastors to call me back. I was horrified and slammed down the receiver without responding, feeling utterly humiliated.

When I collected myself a bit, the only thing I could think to do was to call Deborah. I punched in her number. And waited. The first ring. Nothing. The second. Still nothing. When she picked up on the third ring, I began blurting out my miseries again, so incoherently that she didn't even recognize my voice. I knew that she didn't approve of the way I was living my life—I had seen it in her face the last few times we had been together, which wasn't often, and I heard it in her voice every time we talked on the phone. But I needed to talk to her more than I cared about how she saw me. I needed her to tell me that everything was going to be okay. I needed her to tell me she loved me and would help me.

"Daphene, listen to me carefully," she began once she realized it was me and that I was out of control. "You didn't really think that you could get away with this kind of living, did you? Don't you know that God has seen every last little thing you have thought, said, or done? Good grief, Daphene. You drove your husband into the arms of another woman. You left your kids alone and then lost them. You have tried to kill yourself more than once. What do you expect when you carry on the way you do?"

"Deborah . . ." I sobbed.

"Do you know what the word 'repent' means, Daphene? It's your only hope for any kind of life worth living. Have you repented for the terrible way you have been living your life?"

I could hardly breathe, much less talk. There was a long pause.

"Are you still there, Daphene?" she prodded, then went on without knowing if I was or not. "The Bible says if we confess our sins, He is faithful and just to forgive and cleanse. That's what you need—forgiveness and cleansing. For heaven's sake, Daphene, get down on your knees this very minute and confess your sins." In that moment God seemed far away and my accepting Jesus seemed a distant memory, but I quickly complied—falling hard but not really feeling the pain. She went on speaking to me and I listened, there on my knees, my whole body bent over until my head rested on the floor, sobbing wildly. I managed to get out a few words before I hung up the phone, more devastated than I was before I called her.

After I stopped crying, I sat in a chair, numb, almost until dawn. My mind went back to the conversation I had with my doctor after being released from the hospital. He had called me in to follow up on the tests I'd taken while I was hospitalized several months previously. He explained to me that I had scored very high in intelligence and that I was creative and capable of much more than I seemed to realize. That whole conversation seemed like it had taken place in a kind of echo chamber because I didn't quite grasp what he was saying. *Intelligent? Me? Impossible.* If it were true, then I would have to figure out a whole new way to live, because I knew how to do "dumb and stupid" pretty well. And I continued to prove it by the way I was choosing to live my life. A long-term lie has much more power than a new-found truth. So I continued, for a while, to believe the lie.

* * *

Later that year, I met a man named Michael while managing three service centers for Southern Bell in Atlanta. I had moved out of the little house where I had lived with my kids and into an apartment to try to get myself together enough on the outside to be able to do well at work. Michael was tall, physically fit, and had beautiful blue eyes. What struck me the most, though, was his heavy German accent. He had come into the store on business. I flirted with him a little and then he left the store with the phone he came in to purchase. When he returned the next day, he asked me for a date. I was thrilled.

One date with Michael turned into another and another until, after a short time, he finally moved in with me. He told me that he was from Germany and that he was in the country on business. I guess that was enough to explain why he only had one suitcase and a rental car. Our only friends were his boss and wife who were also from Germany. They spoke German most of the time when we were all together, which made me a little uncomfortable.

It wasn't long before he invited me to go with him to Florida on a short business trip, and I jumped at the chance. I arranged for the time off from work and we were off on our first adventure together. The first night there, while out dancing, I fell and severely reinjured the same ankle that I had injured in high school. The doctor in the emergency room said it was so bad that it would require immediate surgery if I ever wanted to walk on it again. I was horrified. There was no way I was going to have this surgery in Florida, so the next morning we headed back to Atlanta; I was propped up in the back seat in extreme pain and full of narcotics to get me by, and Michael was just driving along as if nothing had happened.

The surgery was a complicated tendon transplant that made the recovery much longer and more painful than I thought it would be. And to make matters worse, my boss at Southern Bell was furious that the long weekend trip turned into a whole month away from work. My position at work seemed to change after that. I had lost my passion for the job.

So, about six months later when Michael asked me to marry him and move to Germany, I was ready to escape what felt like four walls closing in on me. He said he would make all of the arrangements and take care of getting my furniture moved to our new home overseas. That sounded so good to me at the time.

I called my kids and told them what my plans were. They didn't seem to care one way or the other. And I called Deborah to tell her about Michael. She was not happy. By this time my family and friends had all but given up on me ever having a normal life. I was alone and moving to a foreign country with a stranger who was about to become my husband. *What am I doing?*

But the morning the movers arrived to pack my stuff, I woke up with a severe migraine headache. It was so bad that I had to have a friend take me to the emergency room to get a shot. I asked Michael to have the movers pack all my things except what I had set aside to be stored in Atlanta. I didn't want the family treasures inherited from my parents and grandparents moved out of the country because I was saving them for my children. In addition to the inherited pieces, I had also set aside my watercolor paintings for storage in the states. I hadn't painted anything since John and I moved to Atlanta, and I treasured those last pieces along with those I'd done in high school.

When I eventually woke up after sleeping most of that day, my apartment was completely empty except for my couch and the bed I was sleeping on. Michael was gone. Everything in the kitchen was gone. All the family treasures were gone except a small box of jewelry that was tucked under my bed. Even most of my clothes were gone, including a mink jacket that belonged to Deborah. I was dumbfounded—and hung over from all the medication. Two days passed with no word from him. I didn't know what to do and I didn't call anyone. I went to work and I came home. I paced the empty house, alternating between fury and despair.

When he finally showed up on the third day, I came unglued.

"What are you doing? Where are my things? What is going on, Michael?" I demanded.

He stood just inside the door where I had pinned him with my questions. His smugness was beyond irritating.

"I've decided not to move back to Germany, but don't worry about your things—they aren't worth worrying about. And I really don't want to discuss it with you right now, Daphene."

My jaw dropped but no words were there. He tried to step around me to enter further into the house but I stopped him cold.

"Listen to me, Michael. The only thing that isn't important to me right now is you. Now get out of my house this minute or I will call the police."

He spun around on his fancy European shoes and walked out the front door, slamming it behind him. I heard his car pulling away but didn't look out. I was stunned—frozen in my tracks—unable to think at all. It took me days to grasp the fact that I had lost everything . . . again. Everything.

The police, during the Interpol investigation, discovered that Michael was wanted in several states for doing to other women what he had just done to me. The most shocking thing discovered was that he was still married to a woman in Chicago.

I came home one late afternoon from work, sat down on that sofa, and took stock of my life. There I was, living in a nearly empty apartment, going to work day after day, and coming home to nothing night after night. I don't remember even hearing from my kids during that time. It felt like someone had put me on a slow-moving treadmill and I was aimlessly walking my life away—and getting nowhere.

John and his new wife were busy getting on with their lives together. They had John Kevin involved with sports and kept busy entertaining his friends. Denise was now in a sorority at Brenau, a girl's school in Gainesville, Georgia. She had met and was dating a man named Greg Jones and there was talk of them getting married. Life seemed better for both of my kids without me.

When Michael was finally found, he was arrested and put in the county jail near where I lived. Unfortunately, my belongings were long gone and the prospect of getting them back was bleak because his signature was on the form that authorized my furniture and boxes to be sent to Germany. I was told that in order to try to get them, I would have to get a court order. *How could this be happening to me? Deborah was right.* She had told me over and over again that as long as I kept making bad choices I would continue to suffer these harsh consequences. *Will it never end?*

After about a month of living like this, a friend from work set me up with a blind date. Gary lived less than a mile from the apartment I was living in, so we decided that our date would be for drinks at a nearby restaurant. He was tall, slender, and easy to talk to, but he didn't share much about himself. We dated for a while and then I moved into his apartment. Living in my empty apartment was devastating and it seemed the easiest thing for me to do. Nine months into our relationship I began to worry that he would leave me, too, so I started talking about getting married. I got caught up with planning an outdoor wedding gala with catered food and all the trimmings to be held at a friend's house.

My children came to the wedding and had to be introduced to their new step-father. Deborah showed her disappointment by choosing not to attend. The only ones who came were some of my Atlanta friends and girlfriends from work. My closest friends who knew me well saw right away that we were not right for each other.

One of Deborah's sorority sisters, Patty, was married to a Methodist minister who agreed to marry us. It was obvious he didn't approve either but was nice enough to do the ceremony anyway. Once the big "party" was over, I couldn't believe what we had done. We didn't really even know each other that well.

One Sunday afternoon after a late lunch, Gary sprawled out on the couch and said, "I have always wanted to move to the North Carolina Mountains, build a log home, and work from there. I think the time is right. Let's take a trip to Balsam Mountain next weekend so I can show you the place I found."

"What? How can you work from there, Gary?"

"I have put it off long enough and I'm done waiting."

"What about me? What . . . ?"

He had purchased a piece of property several years before and was excited to see it again and show it to me. The drive was nice but I was not prepared for what I saw. Mountains. Trees. Wilderness. I was speechless. We turned left at a gas station and headed up a very steep incline. After about a half mile up the mountainside, he stopped the car and announced: "Here we are. This could be our new home." It was in the middle of nowhere.

It was summertime when we made that first trip to the mountains and there were people scattered throughout the area. Getting away and making some new friends sounded really good to me. I had recently been promoted into a position at work that was way over my head and things were a bit shaky for me there. When Southern Bell announced an early retirement plan in 1985, I jumped on it, even though the funds wouldn't be paid out until I reached sixty-five.

We went back to Atlanta and began making arrangements for our future move to the mountains. Gary wanted to begin building as soon as possible and I needed to find a part-time job to work at until the log house was completed and we could make the big move to North Carolina.

I came home one day, shortly after starting that part-time job, and discovered that our apartment had been burglarized. That box of jewelry that I had collected over the years—the one that had survived the Michael ordeal—was gone. And a $20 gold piece that hung from a solid gold chain that my mother gave me from her grandfather was gone, along with several nice pieces of jewelry that John Weaver had bought me over the years. All gone. They were worth over $10,000, but priceless to me.

Neither Gary nor I had renters insurance. In one short year, I had managed to lose absolutely everything from my past that I treasured. With the loss of that box went the last touch with my past. I felt completely set adrift.

A couple of days after the theft, one of my friends called to say she was concerned with how I was taking the loss of my jewelry. My response was very hateful. "One day when you lose everything you love, call me and we'll talk," I snapped back at her. She quietly responded, "But, Daphene, the one thing that no one can steal is your heart."

I knew that Denise's relationship with Greg Jones was still going strong but was surprised to realize not only was she planning an October wedding, but all of the plans were being made without a certain person. Her mother. I had only been in the North Carolina Mountains about a month when the wedding invitation arrived. The date was set and I was invited. *I'm invited? I am the mother of the bride . . . and I'm just invited?* I called to talk about her plans–I needed to feel a part of it somehow.

Deborah flew in for the wedding, which was held on October 19, 1985. She and Ron were in the middle of negotiations on a 350-acre ranch along the Brazos River outside of Fort Worth that they were really excited about, but because Denise was her godchild, she didn't want to miss it. Gary, Deborah, and I stayed with friends in Atlanta since I was no longer living there, and Denise was still living with her dad and his new wife when she wasn't at school.

I had been left out of the wedding plans completely. John, his new wife, and her family had done everything a mother should have done with her daughter. I was sad beyond words. And seeing John Weaver broke my heart all over again. His presence spoke failure to me. John Kevin was polite to me but didn't seem to miss or need me.

And poor Denise. *Now I know why God abhors divorce. It is the children who suffer.* Her wedding should have been a glorious event, but she was showing signs of great stress. The look on her face when she saw Gary reaffirmed that she was not okay with our marriage. After all . . . my kids didn't really have a chance to get to know him. And it was hard for Denise to introduce her dad's new wife and family to those in my family they hadn't met yet. Greg had his work cut out for him in trying to make sure everyone met everyone else—his parents and four brothers were all there for him. But there were still factions and sides and awkward groupings of people whenever we gathered. At least Denise was marrying into a big happy family. The Jones family hadn't suffered from divorce as her family had.

She looked beautiful as her dad walked her down the aisle that morning. From where I was sitting, I could see both of their profiles and was struck at how much they resembled each other. Their thick dark hair looked like it had been selected from the same batch in heaven. As the pastor began the wedding ceremony by addressing Greg and Denise, she started crying. Then the tears turned to audible sobbing that could not be overlooked. The pastor paused, assessed the situation, and changed course. He began to talk about the tears we have as a gift from God to be used freely whenever needed. As he shared with them in a more personal way there at the altar, Denise was able to relax and focus enough to make it through the remaining ceremony. But it was not the wedding she had longed for.

At the reception I felt more than ever like a guest and not the mother of the bride. The awkwardness continued as groups were gathered for wedding pictures. Since John Weaver was paying for the photographer, he took charge of arranging everything for them. There were to be no pictures of Denise with her mother and her father together. There would be no pictures of our original family: father, mother, daughter, and son. There was still just too much pain for all of us. But Denise was the one suffering the most.

I was so appreciative of John's new wife and her family for working so hard to make the reception nice in spite of the tension. They had spent so much time on the decorations, and the homemade food was far better than any caterer could have provided. My comforter at the wedding was Deborah. She tried hard to stay by my side so that I wasn't standing alone with Gary; she was gracious in her interactions with John Weaver, his new wife, and her family; and she tried to make Gary feel welcome even though I could tell she didn't approve of my marrying someone so different from me. She wasn't comfortable with him as my husband.

"I really don't want you to go back to Texas yet, Deborah. I wish we had more time."

"I wouldn't have missed Denise's wedding for anything—I love her so much, I really do," was her reply.

"She loves you, too, and I know it meant so much to her that you came." I tried to hide my tears but wasn't having much success. *I don't want to be alone. Please don't go.*

* * *

We did move to the mountains but we only lasted about nine months there. What Gary thought of as his lifetime dream was a dreadful nightmare for me. All of those friendly people that were on the mountain when we moved in were long gone. Those people used their cabins in the mountains to get away from the summer heat of Florida or New York or Texas. There was one family who lived above us that we occasionally socialized with. Other than that, the mountain was desolate.

I spent my days there making apple jelly and pickles and cooking big meals that I enjoyed far too much, causing me to gain almost twenty pounds in no time. Gary spent his days working. He was in sales for his company and if he wasn't on the phone setting up appointments, he was gone to meetings that lasted all day. His territory covered an area within a three-hour drive of our place.

Our log cabin had an open floor plan. The only door in the entire house was to the bathroom upstairs. Our bedroom was even open–like a loft. This would have been fine for a weekend get-away, but it did not function well as a home. Gary hated that I made noise while watching TV, and the large mountain across from ours prevented me from getting more than one channel. But I bought earphones that plugged into the TV and sat on the edge of the bed and watched it anyway. In the morning I watched cartoons and in the afternoon, soap operas. This way of life was one hundred percent different from anything I had ever known living anywhere.

Gary was growing tired of the routine his company imposed upon him and began talking about making another move. He hadn't developed into the mountain man that he had envisioned and had grown tired of the solitude, too. I pushed for a return to Atlanta and was thrilled when we decided to move back. Our wilderness life was just not working out.

I set out eagerly to find another "real" job as soon as we got back, which I did quickly. It was at MCI in the sales department. After working only a week, my manager informed all of us new employees that we would be "tested" to see if we would actually be brought on full time. If we didn't pass the test we didn't get the job. Simple enough for most people there. But not so simple for me.

My old fears came rushing back upon me like a big wave in high tide and my test anxiety tossed my whole body around. I hadn't taken a test by myself since the seventh grade. I tried to calm myself down, though. *The doctor did tell me that I wasn't dumb or stupid, didn't he? He did say that I was smarter than I knew and could probably do a lot more than I could imagine, didn't he? Is it possible? Can I do this?*

I tried to talk to a new friend in my training class, Linda Davis, but her response proved she really didn't understand the depths of my fear: "Don't worry," she offered, "the test will be easy." She had no idea that there was not a test on the planet that would have been *easy* for me to take.

The only person that would truly understand my problem was Deborah. So I called her. I was surprised at her sweet response to my cry for help.

"I tell you what. I will let my prayer partner, Patricia Chambers, know what you are facing, so that while you study we will pray for you when we run together. In fact, she has been praying for you for a long time and that's no small thing. She is a *powerful* prayer warrior."

"Oh, Deborah, that would be so wonderful. Thank you, thank you. And tell your friend I am so touched that she would care for me that way."

"When you go in to take that test, I want you to remember that 'He is able,' because He can do anything–especially when you can't." Something had changed her attitude toward me. She encouraged me and prayed with me over the phone and told me not to give up.

But that whole week before the test was tortuous for me. I went over the material again and again but couldn't remember one answer to the next. To make it through the week, I took pills to keep me awake during the day and pills to help me sleep at night. I tried to pray . . . tried to believe that God would help me. And no matter how scared I was, how defeated I already felt, I could not give up because I knew that Deborah and her friend were praying and that God was on my side in this battle because of them.

When test day finally came, I walked into a room filled with people young enough to be my kids. I was holding on to God with all my strength, though, and made it through with the second highest grade in the class. I couldn't wait to get on the phone and tell Deborah the news.

Within a couple of months I was the top salesperson in the department. And when they awarded me a plaque with my name engraved on it, I truly felt like a miracle had occurred. Deborah was always the one who walked across the stage to receive the awards. That first year I was voted into the Chairman's Circle of top sales performers. Something new was happening with me, too.

Back while working at Southern Bell, I had attended a workshop on time management put on by LTS/Time Systems. As I listened to them teach, I began to see for the first time that there was something that could help me organize information and manage my time. Something began stirring that day. It was a new way for me to work and I loved it. I had spent my whole life completely disorganized. I could feel God moving in my heart and drawing me to be brave enough to call the company that did the training. That was my first revelation from God.

So I called them. They said they weren't hiring. So I called them again in a month. They still were not hiring, and the rumor was that they didn't hire female trainers. But I persisted this way for several months until one day, I got an interview. I had been at MCI for a year and had been very successful there. I felt so strongly that I was to move on to the next thing . . . whatever it was. I just couldn't give up.

I started my new career at LTS/Time Systems in 1987. I was so excited about the opportunity to finally do something that seemed to be growing in my heart, something that I felt good about, something that was good, in a new way. I was the only woman in the sales department, and during those early days on the job I felt on the outside of the all-male sales team. But over time I made friends with two men, Bob and Mark, and at least felt welcomed by them. It was the beginning of a lasting friendship. I surprised myself during this time by just taking things as they came without freaking out. I knew that it didn't really matter how these people felt about me because I was where God wanted me. For three years I worked hard, grew a little bolder, and gained some knowledge that would impact my future.

While good things were going on at work, nothing much good was going on outside of work. Mother and Daddy had been moved to a Dallas nursing home near Ron and Deborah's beautiful new home in Park Cities, not far from downtown Dallas. Our parents had not adjusted to the change and were continuing to degenerate, both mentally and emotionally.

Then trouble with the divorce decree from John Weaver surfaced. If I had retained an attorney of my own back then, or if I had read the decree carefully before signing it, I would have discovered that it was my responsibility to pay half of all college expenses for both kids. When I found out, I was not too distressed initially because my parents, right after the kids were born, had purchased an insurance policy that covered the cost of college for both of them. But while we were living in Austin and before John found a job, he forged my name on both of the policies and used the money for other things. I never knew where the money went; just that it was gone, the policies cancelled, and the heavy burden of helping to pay for two kids to go to college was placed squarely on my shoulders. And, to make matters worse, the divorce decree also stated that if the children "elected" to live with their father, I would be responsible to pay child support—to him. And he wanted it. Retroactively . . . all of it. At first I thought that once the judge heard my story about the "missing" insurance checks, I would not have to come up with the money for their college expenses. It was never that I didn't want to help them with college costs; it was just that I didn't have the money.

Gary and I were still married, but very unhappy. I knew in my heart that marrying him was another one of those bad decisions. He didn't understand me at all, and I didn't relate to him, either. His silence had grown irritating and sometimes embarrassing. But there I was—married. I wanted this marriage to work somehow. I did not want to be divorced again.

And I was horrified when the payroll department at LTS notified me that my wages were being garnished. John Weaver was after his money, so I hired an attorney to help me, and the fight was on. I needed a miracle. I needed a couple of miracles.

5
Chapter

At Anaheim

"For I know the plans I have for you," declares the LORD,
"plans to prosper you and not to harm you,
plans to give you hope and a future."

(Jeremiah 29:11)

I answered the phone on the third ring. It was a busy time at work, a troubled time at home, and I was feeling a little frazzled. "Hello, this is Daphene. How may I help you?" I was still loving my sales job with LTS/Time Systems and when the phone rang I was hoping that a client I had been trying to reach about training was calling me back. After a previous eighteen-year career with Southwestern and Southern Bell, I found being in sales was something I really loved–a whole new career for me. After many years of searching, I felt like I had finally found my true gift.

"Daphene, do you have time to talk a minute? I have a great idea for something that we need to do together. There is a conference in Anaheim I want you to go to."

That my twin sister, Deborah, called me at work surprised me because we usually just talked on the weekends. Our last conversation was about a church she found for me in Atlanta, like the one she went to in Dallas, called the Vineyard. I had never been in a Charismatic church before—it was unlike any Baptist or Methodist church that I had ever attended. The people were so free to love each other and the music brought out a depth of emotion that was unexplainable. I attended regularly and felt like the messages preached from the pulpit each Sunday morning could have begun with the phrase, "This word is for Daphene Jones."

"What? What are you talking about, Deborah? I'm at work. How are you, anyway? What's going on?" I stood up from my chair, pushed it back, and edged my way around to the front of my desk so I could shut the door and talk in private. "What conference—when?" I closed my eyes and turned my back on the rest of the world to talk with my twin.

"You've been going to that Vineyard church I found for you, right? Haven't they been announcing this national conference in Anaheim for months now?" She went on, "And I really want you to come with me. I'm anxious for you to meet some of my friends from Dallas and Fort Worth who are also going."

Just thinking about meeting her friends caused many of my insecurities to surface. Deborah's life was very different from mine. She lived in luxury, and I didn't have two nickels to rub together because Gary hadn't had a job since we moved back to Atlanta; I was the only one working at the time. The thought of being around her and her friends for a whole weekend shook me like the first tremors of a small earthquake in the earth's core.

I had heard about the conference—my pastor, Ron Wallace, and his wife Dianne had become good friends of mine and were planning to go—but I hadn't even considered going myself. There was no way I could afford the cost of the conference and the airline ticket. My mind raced ahead as I wondered who the "friends" were and what my already angry husband would say about me running off to California with my sister, leaving him to fend for himself. Living with Gary for the past five years had been difficult for both of us, to say the least. *Maybe being gone for a while will be a good thing— maybe we can find a way to begin again.* I did want my marriage to work; I just didn't know how to make it happen.

"Well, which is it?" Deborah asked impatiently, interrupting my creeping dread. "Where do you want the ticket sent?" She had heard about this healing conference that the Vineyard Church was having in Anaheim, California, and, because she was disgusted with my life and the bad choices that I continually seemed to make, she thought this was something I definitely needed. But she needed it, too. I could tell that she was struggling with something, which probably no one knew about, and I was suffering from a broken life—which everyone seemed to know about.

"I don't know if I can get off work. When did you say it was? Deborah, please give me the details. Can I call you back when I get home? I've got to go into a meeting in a few minutes and I need to gather some—"

"Oh, okay. But I need to know today, so call me back as soon as you can. And, really, Daphene, I want you to do this. I'll pay for everything . . . the conference and your plane ticket. You just need to get off work. Just do it. And call me later, okay?" Deborah Hall hung up the phone without waiting for a response.

Wow. Where did that all come from? I reopened my office door, reached across my desk to hang up the phone, and took a deep breath. *Wow.* The phone rang again, but I walked out the door with files in hand and headed straight for my meeting, the phone still ringing in my office.

* * *

As I boarded the plane several weeks later for Dallas first, then on to Anaheim the next day, my hopes were about as high as we were about to fly. *Maybe God will do a miracle for me while I am at this healing conference with Deborah. Maybe He will heal my heart, my marriage, and even my relationship with my sisters.* Deborah and I had not been close like twins normally are for years and years, and we had never been close to Gretchen, our older sister. God knew what we both needed, even if we didn't. I somehow felt brave for even agreeing to go–brave enough to pray for a life different from what I was living. *There has to be more than this, doesn't there?* I was a Christian, but I felt dull, empty, and unable to get past the pain of my past. I kept making all the same mistakes, going around the same destructive mountain, again and again.

When I arrived at the Dallas/Fort Worth airport, Deborah was waiting–standing straight, arms folded tightly across her chest, lips pursed. I wanted so much to sit and talk for a while, but she was on a mission. We hugged briefly, if you could call it a hug. She had a way of keeping me at arm's length. Glancing at her gold Rolex–a gift from her husband, Ron–she ordered, "We'll drop off all your stuff at the house, say 'Hi' to anyone at home, and then get you some new clothes. I want you to feel good and look good, too. Are you up for some shopping?" Not expecting or waiting for a response, she pushed through the crowd on the concourse, yelling back to me over her left shoulder. "We leave tomorrow for Anaheim—late afternoon—but I don't want to go shopping in the morning. Oh, Daphene, it's going to be wonderful for both of us." I trailed not far behind her, feeling like I had just entered a time warp and was playing our childhood game of follow the leader.

The stores, the clerks, the slacks, the shirts, the scarves and jewelry and shoes—all $800 worth—went by in a blur. When I fell into bed that night in the Halls' guesthouse, I was overwhelmed with gratitude for what she had done for me, and I was excited about what God might have in mind for us. But I was also dreading the next day when I would be faced with being the "odd man out" when all of her friends gathered at the airport to take this trip as a group. She and Ron had money and so did many of their friends. I felt as out-classed as a mutt in a dog show and knew that it would take a lot of smiling and shaking my head sweetly to get through the next few days. *If I can just keep my mouth shut, maybe they won't know how terrified I really am to be with them.* But, really, I had never kept my mouth shut, so I knew that wouldn't work. And I didn't have a Plan B.

The trip from Dallas to Anaheim went by like a movie on fast-forward. Traveling with a group of happy women—all chatting and laughing and discussing experiences I could not relate to—left me out of the conversation most of the time, as I had expected. I listened. I smiled when appropriate. I took deep breaths that I hoped no one noticed. I looked around for someone outside our little group to strike up a conversation with but ended up just trying to quiet my thoughts, slow my beating heart, and get through it the best I could.

On the plane, there was some talk of who was sharing a room with whom, but when we arrived at the hotel in Anaheim, Deborah and I had already been assigned to a room together. This surprised me because I thought she would want to spend this extra time with a couple of her Fort Worth friends that she didn't get to see very often since moving to Dallas. After all that Deborah had done for me, I had high hopes for the relationship I longed for and was excited that we would have some time by ourselves. I could only hope that God was interested in healing our strained relationship.

After the flurry of getting settled and eating dinner, we finally crawled into our respective beds, and she turned out the light. It was dark and quiet. I took another deep breath and began to rehearse the day's events in my mind when she whispered, "Daphene, are you asleep?"

"No. Are you?" At that moment I felt like we were two little school girls at their first sleep-over who were about to share their secrets and then promise to be forever friends. She went on.

"I have something I need to say."

There was a long pause. I held my breath, expecting her to say something wonderful. "I know that you want me to tell you how much I love you . . . but, really, Daphene, I just don't. I know I should, but I can't deal with the way you live your life. I always thought you would change." She hesitated. "But you haven't. I'm so tired of being disappointed."

I muffled a gasp to catch my breath, not wanting to hear another word. The silence intensified. I could feel it. My mind went blank—what could I say to her after that? It was true. My life was a mess. The silence settled in. I don't know when she fell asleep, but I lay weeping far into the night, wondering why in the world she had bothered to buy my ticket, take me shopping, and then drag me all the way to California to break my heart. All I wanted was for her to love me. But instead of loving me, she was disappointed in my character and disgusted with my lifestyle. *Was I really that terrible?*

* * *

Wednesday, February 7, 1990

The first meeting of the conference was amazing. I could feel my heart pounding in my chest and hear my pulse racing through my head as I watched people pour in from the hallway, chatting excitedly while they found a place to sit. There was cool air moving within the ballroom—I could feel it drying my lips, so I mindlessly reached for my lipstick. The lights were muted like the color of the curtains on the stage, and the rows and rows of chairs were so symmetrical as to appear artistic. I looked down at the carpet. I don't know why.

Music played in the background, but it was barely audible above the noise of the crowd. We had met in the lobby early and come in as a group to find a place near the front. I looked around for Deborah but found her several seats away from mine, her head turned the other way as she busily talked to someone behind her. I wanted to reorganize the seating so that I could sit by her—but didn't. I just sat down quietly and waited. We each had been given a packet of information and many around me were rummaging through theirs, but I held tightly to mine with sweaty and shaking hands, like it was the only connection I had left with the real world outside of the building.

When they started, we were asked to stand. A silence fell over the crowd and lasted for what seemed like a long time. Part of me wanted to crawl under a chair and put a bag over my head, but another part of me was itching to jump up and down. Then the real music began . . . and we worshiped the Lord in that place for almost an hour. The excited part of me won out. I could not keep still. It was as if a hundred keys were fitting into a hundred locks deep inside of me.

When the singing ended, a speaker prayed and then welcomed us all to the conference. He explained the sessions that would be offered the next day and introduced the series of speakers for the conference. I had never heard of Leonard Ravenhill, but when he stood to be introduced, the crowd went wild. We were seated close enough to the platform to get a really good look at the men as each took a turn at the microphone to add his welcome to the general one already given. When Ravenhill stood, the man seated next to him stood to help steady and assist him to the podium. His hair was pure white with age, but his eyes were bright, clear, and sparkling, like reflections on water. I was touched by his physical frailty; yet when he spoke, I was struck by the force of his words. He spoke with a British accent, but this was not what set him apart for me. I felt drawn to him and even sat forward in my chair, leaning toward him as I watched his serious expression mixed somehow with such great love and gentleness.

"I only ask that you open your heart . . . so that you can receive . . . what the Lord has to say to you these next few days. You need to hear Him. He wants to speak to you." I didn't want him to stop talking.

When this first meeting was over, a woman sitting behind me tapped me on the shoulder and said, "Do you have a minute to talk?"

"Me?" I asked her incredulously. I looked around to find the person she must be looking for. "Me?"

"I know you don't know me, but can you just talk with me a minute in the lobby?" She was shorter than me and held her Bible close to her chest, like a beloved child. Her hair was red and curly and beautiful beyond words.

"Sure. I'll just follow you." Squeezing between a couple of the women who had moved into the aisle and leaning over another one, I whispered to Deborah, "I'm going to talk with this woman for a minute. Meet you back at the room. Okay?" Deborah was talking to someone else and just waved me on with a quick smile.

When we came to a quiet place in the lobby, she introduced herself to me and said, "During the meeting I kept sensing that God wanted me to share this Scripture with you."

I didn't know what to say, so I said nothing. She flipped through her Bible and began reading Psalm 91 aloud: *"For the Lord says, 'Because you love me, I will rescue you. I will make you great because you trust in my name. When you call on me, I will answer; I will be with you in trouble and rescue you and honor you. I will satisfy you with a full life and give you my salvation.'"* She looked up to see my response.

My reply was so soft that I didn't even hear myself. "Could you read it again?"

She looked at me with so much love in her eyes, and with shaking hands raised her Bible up once more.

When she finished, she hugged me tightly, holding on to me like she was welcoming home a long-lost loved one. I closed my eyes and heard the words again: *'I will satisfy you with a full life and give you my salvation.'* Could this be happening? I felt I had lost all connection with reality, yet nothing had ever felt more real. *Lord, are those words for me?*

I didn't see that woman again even though I looked for her at every meeting. I have often wondered if she was an angel.

Friday, February 9, 1990

The last afternoon of the conference, Pastor Ravenhill, who so touched my heart on that first night, preached a powerful message of redemption and forgiveness. When he finished speaking, people streamed forward, many falling on their knees before reaching the steps leading up to the platform; some cried openly and others prayed aloud. The music seemed to be filling me from the inside out, and before I knew what was happening I found myself in the aisle, on my knees with my head on the floor. It felt like I had been pushed down and held there because I was not able to move.

I was overwhelmed with emotion—awe, fear, confusion, excitement—because nothing, and I mean *nothing*, like this had ever happened to me before. I remained there for quite some time but finally was able to get myself up and back into a chair. Several of the women still sat where they had been before, watching what was happening around them and praying quietly. I moved over to speak to Deborah, who was on her knees praying. I hated to interrupt her, but . . .

"I need to be alone for a while," I whispered to her and headed back to our room, not waiting for a reply. I was desperate to get alone with God and pour out my heart to Him. I unlocked the door to our room and hurried inside.

Alone, with the light off and curtains pulled, I fell on the floor weeping. I wept for my lost innocence and my ruined childhood. I wept for the love that died with my marriage to John Weaver. I wept for the mother I had not been to my babies. I cried out to God about the pain that had driven me to attempt suicide. I just opened up my heart, right there on the floor of that hotel room, and poured out all of the hurt and sorrow and guilt and bitterness until I was completely exhausted, empty, and quieted.

I struggled to sit up and then scooted over a bit to find a box of tissue on the nightstand. I wiped my face several times, blew my nose, and then just took a deep breath and let it out slowly. I took another one, deeper this time, and as I sat there in the dark, I felt those breaths filling me with new life. It felt as if I had been underwater my whole life and had finally broken through to the surface. I rested in the stillness, not wanting the moment to end, just breathing it in like one hungry for air. One by one, I felt the inner, trembling pains of anger and sadness grow still, as well. One by one, those voices fell silent.

I was being filled with God's love—in spite of all I had done. I was being filled with His joy—replacing that great pit full of pain I had carried since childhood. For the first time in my life, I knew that I was His child and that I had been entirely forgiven. A kind of peace settled over me and I knew that I was completely healed of the depression that had crippled me most of my life.

Several hours later, after getting myself together, I attended the worship service that was held to end the conference. I saw our group near the front again and found a chair as close as I could to them. Everyone was standing, singing, and raising their hands in praise to the Lord for all He had done during the meetings. Some were lining up to go forward and share their stories. I stood there at peace with myself for the first time that I could remember. My mind was quiet. My heart was full. My mouth was praising Him for what He was doing right there in Anaheim, California, on this Friday in 1990. It was like no other day in my life.

There's no God like Jehovah. We kept singing that last line of the last song over and over again as if no one in the room wanted the night to end. As we sang on, I felt a tap on my shoulder. It was Deborah. She looked at me and mouthed the words, "I do love you, Daphene." We both burst into tears and wrapped our arms around each other in a way we never had as adults. It was as if God had turned the clock back and we had returned to our mother's womb, feeling the warmth that we had felt wrapped up as one, twins–two halves of a whole. After all those years of feeling like we were strangers, my heart reconnected with hers, and it was almost more happiness than I could bear.

"I'm so mad . . . and sorry . . . about what happened to us as babies, Daphene," Deborah sobbed quietly right into my ear. "Only God can make us new . . . and He *is* making us new." The music was playing and people were singing all around us. *New? God making us new? Incomprehensible.* I just kept hugging her and repeating to myself: *New.* We stood there hugging and crying until the song finally ended. Then we headed toward the door, hand in hand.

As we were leaving the ballroom, a man stopped us and said, "God has given me words to speak to you. Will you receive them?"

Deborah and I looked at each other and then back at him. "Yes, of course," we responded almost in unison. Although the room was buzzing with the voices of hundreds of people, everything for us stood still and quiet as we listened to the man deliver his message:

"The Lord showed me five icebergs. They were very much like people. And the Lord told me there had been a very cold, hard north wind that had blown across your family and had brought a very real hardening of hearts, a hardening of minds, even of wills. The Lord says, from the depths of His love He is about to reach to the very depths of your hurts, from the depths of His compassion He is about to reach the depths of your wound. The Lord says, 'This will begin a season of a southern breeze of blessing that is about to blow across your family.'

I just want to encourage you guys that there are going to be some dramatic changes the first half of this year, but you will look back in December and really see the hardest hearts—the hardest things—have been changed in a more subtle way, subtle meaning delicate, refined.

When the Lord speaks of the depth of His love and compassion, it is like a stream that flows fast and powerfully out of a deep river. By the end of this year some of the hardest things will have been changed in a lasting way that's really going to impact you both for 1991 and throughout the coming decade."

Before he left, he introduced himself to us. His name was Philip Elston—an internationally known prophetic minister. "I will write this all up and send it to you," he told us. "Can you give me your address?" We did and then went on to our room, speechless and deep in thought, still holding hands.

For the first time in a very long time, after getting into our pajamas we both climbed onto one of the double beds in our room, propped ourselves up with a bunch of pillows, and took a deep breath. Neither of us knew exactly where to start, but there were so many things on our minds that we wanted to share.

"How's Daddy doing?" I finally asked, breaking the sweet silence of our togetherness. Daddy had for many years been the topic of conversations that never took place.

"Not good. Neither of them knew who I was when I went to visit them this last time."

"Mother, too? Have you heard from Gretchen lately? How is it being at your ranch? Do you all just love it out there?"

We talked about our husbands and our children, our disappointments and our dreams, crying together far into the night—so much so that the next day our eyes were almost swollen shut.

When we boarded the plane the next morning to return to Dallas, Deborah had the great idea that on the trip home we should put tea bags on our eyes to make the swelling go down. I was in full agreement because both of us looked terrible. The stewardess seemed puzzled but handed over two each. After soaking them in a cup of hot water, we applied them to our eyes and went to sleep. When we landed in Dallas we discovered that the tea bags had burned a square around our eyes. We now resembled two comic raccoons— worse than we did originally. Even though we both looked very funny, we were filled with a joy that was unbelievable. We could not stop smiling.

On the flight from Dallas back to Atlanta I knew my life had been radically changed. I wanted to preserve the details, so I began to write in my journal. I wrote about how God had taken me through a difficult rebirth. I wrote about the pain

I experienced while on the floor of the hotel room, the pain of pouring out my heart in repentance. I realized that before going to the conference, my heart was dead. *Have I only been playing like I was a Christian?* I wrote about the growing hunger to know God's intimacy. I wrote what I heard Him saying in my heart: *Be quiet and learn to rest in Me. I want to be your First Love.* I wrote about how I felt hearing those words spoken over me by people at the conference. I wrote my response: *Lord, let the southern wind blow.* I was no longer praying for myself–my prayer that day was for my Father to use me to glorify His Kingdom.

PART TWO
The Found Life

We once were lost . . . but now we're found.

*Salvation is found in no one else, for there
is no other name under heaven given to
mankind by which we must be saved.*

(Acts 4:12)

Chapter 6

Changing Times

He changes times and seasons; he sets up kings and deposes them.
He gives wisdom to the wise and knowledge to the discerning.

(Daniel 2:21)

I returned to work on Monday, February 12, 1990, after the Anaheim trip with Deborah. As I worked my way through the LTS/Time Systems outer office area to my desk, I exchanged greetings with my coworkers, which was not unusual after being away for almost a week. I unloaded my bag and punched the button on the phone for missed messages, then glanced up to find several of my friends crowding around the doorway.

"What?" I asked, surprised at the gathering. They were all staring at me with questioning looks of their own.

"That's what we want to know. What's going on with you, Daphene?" one of them offered.

I pushed another button on my phone to discontinue the messages and immediately covered my eyes with my hands, thinking that the square burn marks from the tea bags were still visible through the makeup I had carefully applied. "What do you mean? Can you still see them?"

"See what? Did you have a facelift or something?"

"A facelift? Are you kidding?" I laughed at the thought. "I had the most amazing time in Anaheim, but—"

"Well, *something* happened to you because you *look* different. *Really*," one of my friends blurted out.

The phone rang and I answered it, bringing the conversation to an abrupt end. I worked the rest of the day getting caught up on the issues piled on my desk and responding to those phone messages I had received. I didn't have a minute to revisit the whole scene until I was driving home in my car. *I look different? It wasn't the tea bag burns after all?* At the next stoplight I twisted the rearview mirror so that I could get a good look at my face. *Really? Hummm. The tea bag burns around my eyes are completely gone.* I sat smiling at myself in the mirror until my mind jumped ahead to what was facing me when I got home. My smile faded and the light turned green about the same time.

When I was in Anaheim on my face before the Lord, pouring out my heart, I apologized to Him for my conduct with Gary. I knew I received forgiveness at that moment and had hoped that love would spring up in my heart for my husband. But it was not happening. I really wanted my marriage to work and thought that God just might bring about the love between us that was missing. I couldn't quite imagine it, though, because I knew deep in my heart that I had never loved him. Not really how a wife should love a husband.

When we first started living together in his apartment, I was okay, but it didn't take long before I began to fear that if we weren't married I would be asked to leave and I'd have no destination and no belongings. When we sold our home in the mountains and moved back to Georgia, nothing changed; we had built a home near the lake but it still didn't feel like my home, and everything in it was his. I had nothing—no furniture, no household things, no home of my own—just my car and my clothes. Security was the reason I married him in the first place, but it had provided me with anything but that. Now things were a mess between us. He didn't love me and I didn't love him. We didn't really argue that much, but we didn't talk that much either. We lived in the same house. Period. And it was his house. Not good.

"Lord, what should I do? If you will show me what to do, I will do it . . . because I don't know. Please, Lord, just show me."

In early June, the leadership at LTS/Time Systems altered my career path from sales to training. I had often dreamed that I would someday make the switch but was surprised when it was announced. To become a trainer it was mandatory that I go through their training program, but I was up for it. Actually, I was more than up for it—I was thrilled—and couldn't wait to get started.

I was still waiting on the Lord to show me what to do about Gary when the training sessions started. It was mid-morning of the first day of training when the session was interrupted by an announcement over the intercom. "Daphene Jones is wanted in the manager's office for an important phone call."

My mind raced ahead as I scurried down the hall to his office—*This can't be a client, can it? What did I forget?* I was

133

directed to a phone on the receptionist's desk and looked down for the flashing light to see which line to take.

"Yes, this is Daphene Jones. How may I help you?"

"Daphene. Mother died this morning. They just called me from the nursing home. When they went in to wake her up for breakfast, she was . . . gone. I need you to meet me in Luling today, if possible, Daphene. Can you do that? They are transporting her body to the mortuary there sometime today and I am going later this afternoon. Can you?" Arrangements had been made long ago for both Daddy and Mother to be buried in Luling in the Short family plot, even though Mother told me secretly that she longed to go back to Poplar Bluff to be with her people. That conversation flashed through my mind: *What do you mean, your people, Mother? You know, Daphene, my family, my heritage. I left it all but never felt a part of anything else like I did with them. It's like a tribe, a clan, a community—a belonging. It's so much more than just my parents. I didn't ever really "belong" with your daddy's people.*

My mind snapped back to the present moment and I couldn't hold back my tears. I thought that when this finally happened I would only feel relief because she had been suffering in the nursing home for ten years and hadn't known any of us for so long. It was like we had lost her years ago. But the tears flowed.

"I'll see what I can do, Deborah. I will try to fly into San Antonio as soon as I can get a reservation, and then can someone pick me up at the airport?"

"I'll pay for the plane tickets out of the estate, so don't worry about the money. Just come as quickly as you can. Tell reservations that you had a death in the family and see what they can do for you—today, if you can." Deborah sounded tired. I wanted to talk with her a bit more to see how she was doing, and how our daddy was doing, but she had already hung up.

I stood there in the manager's office trying to do the next thing necessary. "Is he available?" I asked my boss's secretary after I hung up the phone. "I have a family emergency."

"Let me see if I can find him for you, Daphene. I will buzz your office when I do and you can meet with him." Instead of returning to the training room, I went to my office and called Gary.

"Hey, I'm sorry to hear that. I want to go with you. Be sure to make reservations for me, too." Gary hadn't had a job since we moved back to Atlanta from the mountains. He was eager for a trip of any kind.

"Uh . . . Sure. Today, late afternoon, if possible. Just to San Antonio. Someone will pick us up at the airport." I disconnected and called both Denise and John Kevin to let them know that Grammy had died. I felt claustrophobic in my office—it was small, stark, and without windows. The pace I worked hadn't left much time for decorating it with anything except a photograph of each of my kids. I sat staring at them while making the calls.

My boss was very sympathetic after hearing that my mother had died. He told me to take the next week off and not to worry about anything because my training would be rescheduled after I returned. I drove home in great sadness . . . I didn't want to say good-bye to her.

By the time Gary and I arrived in Luling, all the arrangements had been made for a graveside service in the Short family plot. We met in the cemetery office so that Gretchen,

Deborah, and I could review the details of the service with the staff there. We had turned to leave the building when I stopped. "I want to see Mother one more time," I said. "Wait for me . . . I will only be a few minutes."

I went into the room where her body was and found a nearby chair to pull up to the casket. Her appearance had changed so much. I tried to find that beautiful young woman of years gone by, but I couldn't see even a trace of her. The only thing I could focus on was the dress Deborah had chosen for her burial. They somehow had been able to uncurl her body from the fetal position she had been in for so long, but just seeing her brought back the smells and sounds of the nursing home where she had spent her last years. That place had been nice, and certainly expensive, but the ugliness of Alzheimer's had covered everything over with such a stench. She didn't have much hair left, but I went searching for a pair of scissors to cut a small lock I could save.

What made me the saddest was how difficult her life had been. I could not remember her ever being happy. Her life started out in such a privileged way—she could have done almost anything with her artistic talent, schooling, and supportive parents. But instead her life ended up to be so pitiful.

"Mother," I whispered over her, "I am so sorry for all of the sadness you experienced in your life." Hearing my own voice and knowing I would never hear hers again caused deep sobbing to well up inside of me. But I continued speaking through it: "You didn't deserve it. I just want you to know that I know how much you loved me and tried to make up for how Daddy treated both of us. The beautiful formals you made for all of us—oh, Mother—you did the best you could. And I love you very much. And I'm sorry for the trouble I caused you, too. I really am." I smoothed out the collar of her dress, touched her cold hard cheek, and backed away from the casket slowly. For a moment, my anxious mind was crowded by memories of another casket, a fall, and people staring, then stepping over me. I pushed the memories back, turned, and hurried out the door to catch up with my sisters.

After the service, we gathered at the home of one of Daddy's relatives who still lived in Luling. I told my sisters that at least now our mother was at peace. They agreed with me that her life could have been so much better, if only . . . I didn't finish it. I didn't need to.

Daddy was in such bad condition that he didn't even know that Mother had died. Before Deborah left for San Antonio, she told him about Mother, but she said that he looked back at her with empty eyes and opened mouth—like a wounded dog curled up in the cage of his own little world.

I don't remember talking much with Gretchen and Deborah during the few days we were together. But just before we left, Deborah took me aside and asked me why I was still married to Gary. "You have absolutely nothing in common with him, Daphene. He was a mistake you made in your past and I don't think you need to keep beating a dead horse." I didn't say anything back but I glanced over at where he was standing and he seemed like a stranger to me.

We all left Luling together and drove quietly to San Antonio so we could each catch our flights back home. It was late when Gary and I arrived back in Atlanta. He never knew my parents, so he felt no emotion at all and was absolutely no comfort to me.

It was a relief to go back to work and enter into the rigorous training I had missed. I was able, for hours at a time, to set aside my grieving for Mother. The instructor was a marvelous speaker and had one story after another that made her points come alive to me. I sat captivated and fully focused as I began to understand not only what she was saying, but more importantly, what she was doing and how she was doing it. More than merely imparting knowledge of the material, she also explained the methods behind it.

When she pulled a volunteer out of the class to demonstrate the procedures on a mock project, I realized that I would have been able to discuss the rationale at each step as he was required to do. I was amazed at how much I had learned and fascinated to see how seamlessly the trainer worked with us. My passion for training was rekindled. Thankful for the distraction, I let myself completely lose track of time. The hours and days flew by.

I had been in the training session for a couple of days when the receptionist walked into our classroom and pulled me aside. "Daphene," she whispered, "you have an important call from your sister in Dallas." She had sympathy written all over her face. I knew Deborah wouldn't have called if it wasn't something bad about Daddy . . . and I think she knew it, too.

We were right. The minute I heard her voice, I knew that Daddy was either dead or soon would be. She told me that she had been at the hospital all night with him and the doctors didn't expect him to live through the day. She needed me to be ready to leave for San Antonio–again. Daddy would be buried next to Mother in Luling.

My mind looped around the strangest things during the next few hours. I thought it was so peculiar that Mother and Daddy had been born two months apart. And now they would die weeks apart. Both my parents would soon be gone. I felt like an orphaned child—even at my age. I was still trying to come to grips with Mother's death and now I had to find a way to say good-bye to Daddy, too. I tried to gather up my emotions about Daddy and understand them. *Could I have done anything to make things better?* One minute I pictured him with belt in hand raised over Deborah and me, and the next minute I heard his softened voice telling me he was proud of me. And then I saw him curled up into a fetal position on his bed in the nursing home. I tried to hold onto those in-between years when I felt loved by him and forget about growing up in fear.

Daddy passed away later that day, and I made the trip to San Antonio and on to Luling. I wasn't able to look at Daddy during the viewing. It was just too hard. The morning of the service, the spring sun was bright and hot already but the slight wind kept us all from breaking out into a sweat. Gretchen, Deborah, and I stood apart from the rest of the family at the cemetery, lost in our own thoughts, suffering in our own way, and hiding our pain behind our sunglasses. What was left of Daddy's family was there, and I could see how difficult it was for them. His two sisters and last living brother were holding onto each other for support as they stood there. Daddy had been their rock. For some reason, he had been the stable brother, a favorite son, a special uncle, the joy of their entire family. My mind skipped around again and landed on a scene from *The Three Faces of Eve.* I wondered if our Daddy had suffered from a multiple personality disorder like the woman in that movie did, because the man he was at work was not the man he was at home; the man he was when alone with us was not the man he was while with his family in San Antonio.

Neither Deborah nor Gretchen wanted to speak at Daddy's service, but I didn't want any of his family to know how we felt about him. I agreed to speak since I had been the one to speak at Mother's graveside service. But to this day I don't remember a thing I said. I kept telling myself that he loved us—I know he did—but also wishing it had been different. I do believe that somewhere along the line . . . sometime over the years . . . he was sorry for what he had done.

I did not invite Gary to come with me to this funeral. It was becoming increasingly uncomfortable to be with him, because we had nothing to talk about. And I was becoming more and more concerned about how I would handle the expected inheritance.

When I came back from Daddy's funeral, Gary sensed a change in me. Our relationship was going from bad to worse, so when Denise and Greg asked me to come and help Denise while they awaited the birth of their first child, I was thankful for a lot of reasons.

I needed to get away for a while to try to figure out what to do. *Is this the help I have been praying for, Lord?* I packed up my few things and by the next morning had moved into the guest room at my daughter's house for an extended visit. They had rearranged the room so that I could have a chair by the window with a small table and lamp next to it. The view of their backyard that I could see from the upstairs window allowed me to see the flower garden. It was just what I needed—sweet-smelling flowers of all colors, with leaves and branches stretching out in all directions. It was a picture of new beginnings to me; I felt a new hope and future springing up in that garden that was my heart. And this heart of mine was exploding with joy at the opportunity to express my love for Greg and Denise. The thought of becoming a grandmother was life jarring, and I was counting down the days until I would add that new title to my name. I had been waiting for five years, hinting all along the way that I was ready for them to have a baby. Finally Greg informed me that when *they* were ready *they* would have one–and *they* would let *me* know. We chuckled at each other during those conversations, but I got the message. Enough said.

Well, the waiting was almost over because the baby was due on July 4. But July 5 came and went. And July 6 . . . and 7 . . . and 8 . . . and 9 . . . until we began to think that we were all just dreaming. Denise was miserable, Greg was worried, and I was counting days, but the doctor was full of assurances each time they called him. I was counting back from my own birthday. The further we moved away from the original due date, the closer we got to July 14–the day Deborah and I were born.

I was beside myself with joy when I followed them to the hospital the afternoon of July 13. They had decided to induce and the labor was long and difficult, but a few minutes past midnight on July 14 their baby girl was born. What a gift from God to me. While Greg and Denise welcomed their new member to the family, I was celebrating out in the hallway nearby. I was so excited that I broke out in a cheer and ended it with the splits . . . something I was known for doing well. Any other time I would have been embarrassed about acting so crazy in front of all the families that had gathered, but I think everyone understood the significance of the day. *Did God really plan it this way?* After Greg and Denise had some time alone with the baby, she called me into her room. I had fully recovered from my cheerleading performance.

"Mom, we named her after you—Millicent *Marie* Jones. Would you like to hold your first grandchild and namesake?" The tenderness of her voice nearly dropped me to my knees. Tears flooded my eyes as I held out my arms to take the little miracle bundle. I sat down next to Greg on a small couch in their room and tried to take into my heart all that was before my eyes. She was beautiful, so much so that I had difficulty breathing. Her little eyes were tightly shut, her little fists were tightly clenched, and the little hair she had was exactly the color of Denise's when she was born. It was as if my heart was parched and this baby was my water—I couldn't get enough of her in through my eyes.

The waiting room was filled with family: all of Greg's family, John Weaver and his wife, and a couple of my friends. John Kevin stayed with me after everyone else left and he and I spent the rest of the night looking at Millicent through the windows of the hospital nursery. The next morning I called Deborah and filled her in on all the details. She was as thrilled as I was that Millicent was born on our birthday. Now there were three of us to celebrate our special day.

When I saw Denise nurse Millicent for the first time after she came home from the hospital, I had to leave the room because I didn't want her to see me crying. *Why does she know how to be a nurturing mother and I never did? Thank you, Lord, for doing for Denise what I was not able to do with her . . . or for her.*

The next week, while I was still at their house—and no one was home—I called John Weaver. I had something I needed to tell him, something that was growing in my heart.

"John, this is Daphene."

"I know the voice, Daphene. What do you need?"

"Actually," I hesitated. "I need to tell you how sorry I am. I'm *so sorry*–for all the things I did to hurt you. I know our marriage failed mostly because of me, and I just need you to forgive me, John." There was a long pause. I thought maybe he had already hung up the phone.

"I'll try to do that–I really will."

"Okay. That's all I can ask. Millicent is our first grandchild, and I never want her to know how things have been. Try to forgive me." I hung up the phone with a new peace in my heart. *A baby changes everything.* I just kept thinking that over and over again. *A baby changes everything.* I stayed at their house until Denise felt comfortable caring for Millicent without help.

I called a good friend of mine, Linda Davis (Friedman), whom I had worked with at MCI, to let her know about Millicent and that I had decided to divorce Gary.

"Daphene, I am so happy for you. Your first grandchild! And I'm sorry about Gary. You know I would love for you to come and live with me, for as long as you want." I agreed that it would make sense to be roommates and made arrangements to do just that. She understood what I was going through.

When I called Gary to break the news that I was filing for divorce and would not be coming home–at all–he couldn't believe it.

"Are you kidding me, Daphene? What the heck are you thinking?"

"I'm thinking that we made a mistake five years ago and I'm trying to undo it. That's what I'm thinking, Gary." I guess he thought that we could just go on in our unhappy life pretending that all was well. But I was determined not to let the men in my past ruin my present . . . or the future I felt stirring in my heart. The Lord was at work changing my mind about almost everything and causing me to look to Him instead of falling apart and giving up. *I forgive him. I forgive both of them. I forgive all of them. And I hope that one day they will forgive me, too, because the Lord has.*

* * *

Gretchen called me one day out of the blue to tell me that she was miserable with the man she had married after divorcing Jimmy Richardson. I felt sorry for her as I listened to her story. Deborah had not invited her to go to Anaheim with us, but we had both prayed that the Lord would touch her heart like he had touched ours. She had worked for the same company for several years with no promotion. And she didn't know who she was and changed on a dime depending on who she was around. We no longer called her "The Queen" behind her back; we now called her "Gretchen, The Great . . . Chameleon." The outside was always changing to match her surroundings: crazy wigs, fake fingernails, and an occasional accent when needed. Her kids disrespected her and treated her like dirt. A successful soap opera could have been written about her life—one drama followed close upon the next. I could have even recommended the title: *The Unfulfilled.* She was the loneliest person I had ever known. She was even more lonely than I was.

I stayed with Linda for almost nine months and then moved into a small one-bedroom apartment not far from my work. My life was settling into a routine that resembled "normal" to most other people that I knew, and I felt happy and secure. It seemed like I was on track for the first time that I could remember.

It had taken a month to get divorced from Gary and end our five-year marriage. After about a year, we finally became the friends we had started out being and should have stayed. The marriage was a mistake, but we both agreed that there was no need to hold on to past hurts or grudges. Having it over was a relief to both of us. He was eventually married again to a woman he loves very much. I was glad that life could go on for both of us.

Our parents' attorney had informed us previously that it could be up to a year before Mother and Daddy's estate would be settled, but we were receiving money regularly from interest on their investments and had been since they died. We called it "free" money since it wasn't taxed. I was operating in completely new territory with this income because now I had two nickels, and I had begun rubbing them together just to hear what money might sound like. That was a step up from not having any nickels at all. I didn't feel worthy of having nice things, so I just settled for rented bedroom furniture and borrowed kitchen furniture. I forced myself to buy a couch and chair, even though I wasn't comfortable doing it. Then one day, several months later, everything changed again.

I rolled over and looked at the clock. It was 4:30 a.m. and still very dark and quiet in my bedroom. I was completely awake and my heart was pounding. I reached for the lamp beside the bed, clicked it on, and pushed back the blanket so that I could sit up and get my feet on the floor. I needed to be anchored. I needed my feet to be on solid ground because my mind was rushing into places it had never been before and my heart was following close behind. *Am I dreaming? Was I dreaming? Did God really speak to me in a dream?*

I flipped on lights as I made my way through the apartment to the workspace I had created for myself. I sat down in the chair, grabbed pencil and paper, and began to write furiously, heading the page with the date: October 19. I did not want to forget one little thing that was racing around in my head. God had spoken and I knew it.

When I finished writing down what I had seen and heard in my dream it was almost 6:00 a.m. and starting to get light outside. What God showed me was the gift He had given me to help people manage time and paper more efficiently. He even showed me the process and steps to follow.

I could hardly wait to get to work and share my dream with the president of the company since he was a Christian and would understand the importance of what God revealed to me. As soon as he walked in the door, I fell in behind him and followed him right into his office. He was dressed in a grey suit with a white shirt and grey tie. He always dressed well and looked sharp.

"Sir," I said, "I just have to tell you what has happened to me." In my passion and excitement I left no detail unspoken so that he would see how important this approach was going to be for his company. I talked about how I could offer an additional service to our clients. If after training they needed more help in customizing the time management book and organizing their paper, I could then help them improve their efficiency and productivity to manage time and information. I even offered a timeline to accomplish the first phase and assurance that we could do it using existing tools that we had available.

"Isn't this just so exciting?" I asked as I finished up my spontaneous presentation.

He hadn't said a word since I began speaking. He hadn't taken off his jacket or unloaded his briefcase, either. He just stood behind his desk looking at me. Kindly. But unmoved. Finally he spoke.

"Daphene, this all sounds good . . . but . . . I don't see this as a critical need for us right now."

"Oh. Okay." I stood there for a minute taking in his response and then turned to go. That uncomfortable silence I knew so well had come in uninvited sometime during our conversation and had taken over his office. This was not how I had pictured the conversation going at all—not even a slight resemblance to what my imagination had created.

"Okay," I repeated, as I gave a little wave of my right hand and clutched my precious notes a little more tightly with my left. As I walked back to my office, I suddenly realized that he didn't have ears to hear what I was saying. *"Well, then,"* I smiled and whispered to God. *"You didn't let him hear me for a reason and I am going to trust You."*

A week or so later I had a late lunch at a nearby café with a man who had attended the training class I had just conducted. He worked for a company that counseled aspiring entrepreneurs. As we sat outside at a little table in their patio section sipping sweet tea, I talked almost nonstop about my dream and about the conversation I had with my current boss at work. Because of the passion that came with my vision, this man suggested that I start my own company. I laughed out loud at his idea, causing several people sitting nearby to look over at us. *Brother, you have no idea who you are talking to: Me—who cheated my way through school and*

147

*stumbled my way though life right to this point. Me—with a stunted
education, little experience, and so little confidence in myself.*

"Seriously, Daphene, you have a great idea here, and you've
got the fire to get it going and really make something of it.
Just go for it." I laughed again but agreed to meet with his
boss just to see what would become of it. I wanted to see if
his boss could "hear" me. As we ate and chatted I thought to
myself, *Well, well, well. Just see how brave I am becoming,* and
laughed once more. He looked at me as if to ask what was so
funny. But I didn't tell him.

Later, when I left my office and walked out into the cool
October evening, I was thinking about the wonderful things
happening inside of me and noticing the beauty of nature
all around me. The leaves on the peach trees that lined our
street were beginning to change from their deepest green of
summer to the reds and oranges and yellows that followed.
Fall in Atlanta was one of my favorite times of the year.

I *did* meet with his boss, though. And he *did* hear me. And
we ended up spending hours and hours together. His office
became our "think tank"—two leather chairs facing each
other with only a small glass coffee table between us. We
drank coffee, rummaged through my handwritten notes,
and shared about our families. I explained that I knew
absolutely nothing about starting a company. Fortunately,
he did, and he had the heart to discover *what* it was that
I would actually be doing for companies that would help
them in time and efficiency. He also pulled out of me the
way to communicate effectively *how* I would go about it.
I cried on and off throughout the time we talked, but he
persevered until he got out of me all he needed in order
to help me create the first business plan. This thin, soft-
spoken, casual dresser became my hero.

* * *

In early December, I gave my thirty day notice to leave my job because I was drawn to something else. I wanted to follow God's calling on my life even though I didn't fully understand what that meant and in spite of the fear I felt.

It felt so good, even in my fear, to be following God. I had faithfully been writing in my journal since that plane ride home from Anaheim. Now I began to document everything that was taking place inwardly and outwardly as I saw God leading me into a new career. When the fear attempted to paralyze me, I went back and read in my journal what the Lord had been saying to me and doing with me. I had to constantly remind myself that I was in His hands now and everything was going to be alright, no matter what.

I had so much to learn and needed to learn it on the run because I was determined to build my new business. I turned to the yellow pages of the local phone book to look for potential clients. I figured that if they had money for large ads, maybe they would have money to hire me. But every time I picked up the phone to make a call to someone I didn't know, I had to battle through my fear. And every time I sat down to write a business letter to one of those potential clients, I had to battle through my fear again, because I hadn't grasped the most basic things in school—the things most people took for granted. Those days were busy ones as I faithfully documented everything that happened during each day and then fell into bed, exhausted from the battle. I was scared, but I was happier than I had ever been in my life. And, of course, I shared what I was doing with my family and friends. Deborah was thrilled.

My first real client was the president of a small company who needed help managing both time and paper. It was an exciting time in my life–discovering and implementing what God was showing me. I had just what they needed and it set them on a course for success.

And I was so excited when my dear friend, Marilyn Callahan-Draper, offered to help me grow my business, because I needed help with technology and with marketing and she had connections. She took me under her wing and helped me get involved in different organizations that she belonged to in the Atlanta area. It was an amazing thing to watch her explain to all of her contacts what I was doing. God was moving on my behalf in all kinds of ways and in all kinds of places.

It didn't take long for me to become quite confident with the marketing letters that I was now writing. The template I used began with "Dear [Name]," and ended with "Thank you, [Name]." I chose to do it that way because I felt the letter would sound friendlier and more personal. One day I got a call from a client who had received one of my follow-up letters.

"Hey, Daphene. How did you know I had a brother?" His question confused me and I stumbled around a bit until he said that the letter I sent him started out as "Dear Bill," and ended with "Thank you, Tom." Rather than trying to excuse my mistake with a bumbling apology, I just told him that what I desperately needed was a secretary. We both had a good laugh, and I continued working with him in his business. In fact, we chuckled over that little scene many times over the next couple of months. I shared this story with Deborah during our next phone conversation. She just laughed and assured me again that God protects the foolish. When I told Denise, she thought it was funny, too. It felt so good to laugh with the people I loved.

It was one thing to share what God had shown me about solving organizational problems for people—I saw them simply and clearly and presented them to clients in just that way, with great confidence. However, my insecurities always kicked in and left me feeling totally inadequate to actually implement the solutions. In my fear, I often secretly wished that someone had stuck a big sock in my mouth. But God was moving me forward and giving me courage, so when Janet Reese, a trainer at a large company, approached me about designing a program for her, I plunged ahead and was successful in helping to accomplish her goal. During those days I had the strong sense of God's presence and His control over the success of my business. Deborah continued to encourage me all along the way in those early days and I knew that she and her friends were praying for His protection over me.

Many of those initial concepts and techniques that God gave me when the company first started are still being used today. God is truly amazing. A copy of the check I received for that first week's work hangs on my wall today and occupies a treasured position among the many artifacts I've kept over the years to document the history of DJ Consultants, Inc. I'm thankful that God unfolded only a small bit at a time of all that He had in store for me, because I would have been scared to death to see it all at once.

One of those small steps occurred when I met Diane Coleman. She was a woman I became friends with when we both signed up for a tap dancing class. After finding out what I did for a living, she hired me to help her train people in the Estée Lauder regional office where she worked. I had only been working there for a week when I got another call from her.

"Daphene, Diane here. Do you have a minute?"

"Sure. What's up?"

"I just got off the phone with my boss and she would like to talk with you about replicating the training you are doing for me in all the regional offices throughout the country."

I was stunned but thrilled. "Wow, that's incredible!" I took a deep breath and asked her some additional questions that she was not able to answer.

"I'll set up the meeting for us and you can get all the answers then. What day next week do you have available?" We talked a little more and then hung up. I was very excited that her company wanted to have a system in place throughout the region that would make it easier for people to transfer from one regional office to another.

The meeting went well and I began immediately to implement the training. No matter where I went as I travelled for them, I always stayed in beautiful hotels and was made to feel like a princess. My life was changing rapidly. After a year of working alongside a corporate trainer in the regional offices, I was asked to work in the corporate office in Manhattan . . . alone. *Manhattan. Me? I have got to call Deborah. She's not going to believe this.*

"Deborah, I couldn't wait to fill you in on all that's happening."

"So what's up?"

"Did you remember I went to court this morning? After all these years of fighting in court, today was the final day. But John Weaver didn't even show up." I started to pace my apartment, feeling the frustration all over again. "I met my lawyer there, and when the case was called we went in and sat at the table in the front of the courtroom–just like on TV. It was weird and I was nervous, but my attorney handled everything. John's attorney seemed so smug to me. It was really irritating."

"What did the judge say?"

"Well, at least it's over, but I do have to pay the large sum that John asked for."

"I think–" Deborah began and then stopped. I waited.

"What?" I finally asked.

"It's good that it is over. You need to be okay with that. Just move on."

"There's nothing else to be done. Our case went all the way to the Georgia Supreme Court in Gwinnett County. So it really *is* done, and I'm glad."

"Did you cry?" Deborah asked.

"Wept like a baby, but mostly I'm just thankful to have it over and done with. My eyes are swollen and I have a headache. Maybe I should get out the tea bags again."

"Yes, why don't you?" We laughed together over that sweet memory.

"But I have good news, too," I said. "Guess what I have been asked to do? Guess where I'm going to work for Estée Lauder? Manhattan. Can you believe it? Me–in Manhattan."

"Well, that's pretty cool," she said with enthusiasm. "Congratulations. How's that going to work?"

I explained to her that I would travel there and work during the week with individuals in the company, teaching them how to manage their time and paper. She was impressed with how my business was growing, but we had a good laugh remembering how out of control my side of "The Twins' Room" always was.

"Can you believe it? I am so excited. And a little nervous. I mean, Manhattan! Do you like it there? Where do you stay when you go with Ron?"

We chatted back and forth a bit more about Manhattan and then I asked about her kids.

"Teenagers, you know," she said. "Great. Busy. Wonderful. How about yours?"

"Denise is such a wonderful mother, Deborah. It is amazing to see, really. Millicent is precious and growing so much. I don't hear much from John Kevin but he's doing fine for a college student. Denise mostly fills me in on what he's doing. I called and told them both about traveling to Manhattan and they were really excited. They want me to stay in a hotel big enough for them to come and visit once in a while."

"How are they going to do that with Denise's kids and John Kevin's classes?"

"Oh, they want me to spend some weekends there too—instead of coming back home—and they will come then. We'll see how it works."

"Well, I'll see when Ron plans another trip there. When are you starting this job?"

We finished our conversation after a few more topics and promised to keep each other posted on any more updates about . . . well . . . everything.

* * *

At the end of my first year in business, I decided to go through all of my invoices and write a "Thank you" note to each client and person who had helped make it a success. What I discovered made me laugh. I found at least one mistake on every single invoice I had sent out to my clients. Every single one. Deborah's prayer for me had always been that I would be protected from myself, and apparently her prayers had been abundantly answered. Even with all of the mistakes I made, each invoice had been paid on time.

As I considered that first year, I realized how tired I was from trying to do the daily administrative tasks after teaching all day, sometimes until 2:00 a.m., and even while traveling around the country. I realized I needed help. So I hired Melissa Rice, the accountant who had helped me with my personal taxes for several years. She worked for an accountant who owned the company and had been recommended to me after Mother and Daddy died. We all agreed that she would do my accounting and manage my office—basically do the administrative side of the business. Although Melissa only worked part time, she soon became invaluable to the company.

And it wasn't long before other people approached me about coming on board. Word of mouth is a powerful tool and the word had spread from friend to friend that I needed help. Each of them that applied for a position with me believed she could do what I did in her own state. After I hired them, several of my close friends suggested I hire a consultant to help me with a business plan that would give the company the structure that we so desperately needed. So, not only did I hire a consultant, but I also paid for a conference room at a hotel, airline tickets, and accommodations for six of the people who came from out of town. About halfway through the first day, everyone started arguing about what titles I would give them and what part of the United States they could call their own. I thought for sure that I was about to be rolling in big bucks with these people working as hard as I was and making money for the company. But to my surprise, other than titles and territories, they went home and did absolutely nothing. Nothing. Over time, they all disappeared. Linda was the only one who persevered through those early years. Then, at some point, she decided she needed a "real" job, too. Although she left the company, we retained our friendship.

One day, out of nowhere, I got a phone call from a man who had worked with me at LTS/Time Systems as a trainer before I started my company. He knew I was traveling to Manhattan nearly every week to work with Estée Lauder and thought I might be interested in meeting with a department at the Pfizer Pharmaceutical corporate office there. I assured him I was very interested and thanked him for thinking of me. *And, thank you, Lord. This can only be by Your hand.*

Once I got the Pfizer Pharmaceutical contract, I realized that there was more work than one person could do. Melissa was still doing the accounting and managing my office, but I was the only one out there doing the work. Pfizer didn't want training but needed individual coaching instead.

As the money came in, I hired two sisters from Minneapolis, Jennifer (Schwieters) Eibensteiner and Kay Duffney, who had the same passion for helping people as I did. They worked hard for me and made a huge difference in the growth of the company. Our clients loved them and so did I. Our business grew, so we stayed busy and made good money. It was an exciting time for all of us and I marveled at God's blessing.

* * *

In the fall of 1994, I bought my first condo in Atlanta with the money I had inherited from my parents because I was tired of wasting money on rent. Deborah flew in to help me find it and then, after it closed, came back to help me decorate it. She had good taste. And she didn't seem to mind spending my money: "Daphene, it is time for you to stop acting like you are a poor Texas girl who doesn't have two nickels to rub together, and start enjoying having nice things around you." Some of the furniture was bought in Dallas and the rest of it in Atlanta. She ordered a beautiful custom-made light beige couch, two purple and green printed wing-backed chairs, two stone tables like she had—one for behind the couch and the other for my coffee table—several custom lamps, a beautiful iron bed with two antique chests, and a small oak dining room set. For the guest bedroom she chose iron twin beds, a black dresser, and a small antique chest. Everything was beautiful. Of course she made sure I had all the accessories to make it look fabulous.

Just as we were leaving the last furniture store, Deborah spotted a chair and ottoman that she said I just couldn't live without. It was a pale cream-colored overstuff—very comfortable—with a soft brocade design that that brought all of the colors in my living room together.

"Daphene, this chair is *just* what you need in your house." She plopped down in it, pulled the ottoman over enough to prop her feet up, and rested her head back on the cushion. "I can picture you in it when we talk—feet propped up, coffee in hand . . . it's just perfect." I agreed and took a mental snapshot of her, there, in my chair. It seemed like the finishing touch and she and I went out of that store laughing and talking and having the most wonderful time together. We were almost giddy.

Deborah had seen to all the details; since some of the pieces had to be ordered from the factory, she decided that on one of Ron's trips, he would fly into Atlanta to help arrange delivery and setup for me. She had drawn out the floor plan of my condo and given him instructions on where everything was to be placed. Ron's mother made all of my drapes, bedspreads, and covers for side tables so that everything matched perfectly.

I was a happy woman. And I wasn't the only one. Because Ron did all of the decorating at their house, Deborah hadn't had the chance to spread her creative wings until now. She really loved doing it and surprised both of us with how high she could soar.

In December 1994, I got a call from Denise telling me that she and Greg were expecting another child. I was overjoyed that it was another girl because I was all settled into my new home and anxious to host slumber parties with my two little granddaughters as soon as possible.

Denise was induced on April 1, so she and Greg asked me to keep Millicent the night before she was to go in. Neither one of us felt like going to bed, so we made out the couch in the den and watched TV all night. She was now close to five and so much fun to be with. We finally did fall asleep at some point but were awakened by a call from Greg telling us that Madison Leigh Jones had arrived at 2:30 that morning and for us to get dressed and head to the hospital when the sun came up. We were both so excited that we had trouble falling back to sleep.

When we walked into the hospital room, we joined the excitement and stood in line to hold little Madison, who soon became known as Madi, Padi, Pumpkin Pie. We could tell right away that these two little girls were going to be very much their own persons—Millicent the shy one, and Madi ready to take on the world. It had been five years since I had held a newborn, and I had forgotten just how tiny they were. It was wonderful to have her in my arms and to begin making plans for our sleepovers. I could have sat there holding her for a week.

I couldn't believe how sweet it was to see *my* little girl with *her* two little girls. This was the kind of family I had needed as a child; it was the kind of family that I wanted for my children; it was the kind of love and caring that my grandchildren would grow up with.

On May 17, 1997, John Kevin and Melissa (Missy) Rose were married in Athens, Georgia. Seeing him standing at the altar watching his bride approach flooded me with memories . . . of my wedding day with John Weaver . . . and of Denise's wedding day . . . and how much things had changed. I saw the absolute joy on his face, the tears that had welled up in his eyes, and I could not hold mine back. As the wedding march filled the sanctuary, I took a deep breath and scanned the family section where we were all gathered. *The family.* What a precious word. Deborah, Ron, Regan, and Carson had all come; John Weaver and his wife were there; Denise, Greg, and the little girls had also come. And we were *together* for John Kevin at this special time. I felt the gentle southern breeze stirring that day.

Chapter

Moving East

He will yet fill your mouth with laughter
and your lips with shouts of joy.

(Job 8:21)

We were sitting around the dining room table after devouring a wonderful Thanksgiving meal. A fire crackled in the fireplace and a football game played quietly on the television. It was 1997, late afternoon, and the view from the dining room at Rocky Top Ranch was spectacular: waning sunlight, rolling Texas hills, and the Brazos River gliding by the south edge of their property. We sat quietly for a little while, all lost in our own worlds.

Deborah, Regan, and I had spent the last two days cooking, so Ron and Carson had been volunteered to do at least some of the cleanup. We were all stuffed and not eager to tackle the work in the kitchen. We were thinking about dessert but had no room whatsoever for it.

The conversation drifted from the food on the table, to the view out the window, to the travel plans for returning to our respective places of employment at the end of the long weekend. I stretched my legs out under the table and squirmed a bit, trying to get comfortable. "I am exhausted after every trip to Manhattan. I've been doing it almost every week for the past several years now and I'm sick of living in a hotel while I'm there—except when you come over to stay with me, Regan. I love that."

"Well, Daphene, you know how you can solve your problem, don't you?" Ron piped in as he leaned back in his chair the way Deborah hated. He just looked at me and waited to see if I would try to guess what he was thinking. I didn't. Glances were exchanged around the table. Deborah shifted in her seat. Ron sat his chair back down and I waited, not knowing if I wanted to hear the solution. He rubbed his face with both hands as if trying to change expressions.

"Well, you could move there," he finally said quietly. When he suggested that, I nearly hyperventilated.

"You've got to be kidding, right? All by myself? I can't even imagine it. Deborah?"

I needed to hear from her on this, but she just shrugged and smiled sheepishly at me as if they had planned the conversation. I didn't really believe that they had, but it did cross my mind. She sat cross-armed, like Regan, and flashes from the large hanging lamp above the table bounced off the Rolex watch she always wore—like sparks from a campfire.

"Are you kidding?" I repeated, looking back at Ron. "Don't you remember who I am? I am Daffney Snort, and I was a Snior from Sider. I can't move to Manhattan." We all burst out laughing at the now famous family joke. Regan and Carson had heard it many times before but both of them laughed again anyway.

"Yep, Snort from Sider, that's who you are, alright, Daphene," Ron confirmed, grinning from ear to ear.

Instead of getting into the conversation, Deborah stood up and began to gather the dishes of food that were nearest her on the table. That was the family cue to get up and get the cleanup underway. We all obeyed the unspoken order and set about doing our pre-assigned chores. The conversation shifted back and forth between what to do with what in the kitchen and chitchat between the kids. But I was thinking about Manhattan.

On Friday I was curled up by the fire in the den when Regan came in looking for me. She had flourished and become more physically fit than she had ever been. Her hair was thick and shiny and her smile bright. Her voice had lost none of its Texas twang.

"You know, Daphene, it was hard for me when I first moved to Manhattan. I like the program I'm in at Christie's, but I understand why you are hesitant. Dad thinks the place is the next best thing to heaven, but what a culture shock for me after being on campus at TCU. But I *am adjusting*. And you would, too."

"I know, but—"

"You've already won half the battle by being there so much for work."

"Yes, but—"

"And you have people there. I'm there, and we have Times Square Church."

Times Square Church had become a home away from home for both of us. It wasn't far from her apartment on Central Park South or from UN Plaza where I stayed most of the time while traveling there for work. It was our spiritual nourishment and our social outlet combined.

"I'd love having you there all the time, Daphene. I really would."

Before the Thanksgiving weekend was over, the decision had been made that I was moving to New York City. My flight back to Atlanta went by fast because I spent the whole time making lists of tasks to do, people to contact, and things to sell. When I stepped off the plane late Sunday night, I felt like a whole new woman. Again.

The first order of business was to break the news to my two children, which is what I did early the next morning.

"Mom, I think it's great," Denise said. "Really. I have always wanted to see New York City and now I can come and visit you. The girls are not going to be happy about this, though. They love your sleepovers." Sadness welled up in me at the thought of Millicent and Madi. I had worked hard to create memories for my two granddaughters over the past few years and would need to figure out a way to continue to do it.

"What do you think John Kevin will say?"

"Oh, he'll be happy, too, for sure. We're proud of you, Mom. Your company is flourishing and you are doing so well."

After delivering the news to John Kevin, I hung up the phone and felt a sense of relief. I needed their blessing on this and I had gotten it.

* * *

I spent the next three months preparing to make the transition to buses, honking horns, and crowded subways. As the big day approached, I grew more and more apprehensive, even though Deborah had assured me that she would help and seemed so excited for me. She said it was a "big girl" thing to do and that she was proud of me for doing it. Regan was thrilled that I was joining her in the Big Apple, and together they kept me moving forward.

A week before the movers were scheduled to pack up my things, Jennifer, who worked with me, threw me a wonderful going away party. She invited many of my friends over, ordered a specially designed cake in the shape of a big red apple, and purchased a beautiful book for them to write notes in for me to keep. I felt so loved by everyone that I began to second guess my decision to leave, though I tried not to focus on it.

On the Friday before the move, my dear friends Patty and Tommy Green came to pick up my nearly new Camry. I was thankful that they wanted to buy it for their daughter because I knew it would have a good home. But as they pulled away from the curb, I felt panic rising in my chest. My car . . . my freedom . . . turned the corner and disappeared. I knew, of course, that there was absolutely no reason for me to have a car in Manhattan. No girl drove her own car there unless she wanted to pay a fortune to park it. I had to start thinking like a "city girl" and leave the Texas girl behind—at least for now.

Then the day came to load all my things into the moving van. It was February 28, 1998. I will never forget it. When the movers arrived that morning, everything was in turmoil. I had worked so hard to maintain order, but somewhere along the way things had gotten completely out of hand. I had planned that the movers would keep each room's content together in the truck so that unloading would be easier. But people were trying to be helpful by carrying out the smaller things from inside to make room for the removal of furniture. I felt like there was a crazy game of musical chairs being played with my possessions. I could almost hear the music.

My security–the very first home of my own and one that Deborah had helped me decorate so beautifully–now would be home to someone else. At least I knew that Jennifer would take good care of it; she worked for me and was willing to rent it until I was sure I wanted to make Manhattan my permanent home. This arrangement kept the door open just in case living in Manhattan didn't work out. I had struggled for weeks trying to pare down and say good-bye to so many things that I had grown to love. My *new* things. My *own* treasures.

When Denise and my granddaughters stopped by to help me with the last few things, Madi, the youngest, saw my empty bedroom and started to cry. "Mimi, where are you sleeping?" I could tell by the look on her face she was wondering how we would have those fun sleepovers at my house without my bed. My big bed was our favorite spot to talk, play, eat, and watch movies. Now it was gone.

Her mom tried to explain to her what was happening, but when she saw the headboard to my bed being loaded into the moving van, she let out a yelp and ran to me.

"Where's it going? Where's your bed going, Mimi?" She was not the only one struggling with the idea of me not being in my own bedroom and in my own bed. I picked her up and hugged her, hoping that would bring some reassurance to her heart. "I'm right here, sweetie. I'm right here. Your mommy and daddy will bring you and Millicent to my new house and we can have sleepovers there, too. And I'll come visit you." I fought back tears of my own.

As I watched the last of my belongings being loaded onto the moving van, I found myself talking more and more in a kind of nonsense babble. Several friends stopped by to wish me well but saying good-bye to them that day was not easy. And I have to admit that as we all stood there and watched the moving van drive off, I had a sinking feeling in the pit of my stomach.

Two days later, a cloudy and windy Sunday afternoon, Greg, Denise, and the girls drove me to the Atlanta airport. We had spent a wonderful few days together—special time in so many ways—and thought we would be fine saying good-bye. But when the time came, the tears flowed.

"Good-bye, Millicent. Mimi loves you dearly." I hugged her fully and didn't want to let her go. "Sweet Madi, I love you, too. We will talk on the phone often, okay?" I had picked her up and she had wrapped her arms and legs around me so tightly that I couldn't put her down. Denise pulled her from me, I leaned over and kissed Greg on the cheek, and then I fled into the crowd in the terminal, hoping that I wouldn't see anyone I knew until I could calm down. What kept me from completely falling apart was the knowledge that when I arrived at LaGuardia, Deborah would be there waiting for me.

And there she was. When I walked off the plane I saw her immediately. She waved wildly at me, thinking I had not seen her. I returned her wave and we were in each other's arms before you could count to five. I closed my eyes and let her hold me for as long as she would because I needed it desperately. When she started into an excited explanation of a catastrophe of some magnitude, I drew back just a little so that I could look her right in the eyes.

"Daphene, do you remember me telling you about that incredible belt Ron gave me for Christmas?" She released me and took my hand to pull me along more quickly. "Well, I took it off to go through security in Dallas and I didn't pick it up. We have *got* to find someone to get them on the phone and find it for me." She looked down at her watch as if she could will it to stop time completely until she could retrieve her belt.

I followed along, still holding her hand. I loved feeling her hand in mine. I wouldn't have let it go for anything, even though I was struggling with the carry-on and my purse that were both hanging uncomfortably off my right shoulder.

"Ron will have a fit if I don't find it. Seriously." She was walking very fast and talking without looking my way. I could hardly hear her over the airport rumble. But we got some help and the belt was found. She would have it on when she returned to Dallas, and Ron would never know. "Thank you, Lord, for overnight Federal Express," was her last word on the subject.

Our plan was to spend our first few nights with Regan in her efficiency apartment. It was efficient for one, very inefficient for two, and completely untenable for three. When we finally got a bed made for each of us that first night, we were in wall-to-wall beds: Regan in her single bed, Deborah on the couch right next to her, and me on an air mattress placed on the only open spot on the floor. We looked like puzzle pieces fitted into a completed picture—no space unfilled.

Deborah and Regan both fell asleep as soon as their heads hit their pillows, but I couldn't. I lay there listening to their breathing and following my thoughts as they raced from one coast to the other. So much had happened since that night eight years ago when Deborah and I had been together in Anaheim. Now I was on what seemed like the other side of the world. I got tears in my eyes just thinking about it. A realization—*The Lord has done great things for me*—rose up from my heart. *Yes, Lord, You have done great things for me . . . and I am glad. I'm afraid. I'm excited. And I am completely exhausted. But I am so thankful. Thank you, Lord.* I kept whispering "Thank you" until I slipped off to sleep.

On Monday morning, Deborah and I headed off to my new home—a one bedroom, one and a half bathrooms apartment I had leased weeks ago—to wait for the movers whom we expected to arrive at 8:00 a.m. sharp. When we opened the front door of the apartment, I saw the desk I had ordered sitting in the middle of the entry area. I knew my apartment was small, but I really thought the desk would fit into the small space in the wide entry hall that I had set aside for my office. It didn't. It took up the whole space with no room to pass by. And it looked awful. I called and requested a return, but getting it picked up wasn't easy. We knew that, at least until the movers left, it would have to be moved outside of my apartment and into the hallway. Nothing was easy in New York, I had decided already.

I wished I had brought my old desk but had left it in the house for Jennifer to use for work. It was one less thing to mess with. But now I had to start over and didn't have a clue where to begin looking for a new one in Manhattan. Deborah got on the phone and found me one.

"They will deliver it next Friday and it will definitely fit in that space. So don't worry any more about it, Daphene. It will be fine."

We waited and waited for the movers, but they didn't show up until 11:00. Deborah and I spent those three hours standing at the windows watching for them. As the minutes ticked by and time slipped away, we grew more anxious. *What in the world would we do if they didn't deliver the stuff, and soon?* The manager of the apartment said that no moving could be done after 7:00 p.m. to keep from bothering others.

When they did finally arrive, there were only two men to unload the whole truck. They worked hard for almost seven hours because I had brought way more from Atlanta than would fit into my apartment in New York. Way more. Decisions had to be made, and Deborah voted herself to be the one to make them. She positioned herself at my front door and—ever the boss that she was—made executive decisions as to what would make it in and what would be given away to the movers. It was out of the question for me to pay for storage. *Deborah, these are my things and I want to choose what I want and what I don't,* I thought more than once . . . but never uttered. After all, she was accustomed to calling the shots and she was kind enough to be here to help me. *Just be thankful,* I told myself. *Okay, I will. I will.*

One of the last things the two men carried in was the beautiful iron bed that Deborah had picked out for my first home. It didn't take but a minute to notice that the footboard was missing. Now, normally I consider myself to be an easygoing and kind person, but I had reached the end of my patience and I lost control.

"I don't really care what your boss will say—you are not leaving this spot until you produce the footboard for my bed. Period," I shouted. "Why would you have just two guys to unload all this stuff and then leave the truck unguarded when you were inside? That makes no sense whatsoever." There were two other families moving at the same time, one into the building and one out of the building. It was logical to conclude that my footboard left with another family's belongings on one of their vans. I was fuming. I picked up the phone and called the corporate headquarters for the moving company in Atlanta and threw a complete fit over the phone. It was not pretty.

Of course, there was nothing they could do. They apologized but it was getting late. So we demanded that the two men at least attempt to assemble the bed without the footboard. They said they would be happy to try and as they began working on it, one of the men looked up at me and said, "Lady, I don't think this bed ever had a footboard."

My head jerked around to look at Deborah and her head jerked around to look at the bed. *No footboard? No footboard.* We both knew instantly that he was right.

"Oh, I am *so* sorry. I think you are right. No footboard." Tears came immediately to my eyes and I could not think of anything else to do except apologize. We had kept those two men working for two extra hours over the footboard issue. After they finished putting the bed together Deborah walked them out to their truck and tipped them *very* well . . . with my money. When she came back in, she let out a huge sigh, moved a stack of boxes from the couch and flopped down, looking as exhausted as I felt.

"I'm done for the day. How about you?" We had planned to have everything put away by that time but hadn't even started. What a day it had been. Day One.

The next morning, Deborah contacted the maintenance men in the apartment building to see if they would be willing to help us with a few things. And, of course, they were willing—at the tune of $50 an hour.

"I am fully capable of hanging a few lamps. Daphene, get the tape measure and measure from here to here," she ordered me. We were off and running. Deborah knew the exact placement of the wall lamps that were to hang on each side of my bed. I got out the tape measure and pencil and went to work. Then Deborah got out the electric drill. I was thankful that I had been smart enough to include an electric drill in my first toolbox, though I hadn't really believed that I would ever need it.

"Why don't you use molly bolts on that?" I suggested. I wasn't even sure what a molly bolt was but had heard the term. After drilling a hole nearly big enough to crawl through, she realized the plate was upside down and the holes were in the wrong spot. That sent sparks flying, and not from the drill. A few choice words and a couple of dirty looks were exchanged before we got back to work. We did eventually get them hung, but they were so high on the wall that in order to turn those lamps on or off I had to stand on the bed and stretch to the full 5 feet 8 inches that I was. *Let there be light. Amen.*

On Tuesday we decided to buy shelves to put in the walk-in closet to maximize storage space. Step by step, we went through the process and finally completed that task, too. By then we proudly pronounced ourselves professional carpenters and no longer dependent on the $50 men. We got many of the boxes unpacked and much of the contents put away that day. I felt wonderful.

"We need curtain rods for the living room and bedroom windows, don't we?" Deborah asked. I brought the beautiful drapes that Ron's mother had made for my home in Atlanta with me to Manhattan but not the rods to hang them from. We searched until we found a Pottery Barn not too far away and went out to buy them. We considered our options: we could either walk or take the bus, subway, or a cab. We decided to walk, but that meant we would have to carry several sets of long curtain rods back to the apartment. "We can do that," Deborah announced.

On our way back to the apartment, though, we stopped at Starbucks to get coffee as a way to celebrate our success at Pottery Barn.

"Daphene, you are going to love living in Manhattan. There is so much to do. And I'm happy that you have Regan to go with you places. Ron told me he needs to come to New York week after next and I may come with him. It's great to have both of you to visit here. Carson—"

"I'm ready to go . . . shall we?" I interrupted her. People were packed in all around us waiting for a place to sit and I was growing uncomfortable from their stares. We both had curtain rods in our hands and sat holding them like ski poles in one hand with our coffee in the other. We must have looked like woman warriors with spears.

As we were gathering up our purses and adjusting the packages to leave, one of the rods fell out of a bag and hit the man sitting next to us on the head. We looked like a couple of bumbling fools. And our apologies in Texas twangs drew a lot of attention. We were so relieved to get out of there.

"Daphene, there's a reason that most people have everything delivered in Manhattan," was Deborah's parting comment as we stepped out into the street.

When we got back, we discovered that the living room curtains that I had in Atlanta fit the living room windows perfectly, but the bedroom curtains needed to be altered. Deborah, now close to being a certifiable all-purpose handywoman, said she could make them fit. But she couldn't. After about an hour of trying, we ended up hiring the $50 maintenance man to hang the curtain rods for us. *What stories we'll be able to tell when this is over.*

Day three of unpacking ended peaceably with a nice dinner out with Regan and a couple that I had made friends with from Estée Lauder. They came in to see my apartment and were surprised to see that there were no boxes stacked around and that the paintings had been hung. It was wonderful. I knew that it was the last night that Deborah would stay at my apartment with me because she was leaving on Friday and would spend Thursday night at Regan's place. The week of getting settled went by way too fast for me. I didn't feel quite ready to face my new life alone.

It helped that Friday was my first day back to work with a client at Pfizer. I really wanted to blend in with everyone else there—to become a "real New Yorker"—so I decided to walk to work and use my new CD player. My intentions were good, but what I didn't realize was that it was a thirty-block walk one way. I made it to work and the day went well but by the time I made it to my front door I was nearly crawling. I was too tired and sore to even notice how quiet my new place was without Deborah. And I needed to get busy with the next project that I faced.

My new desk had been delivered as expected that afternoon, so after resting a bit and eating something for strength, I pushed it to one side so I could sit down on the floor and sort out all the connecting cords to my computer and printer. It soon became obvious to me that a hole needed to be drilled in the back of the desk so the keyboard and mouse cords could be plugged into the wall outlet.

I did not consider asking the maintenance men for help; after all, I still had the electric drill that could do the job for me. But the bit–at least, I think it's called the bit–was too small and after nearly thirty minutes trying to drill through Formica, I stopped to rest. I was sweating and wishing I knew what I was doing. As I set down the drill and leaned back against the wall, I ran my hand over the back of the desk–and found holes. My new desk had two holes in the back, one small and one large. *I better hide the drill and forget where I put it.* When I finished setting up my work space, I was done. Really done. I needed a good night's sleep, so I poured myself a glass of wine and crawled into a hot bath to unwind. I slept like a baby that night.

After a week of moving in and returning to work, my laundry was piling up. I gathered it all up and made my way to the laundry room. I had plenty of quarters with me, but when I filled the first washer with my first load of whites, I discovered that the washers and dryers required a card key, not coins. I marched myself to the front desk and told the man on duty that I needed to purchase a key. *Good grief, people . . . wouldn't it be easier just to use coins? But . . . what do I know.* Why someone hadn't told me about this when I moved in, I will never know. But now I was faced with a choice: purchase a $20 or $40 card key. Back I went to my apartment to get money. I decided to splurge for the $40 key so it would last several weeks. I was reassured that the laundry facilities were simple to use and off I went.

I spent $10 to wash several small loads. The washers were extremely small and I had to use several. Instead of going back to my apartment, I decided to spend the time between washing and drying in the health club, which was on the same level as the laundry room. I knew that the rising stress level in my body needed some form of outlet that it wasn't getting. But I should have known that you had to pay big bucks to join that health club. *Do I or do I not want to pay this fee?* It irritated me quite a bit, but I just paid it and went in to work out anyway. By then I knew that I needed it more than ever. *Everything costs money in Manhattan.* I didn't have pockets in the workout pants I had on, so I tucked the laundry card key in my bra and jumped on the treadmill. I turned it to incline, set it to a brisk pace, and lost myself for a little while in the focus it took to get a good burn going.

My workout went great and I was feeling much better about everything when I returned to the laundry room to switch my clothes from the washer to the dryer. When I inserted the card key into the first dryer, nothing happened. I tried it again. Still nothing. It didn't work. I could feel my stress level begin to rise again. I marched straight to the doorman. "This thing is not working. I used it once and now it stopped." I had put the key back into the holder I was given and flashed it around like a sword in front of his eyes. He reached out and took it from my hand to examine it more closely to see why it wasn't functioning.

"Why is the cover of the card key wet? You ruined it."

"I . . ." I opened my mouth to explain, and then shut it again. I didn't offer an explanation as to how it got wet–I thought it was obvious. I was sweating from head to foot.

"I can sell you another card for $40, and you will get a refund for it. But you'll have to wait for it to go through the administrative process–could take weeks. What do you want to do, Ms. Jones?" The look on the man's face told me he thought I was a complete dunce. *Who cares what these people think. I know who I am now. I'm a professional businesswoman. And the Lord loves me, anyway.*

* * *

It was raining hard on Monday morning, so walking to work wasn't an option. I would have to ride the bus. Thankfully, I had purchased an umbrella, but I couldn't figure out how to make it open. When I stepped out of the building into the rain, I gave it a hard yank at the top to pull it open and had to hold it that way to keep from getting wet the two and a half blocks to the bus stop. When I arrived, only one other person was waiting there; but once the bus pulled up, hoards of people appeared out of nowhere.

Being the polite Southern woman I am, I stepped aside to let people go in front of me and climb aboard. Just as I was about to lift my foot to climb on, the door to the bus shut and I was left standing there. I stood there until the next bus arrived and then climbed on first after a little jostling of my own. I now understood why New Yorkers push and shove . . . it's done for survival. Once safely on the bus, I tried to close my umbrella. But instead of closing as it should, it popped all the way open, sending rainwater out over everyone within five feet of me–like some kind of big dog trying to shake himself dry after a drenching bath. If looks could kill, this Texas girl would have been dead.

I struggled to get around in NYC because, unfortunately, I was born with a terrible sense of direction that made it quite difficult to learn the subway system. But I had tried all the other possibilities and needed to conquer the subway, too. I got brave and began using it to save money. After much practice, I eventually became quite confident and more than proud of my accomplishments.

One day, while waiting for my train in Grand Central Station, a tourist asked me for directions. I pushed aside the fact that I was still a little overwhelmed with it myself and stated boldly: "Yes, that's right. Just take the Number 4 and it will get you there." I pointed out the route on her map. Just then her train pulled up and she got on. We parted— both smiling and happy that I was able to help her and she knew where she was going. Then I boarded my train. But at the first stop I realized, with horror, that I directed her to the right train, but sent her Uptown instead of Downtown. I had put her on my train and I had jumped on the one she should have been on. I felt badly that I had led her astray, but I couldn't help but burst into tears of laughter at my overzealous behavior with that poor tourist. As the tears flowed and the laughter continued, I must have looked like one of the many crazy people that ride the trains every day. *Lord, please help that poor lady find her way.*

After several weekends of getting settled, Regan and I attended Times Square Church together. We knew from experience that in order to find a seat together we would need to get there at least thirty minutes early. We tried to arrive early that morning, but the traffic was bad and we arrived late. So late, in fact, that we thought we would have to join the standing-room-only crowd that was common no matter what service you attended. But the nice usher found two seats together between two men. The one next to Regan was about her age and nice looking. The one on my side was homeless and smelly. Throughout the entire service I tried hard to ignore the stench and remember that he was also a child of God. At the close of the service the pastor announced from the pulpit: "What I want each of you to do today before you leave is turn to the person standing to your right and give him or her a 'godly' hug." I gasped and snapped my head around to look at Regan. She had also snapped her head around to look at me, but she was smiling broadly. I was not. I turned back around to do my Christian duty and, just in the nick of time, turned my head to avoid a big kiss right on my mouth.

I was so flustered by all of that commotion right at the end of the service that I could hardly wait to get outside and let it out. "Oh, my gosh. I could have died. How embarrassing." Regan and I made our way back to her apartment and dove right into cooking Mexican cornbread with creamed corn, cheese, jalapenos, and sour cream, along with a big pan of brownies that she had planned for us. Her cooking could erase any bad memory with one bite. We ate heartily and ignored Deborah's suggestion that we might want to purchase scales to keep up with our weight.

* * *

After I had spent a wonderful Christmas holiday together with everyone in Atlanta, I invited them all—John and Missy, Denise and Greg, and the girls—to come to New York to celebrate New Year's Eve with me in the Big Apple. During the days leading up to the big night, we spent time visiting parks, shopping, and sightseeing. On one occasion

I slipped off with little Madi. She and I went for a grownup manicure and had the time of our lives, making memories for both of us. Unfortunately, within a couple of hours she had chewed off nearly all of the polish and was afraid her Mimi would be mad. I certainly had no intention of taking her back, but I assured her it was okay. Then, on New Year's Eve, when the rest of the family went to Times Square, she and I got all dressed up and went out to dinner. What a glorious time we had together that night. We didn't make it to midnight, however. But neither of us cared a bit. Having my family together was healing my heart.

* * *

I had been in New York about a year and was comfortable and in the swing of things in my new environment. The business was growing and I was adjusting nicely, but I needed some help in New York on a special project at Pfizer. Jennifer still lived in my condo in Atlanta and worked for me from there. She agreed to travel to Manhattan to help me with it.

The second day she was there, we went to Kinko's to get some printing done. While we waited, we decided to walk around the area, and we talked about how working together long distance was going. She mentioned that she thought we should each get a cell phone. When we passed by a store, she recommended that we take action.

"Why not get it now?" she asked. With the below average technical aptitude that I was born with, I didn't realize that not only could I get one that very day, but I also could have the service working immediately. Because I don't do well with any kind of equipment, I asked Jen to do all of the talking, pick out the phones for us, and have the service connected. Once the salesperson started giving multiple options, my eyes glazed over and I went numb on the ends of all my limbs. We made it out of the store and back to Kinko's before I returned to normal.

Then, once I got home I had to plug my new phone in so it would charge and be ready for use the next morning. I tried to approach this whole thing with the cell phone as just another adventure, so I got brave and tried to set the safety lock. I got it locked but then I couldn't get it unlocked. I pushed every single button on the entire phone and ended up with what must have been a terribly tangled virtual mess somewhere out *there*. I could almost see it–invisible wires sending silent messages into clouds and bouncing off rainbows. I looked through the little booklet that came with the phone and ended up calling the 800 number for customer support in acute anxiety. I explained to the person on the line what I had done as best I could. No small task.

"Lady, I think the best thing for you to do at this point," the support representative said, "is just take out the battery and let it rest a while before putting it back in. Can you do that? That should unlock the phone."

I spent the next thirty minutes trying to get the stupid battery out. When I did finally think I had it working, I decided to call a friend to verify that it worked. In my haste, I hit the mute button by mistake and she couldn't hear me. I was frantic. *This phone is going back to the store on Saturday.* I was sure that I could use two cans and string more easily and efficiently than this cell phone that was causing me so much grief and frustration. I eventually figured out what I had done. What a humbling experience for someone who thought that she could teach people how to use a computer. *Really, Daphene, you are clueless about how to make things work and follow simple directions. Physician, heal thyself, for heaven's sake. Good grief.* I sat down in my comfortable chair and called Deborah with my new cell phone.

"Deborah, guess what? I just got a cell phone. I'm talking on it right now. Do you want my new number?"

"Wait. Are you sitting in your chair with your feet propped up like I showed you?" I wasn't, so I pulled the ottoman over immediately and complied.

"Okay, now I am." I just had to tell her all about the misadventure and we had such a good laugh together. And I told her about my homeless man encounter at Times Square Church, too. We laughed some more.

"I really believe, Daphene, that being at Times Square Church is a preview of what heaven will be like, don't you?" She and Ron loved it so much that they never missed a Sunday while in New York on his business trips.

"And I wanted to let you know that Denise and a friend are planning a trip here to visit me." They had been making jewelry and since they could get beads much cheaper here, we planned a shopping trip to buy beads. I was excited to see if this could possibly grow into a new hobby for Denise and me.

"Great. Let me know how she does in the big city. Who's the friend? Do I know her? How come Greg and the girls aren't going with her this time?"

We chatted for a while longer, and after I said good-bye, I looked at the cell phone for the "hang up" button. I didn't see one. *Oh, good grief. How do you turn this thing off, now?* I finally just pulled the battery out again and went to bed.

Not long after my cell phone ordeal, I received a call from one of my consultants in Atlanta. She told me that Debbie Kirtland, whom I had met when I was thinking about creating a multimedia program, had just lost her job when the company she worked for closed. She had a background in marketing and sales, and since I felt it was time that we expanded our company to include a dedicated salesperson, I decided to hire her.

Debbie set up a home office in Atlanta and went to work. After a couple of months, I sensed something was not right and, because I had plenty of frequent flyer points, I asked her to come to New York. I had just moved to my new apartment—one floor below my original one—and now had two bedrooms, so I invited her to stay with me. Even though the second bedroom was my office, I had purchased a sofa bed for any company I would have.

When she arrived two weeks later, we sat in my home office. Not long into the conversation Debbie began to cry. "I don't know why you hired me—and I don't know what to do." I could feel her pain and started crying, too. Our hearts had connected and we shared a passion for the work.

"Debbie, it's going to be okay. We just need to figure out how we can work together." I felt confident and wanted to comfort her. The problem was twofold: her expertise was selling products, but I didn't have products; and I only did consulting work. We both knew selling a consulting person was much different than selling a product, so we had to trust that God had something in mind that we didn't yet see. "I know that He will show us how this is going to work, Debbie; just go back to Atlanta with peace in your heart and wait for things to unfold." So that's what she did.

When I got word that my aunt and uncle from Texas were planning a visit to New York City to celebrate their fiftieth wedding anniversary, I got busy the next weekend getting my house ready for company. I had just turned on the water in the kitchen sink when I heard my office phone ringing. I turned and went into my office to take the phone call. When I hung up, I picked up a stack of papers in my in-basket and began to sort them according to priority. I decided to tackle a couple of the critical ones.

After working for a while I felt hungry, so I got up and headed toward the kitchen. When I made it about halfway through the living room, I looked down and was standing in water. I was horrified. I rushed into the kitchen, turned off the faucet, and began sopping up water with everything dry in my linen closet–sheets, towels, blankets, and even tablecloths. The mop was of little use in this wading pool I had created.

Not long into my harried cleanup, I received a visit from the building superintendent and three maintenance men. I just couldn't bring myself to tell them what I had done, so I allowed them to search for the leak. I retreated into my office and pretended to talk on the phone to a client who needed my immediate attention. The maintenance men were frantic because the apartment beneath me was flooding. It was some kind of medical office, and they were concerned about their expensive equipment, their records, and their patients. They had to stop working until the leak was fixed and the mess cleaned up.

When the workers could find no leak in my apartment, the superintendent returned and knocked on my door.

"Are you sure, Ms. Jones, that you didn't leave the water running in your kitchen sink?"

Of course, I had to tell the truth. I was horrified. I apologized all over the place and for the next several days felt like a hostage in my own apartment—not wanting to show my face to anyone in the building. To make matters worse, I had broken my middle toe in the flurried cleanup.

I was still limping around when my family arrived from Texas. They asked what had happened but I told them that they really didn't want to know and changed the subject.

* * *

Denise and her friend finally arrived from Dallas for their weekend visit. I was so excited to see them both. They wanted to shop while in New York, so we decided to grab a cab, head to the jewelry district to get some supplies, and then return to my apartment and make jewelry. We were riding in the cab down 59th Street when Denise yelled out, "Hey, Mom, let's stop at FAO Schwarz so I can get something for the girls." About that time, the cab driver pulled up behind a line of cars at a red light. I thought we were at the curb so, without checking, I opened the cab door. The car in the lane next to my side of the car whizzed by, clipping the door and bending it back beyond its natural range. It didn't sound good when I tried to close it. Denise whipped out her cell phone and quietly called Greg to see what we should do. He told her to say as little as possible, so when the driver asked if we were from Manhattan, we all said "NO" in unison. I dug around in my purse and came up with $50 cash—all that I had with me.

"Will you settle for this cash and let us leave?" I asked him. He nodded his head yes, so we jumped out before he changed his mind. The three of us took off running and laughing so hard that I thought we would surely be arrested for causing a public disturbance of some kind. Jewelry making was fun but paled in comparison to our shopping adventure.

About a week after they left, I was working in my home office one morning but was unable to connect to my email. I called a technical person and was told the modem probably needed to be replaced. So I called and spoke at length with my computer person in Atlanta, who said the computer needed to be taken to a nearby computer store to have another modem installed. He had me open the box that stands up to see what type of modem was needed. Of course, this scared me to death, as screwing in a light bulb was difficult for me. I did it, though, and was very proud of myself. In order to get my computer to the store, I had to lug that big box across the city either in a cab or on the subway.

After we hung up, I called a computer company to see if they would help me right away if I made the trip to their store. They said they could, but I was dreading the trip and put it off as long as I could.

I decided to pull out everything that was under my desk and have another look. When I did, I discovered the reason I had no internet service. I had mopped my office early that morning and somehow the phone line had become unplugged. I was extremely relieved, but there was no way I would call back to Atlanta and admit my mistake. *Maybe I will just never mop again.*

Spring came creeping into my second year in New York with hints of hope and possibilities for new life. My business was flourishing and I was beginning to feel at home—something that surprised this Texas wildflower. And I *did* mop again because when spring came around, the time for spring cleaning came with it. But I never mopped again without thinking of my little adventure with the internet.

Chapter 8

Standing Strong

Finally, be strong in the Lord and in his mighty power.
(Ephesians 6:10)

Journaling had become a way of life for me and I had grown
more faithful to it with each passing year since Anaheim.
I even carried my journal with me sometimes when I went
to work. Otherwise, I just curled up in my chair at home
with my Bible and my journal and went back and forth
between the two, spending hours reading, thinking, and
writing about what was going on in my life–how I felt, what
I thought, and things that were troubling me. I could not
have known just how important my journal would become
in the dark days that were upon me.

*Journal Entry for: **Thursday, April 1, 1999***
5:20 p.m. (at home)

*I got a call from Deborah today on my cell phone as I was
leaving work at Pfizer. It was raining lightly and I juggled my*

purse, cell phone, and umbrella as I walked and talked to her. I'm sure it wasn't a pretty sight.

She told me that she had gone in for her annual physical and the doctor was concerned enough that he has ordered a CAT scan for tomorrow. She said when he pressed on her lower stomach she winced, it hurt her that much. And this is Deborah. She told me not to worry but I could hear worry in her voice, and I've never heard it before—not like this. When she asked me to pray for her I knew something was different. I am praying.

Friday, April 2, 1999
7:00 p.m. (at home at the kitchen table)

Another call from Deborah today but I didn't get it until just now. She left a voice message that said she was at the ranch and would be there until Monday. The doctor read the scan and he detected a mass in her colon. I could tell she was struggling to sound strong for me, but I heard fear in her voice. She said she had another appointment with her doctor on Monday morning and she would keep me posted.

Monday, April 5, 1999
10:45 a.m. (at work; glad I have my journal with me)

Deborah met with her doctor and called to let me know that he had ordered a colonoscopy for Wednesday morning. Oh, Deborah. I am so sorry we didn't get that test done when we were talking about it several years ago. I am so afraid for you.

Wednesday, April 7, 1999

2:10 p.m. (at work; I now carry my journal in my purse—everywhere)

Ron left me a voice message that the colonoscopy showed that the mass was malignant and she will have surgery at 10:30 a.m. tomorrow to remove the lower part of her colon. My heart is breaking just thinking about what she will have to go through in surgery. Oh, God, let the tumor be easy to remove and make her heal quickly and be well. She is a picture of health, after all.

Thursday, April 8, 1999

6:15 p.m. (at home in my "prayer chair")

Regan left me a voice message that the doctor had removed the part of the colon that was malignant, but it had spread to her pelvic area and liver. I can't take it in. This can't be happening to my sister. I need to write you a letter, sweet Deborah, to let you know how much I love you and how precious you are to me. A phone call just won't do this time.

My dear precious Deborah,

I'm sitting in that special chair you picked out for me. I now call it my "prayer chair" because I keep my Bible right beside it and have my quiet times there. It makes me feel close to you. I just propped my feet up, so you can picture me now . . . like you said you wanted to.

I've told you many times how much I love you, but maybe I've never expressed it in a letter. I want you to know what you mean to me.

I am honored not only to be your sister but your twin. When I think back over the many years we didn't even know how to be sisters, I am awed with what God has done for us. You probably don't remember that weekend in February of 1990 at Anaheim the same way I do. That first night when you told me you didn't love me, it certainly wasn't what I wanted to hear, but I realized later that it wasn't easy for you to say, either. Then everything changed.

When I poured out my heart to the Lord, He completely transformed it and changed my life—in one afternoon. Then when I saw you later that evening, I realized that you had been changed, too. I can still feel your sweet hug and hear your soft voice telling me that you loved me, as if it were yesterday.

I kept the letter that Philip Elston sent to us about what God was going to do. Isn't it amazing that the southern breeze is actually at work, melting hearts? And it started with us—right there in Anaheim—even before the words had been spoken.

I think having you proud of me is more important than anything else in my life. For so many years I was nothing more than a big disappointment to you and to everyone else in our family. But since Anaheim, the Lord has used you in such a powerful way to influence my life more than anyone or anything else. I'm sure you didn't realize how much I needed your approval. I am so thankful that you are now proud of me, Deborah.

I've always wanted to be like you, my dear sister. When I look at you, I see Jesus. The changes I've seen in both you and Ron have been nothing less than miraculous—all by the grace of God.

Now to Ron—Deborah, he adores you. Every time he's been here in NY and we've had dinner, either with people or by ourselves, he does nothing but talk about how much he loves you and how precious you are to him and to everyone who knows you. I've watched you both fall in love again over the past several years, which is a huge testimony of what God's healing grace can do. I just hope that, if it is God's will, someday a man will love me the way that Ron loves you.

You've touched so many people's lives and I don't think you even know it. I've seen your heart change in such an amazing way. Once you were so afraid to love. Now you love so freely. I am honored to be your sister, your twin, and your "best" friend. Thank you for loving me and being such a gift of life. I look in my closet, around my apartment, and at my thinner, healthier body and know that you have touched every part of my life. You are so much a part of me, and I love you with all of my heart.

Please know that you, Ron, and the kids are constantly in my prayers. Our wonderful and mighty God is in control. When I think of how much I love you and then realize that it isn't nearly as much as God does, I am amazed.

I want to see you so badly but will wait until you are ready for me to come. I can feel your arms around me as I write this letter and am comforted. Our God is in the business of healing. I come boldly to Him expecting miracles for you. He has such wonderful plans for you and Ron.

I pray that God's love and presence will be a comfort to you these next few days. Many people of God are praying for you, and we have the assurance that He hears us. I claim in the name of Jesus your complete healing. Because you are a child of God, and belong to Him, Satan has no right to touch you. Deuteronomy 18:21-22 says, "You may be asking yourselves, 'How can we tell if a prophet's message really comes from the Lord?' You will know, because if the Lord says something will happen, it will happen."

I will close for now.

Daphene

Friday, April 9, 1999
8:15 p.m. (at home, propped up in my bed)

Before I call Gretchen, I need to update this journal. My journals have always given me comfort and I know this is something I need to do for myself with what we are all facing.

What a long day . . . most of the morning I spent in a state of shock. How many tears will I cry before I am completely dried up? I finally was able to start packing for my trip to Fort Worth after going to Bloomingdale's to get Deborah some pajamas. I found the softest pair that I have ever seen; they reminded me of cotton candy. Since she spends so much time in bed now I know she would like having some new "jommies," as we like to call them. Then I went to Estée Lauder to get the special cream she loves for her face and eyes. It seemed to help to be out with people. I wandered around in those stores for what seemed like hours, picking things up and then putting them back down, even circling around to look at something only to realize I had been there before. As I walked around, trying to act normal, in my heart I was trying to figure out how I can be strong for the one person who has always been my strength.

I called Gretchen after I got home from shopping and can't believe the conversation we just had. She is so absorbed with herself and her problems that I don't think she realizes how critical the situation with Deborah is. How can she talk about trouble with her kids when our sister is so sick? She reminds me of a wind-up doll with only one recording: "Me . . . me . . . me." I know the resentment I feel toward her is wrong, but I can't help it.

I leave for Fort Worth at 11:40 tomorrow morning. I'm packed and ready to go, but I'm so nervous about seeing Deborah. I haven't seen her for a little over four months—since Thanksgiving at Rocky Top—and I don't know what to expect. She's been through so much in the last ten days. Lord, help me to be strong for her. I don't feel strong.

* * *

"Thanks for picking me up this afternoon, Regan. I'm glad my flight was on time so you didn't have to wait for me." Regan didn't quite look herself—her hair was pulled up in a ponytail and her eyes had dark circles under them—but her hugs were genuine and comforting and her voice strong. She had recently moved back to Texas after completing her internship at Christie's and was working with her dad at Hall Gallery in Dallas.

"They finally took the tube out of Mother's nose this morning. She looks so much better with it off her face. They also removed the catheter—she hated having that thing in her so much."

"How's she doing, Regan? I am so afraid I will cry when I see her. My heart is just aching." I pulled at the hem of my new red shirt to make sure it was falling right over my skirt. I bought a new outfit to wear to the hospital because I wanted Deborah to be proud of me. I checked my earrings and fluffed my hair nervously with both hands before lifting my suitcase into the back of Regan's car.

"Do you want to drop your things off at the house before we go to the hospital, or—"

"To the hospital," I ordered as if I were speaking to my chauffeur. Then I softened: "We can do all that other stuff later. Does that work for you?"

I was determined that when I walked into the hospital room I would be as strong as I could be for Deborah. She had always been the backbone for everyone around her. Now it was payback time. I've never had control over when I cry and when I don't, but I fought back tears with every click of my pumps down the hospital corridor toward her door.

"Hey, sweet Debbie, I am so thankful to be here." My voice quivered a little but I hoped that nobody noticed. Ron came over and hugged me, and then he and Regan left us alone. Deborah was sitting propped up on pillows with a light blanket folded across her lap. She looked thin and pale and her hair was pulled up in a ponytail like she always wore it. I slipped out of my shoes, moved right up to the bed, and wrapped one arm around her the best I could. Then I laid my head on her shoulder.

"Cancer," she whispered right into my ear. "And I'm scared." Her words sank into my heart like bodies weighted for sea burial. I kept my head on her shoulder so she wouldn't see my face. Those last words had never before crossed the lips of Deborah Louise Hall. Never.

"I know. So am I," I whispered back. Tears were running down my face, so I turned and wiped them away before I sat down by her bed. I could not imagine what must have been going through her mind.

"You are loved by so many people—you just know that there are tons of people praying for your healing, don't you?"

"Daphene, this is an amazing hospital. Even the doctors pray with me when they make their rounds. Yesterday there were so many flowers delivered to me that they lined both sides of the hallway with them. The nurse said it looked like a garden pathway out there." She was smiling, and it was good to see her smile. "I finally told them to take them to the Union Gospel Mission."

"You should have seen this place on Wednesday," Ron added as he re-entered the room. "We had about thirty of our friends from church in the pre-op room before she went into surgery–praying, laying hands on her, and singing. It was amazing."

"You've heard me talk about that group I'm in called 'The Wednesday Watchmen,' haven't you?" Deborah asked. "And those women brought their husbands, too." Before I could answer either way, she continued. "They had given me something to make me sleepy but it hadn't fully kicked in yet. I felt like I was in heaven, surrounded by angels. The nurses told me later that the music could be heard all over this part of the hospital . . . and . . ." She seemed out of breath.

"Christian doctors we know gathered to pray for the surgeon. Can you believe that?" Ron was pressing himself to be upbeat and optimistic for both of us. I could tell.

"And they even prayed over my liver. I wonder if that was a first for them." She forced a weak smile and then let out a deep sigh. She looked weary from worry.

"Sounds like heaven is being bombarded with prayer, doesn't it? I love that." I tried to match Ron's enthusiasm. Regan and Carson had both come into the room and stood silently behind Ron. *God, we ask you to heal her body. Please let us have her for now. Her ministry is just beginning.*

Because everyone else was so tired, I offered to spend the night at the hospital with her. No one considered leaving her alone there. I was thankful for the time we had to talk, to pray together, and to listen to praise music. Even when people came in to see her, we ended up praying again and speaking words of healing over her. Everyone that walked into her room experienced God's Spirit as it filled the place with peace and comfort.

We rejoiced later that night as her tummy came alive and she had to get up several times with my help to go to the bathroom. The nurse said that was a good sign after the surgery. Even so, my heart was breaking, and I couldn't stop the tears. The best I could do was to hide them so she didn't know.

This is my precious sister, Lord, and she is so sick. Thank You, Lord, for the nine months we had in the womb—wrapped around each other—growing, developing, preparing for life together.

"I want to go home tomorrow, Daphene. Do you think it's possible? Will you ask the nurse to check with my doctor? Maybe Ron already has . . . we can just wait and see until, he gets back."

"Deborah, did you hear what that nurse said? She wants to know if you are somebody famous or something because everyone is talking about you around the hospital."

"Oh, brother. Just run and tell her that *I know Jesus* and *He knows me.* That's about as famous as it gets."

The next morning, as soon as we heard people stirring in the room next to hers, Deborah turned to me and asked, "Daphene, I want you to do something for me. Will you?"

"Of course. What—"

"God wants me to pray with that family in the next room, but obviously I can't do that very easily. Would you do it for me?"

"Me? You want—"

"Yes, you. Just go on in there and tell them that the Lord has seen their trouble and wants you to pray for them. Just go."

I stood in obedience to her command but my heart was beating wildly and I was scared to death to do it. She was the one who thought nothing of praying for strangers, not me. I walked toward the door slowly. I stopped, trying to get a prayer together in my head, rehearsing what I would say when I walked into the room of total strangers who might think I was a complete dunce.

"Go," she said again. "Go on." Of course, I always did what she told me to do. I had a sudden flashback of two little girls pouring chicken feed into a bathtub full of water to make oatmeal. I couldn't help but smile.

When I came back into her room she was grinning from ear to ear. "Now, tell me everything."

"Well, the patient is a child with cancer–a girl. She's about fourteen, I think. Her mom and dad were both there and they seemed touched that a stranger would care about their family. I told them about you, and they said they had heard the singing."

"Did they let you pray?" Deborah was never one to let the teller tell the story. I often thought she should have been a detective–she was always pressing for different answers from what she was getting.

"I felt such sorrow in that room that I asked the Lord to swallow up that sorrow with His peace and joy. I don't know if they got any of it, but I sure felt it. My heart is full right now."

"I knew you could do it. Wasn't it wonderful?" She took a deep breath and then continued. "You just need to step out of your comfort zone and trust the Lord to use you, Daphene, and He will." She had raised herself halfway and had propped herself up on one arm as she spoke to me, and when she finished she eased herself back down on the pillow and closed her eyes in exhaustion. But she was still smiling.

Over the next few days, we prayed constantly that God would begin to heal her body. She was already off morphine and was pressing the doctors to let her go home. What a testimony of a strong body and mind. The doctors told us they would release her on Tuesday—just five days after her surgery—and Ron planned the homecoming.

He invited all of their friends over to their house to welcome Deborah home. They were living in a friend's home that they had rented while their new one was under construction. The homecoming was an amazing celebration, with a huge "Welcome Home" sign hung from the second floor loft and baskets of white silk roses covering the buffet table in the dining room. Among the guests was a local musician named Katherine Barnes whom Deborah adored. They had a special bond because Deborah had helped finance her first CD.

When she began to play her guitar and sing Deborah's favorite song, "Shout to the Lord," right there in her bedroom, Deborah leaned over and whispered to Ron, "Help me stand up, would you?" I was watching so I moved closer to the bed and helped lift from the other side. It broke my heart to feel how weak she was, but I was so touched to see her break free from our grasp enough to lift her hands to worship the Lord as she sang. I closed my eyes and only mouthed the words so that I could hear her voice. It was true . . . and simple . . . and bold.

As the singing continued, people began to either kneel or go face down on the floor in worship in her bedroom, and there was not a dry eye in the place. I knew that my twin had been my strength, my mentor, my . . . everything. I began to suspect that she was the pillar for most of the people in that room, too. It was hard for all of us to see her unable to stand alone.

Wednesday, April 14, 1999

I really hated to leave Deborah, but I needed to go back home to Manhattan because of work. I decided to stop over in Atlanta to see Denise and her family, though, because Deborah is her godmother and Denise is really upset over this illness. I sensed that she needed her mom, and because I haven't always been there for her, I wanted to be there for her now . . . for this. Even though Denise and I had never prayed together, I knew it was time to break down the barriers and pray for our Deborah. It was such a special time and one more way for God to bring us even closer together.

Friday, April 16, 1999
6:45 a.m. (at home in my prayer chair)

My dear wonderful Deborah,

I have so many things to say but will wait until I have time to really write to you. It seems a little strange for me to send you things that you can get in Fort Worth but I just want to do something for my dear sister. Hope you like the Estée Lauder goodies I found for you. I hated the winter jommies Regan had on and told her I'd get her some like mine. If they don't fit, she can take them back to a store there. Tell Carson I'll find a treat for him, too. Tell Ron that all I have for him is a bunch of love.

I feel so different—and I can't really explain it—since I came home from this last trip there. The glorious time I spent with you, Ron, Regan, Carson, and all your precious, godly friends has changed me somehow. My relationship with God has been growing stronger this past year since I've been in Manhattan and attending Times Square Church. And now, after being with you all, I feel I've been touched by heaven.

I wanted to let you know that I had a really wonderful time with Denise after I left Fort Worth. God is certainly working in her life in a mighty way. She has such a hunger in her heart and we had time to pray together. I'll tell you everything when I see you again, which I hope will be soon. God is so good. His promises are coming true.

I hope you are checking the beeper that was set up for you to let you know when people are praying for you. So many of us are thrilled that we can let you know you are being prayed for. What a wonderful idea. It gives me a way to feel close to you during the night when I can't sleep.

Please know my tears are because I hate seeing you so sick. On the outside you look wonderful and peaceful. That is Christ shining through you—like a lamp on a dark street—bright, steady, and comforting. If I could come up with the ultimate way to say I love you, I would. I'm at such a loss for words.

I can't take your suffering away, but I can be there for you and your wonderful family. It is my joy to care for the one I love so very much.

I am soaking myself in the Word, as I need to now look for strength from Him. I've leaned on you so many times and for so many years that now He is calling me to lean on HIM. I pray constantly, my precious sister, for His healing hand to be upon you as you go through this difficult "challenge."

May God's grace be sufficient in all things.

Your loving sister in Christ,

Daphene

Friday, April 16, 1999
8:30 p.m. (at home, curled up in my bed)

I am exhausted but happy to be home in Manhattan. It is nice having my little kitty, Lucy, greet me and knowing how much she misses me. I called John Kevin and Missy when I finally crawled into bed. I love them both so much. I pray that through this crisis in our family he will open his heart to receive and experience the love of Jesus Christ. Missy said his friend, Chris, is beginning to minister to him. Praise God. I prayed for my sweet son as he has a big presentation at 3:00 p.m. tomorrow that he has worked so hard on. How could I be any more blessed?

While I was traveling, I received a call from a client in

Atlanta who asked me if our company would be interested in doing business in California. *Not knowing if she was even a Christian, I asked her to pray for Deborah. She told me her mom had been diagnosed with colon cancer and given from two to six months to live. They came together as a family and prayed for God to help them with the decisions regarding her treatment plan. Instead of chemo and radiation, they chose the holistic approach. That makes me nervous—maybe because I know nothing about it. We didn't make any decision about the job they needed done in California.*

Saturday, April 17, 1999
9:20 a.m.

I spoke with Deborah this morning. She is at the ranch with Ron, Regan, Carson, and Megan (his long-time girlfriend). It is always so wonderful to hear Deborah's voice. It comforts my soul. She didn't sleep well last night—she's worried about going to the oncologist on Monday. Her family helps to comfort her and she draws so much love from them as they all crawl up in the "big bed" with her. I love our family tradition of turning our king-sized beds into family gathering spots. God, we are praying for a good report. Please make this next mountain easier for her to climb.

4:15 p.m.

I have been crying all day. When will the tears stop? Other than getting on the treadmill for thirty minutes, I stayed at home. I have found that journaling helps me deal with the sadness. I wrote to several of Deborah and Ron's dear friends and sent Mary Ellen, her best friend, a compact from Estée Lauder with a note to say thank you for being such a dear friend to Deborah.

I received a package from a friend today that had a newsletter about a holistic approach to healing cancer in it. Two times in two days I've received the same information. I made myself a copy and then sent the original overnight to Deborah and Ron. When I got ready to go to bed I read it again, and I was amazed at the stories they shared. It gives me hope. I know they will prayerfully consider all of their options because they know that chemo and radiation will destroy her frail body. Oh, God, please show them the right path to follow. We're claiming healing for our Deborah.

Sunday, April 18, 1999
7:30 a.m.

This song keeps playing in my head: Give thanks with a grateful heart, give thanks to the Holy One, and give thanks because of what He's done for us. He's given Jesus Christ, His Son. Music is so healing to my heart.

Jesus, I come to you this morning asking you to watch over my dear Deborah. My heart is breaking from the pain she is suffering. Please heal her and make her well again. What on earth would I do without her? My love for her is so strong—I am at a loss to say what my life would be without her. She brings me so much joy. I know that today they are bathing in Your love and presence, as am I. Thank you. You are our Hope, our Joy, and our Comfort.

I called Deborah at the ranch before I left for church. She said she slept most of the night and felt great this morning. Her strength is so contagious. When I hung up the phone, I put on the new CD she sent me while I got ready for church and nearly danced all the way there. My heart feels so much lighter now. Thank You, Jesus. I will take one day at a time—one hour at a time—and be thankful for each miracle You give us. It serves no purpose to cry all the time.

6:20 p.m. (at home)

Denise called a few minutes ago. The Holy Spirit is at work in her heart. She has been weeping for days now, and my heart feels Jesus calling her to experience an intimacy with Him we're all longing for. Thank you, God, for sending my sweet daughter two godly friends. I expect her to be raising her hands in church before long. More and more I feel the southern breeze blowing over our family. I rejoice in the changes I see in my own children. My heart is smiling.

Monday, April 19, 1999
6:30 a.m.

I woke up crying. I'm depressed and hate to admit it, but it's hard to live in Manhattan so far from my family. I called

Denise to see if she wanted to come see me next weekend. When she called me back to say she did, I was thrilled. Unfortunately, I can't get her a flight with frequent flyer points so I will just have to cover the cost myself. It's worth it—I miss my kids so much. I need them.

11:00 p.m. (at home, in my prayer chair)

Today was a horrible day. Deborah and Ron had an appointment with the oncologist. When I talked with Deborah this morning before they left, she said they had decided not to ask the doctor the dreaded question. If he says anything about that, they are praying God would deafen their ears. All day I felt like I was having a panic attack—unable to breathe, ready to throw up. The appointment was at 2:30 p.m. By 4:30, I couldn't wait any longer for a phone call from them, so I called Regan to see if she had talked to her mom. The conversation is still rolling around in my head:

"Regan, I don't want to know but I can't help but ask. Did the doctor tell them?"

"You mean about how long she has? Daddy said they didn't ask and he didn't say."

"Oh, I am so thankful, sweetie. Don't you think that's best? How could we—what would we—"

"I know. Either way it's terrible."

My heart felt somewhat better after our conversation, but now

I can't stop crying. I want to feel what I know by faith: she will live. But I'm so afraid of losing her and can't even imagine what life might be like without her. Just thinking that way makes me wonder if I even have any faith. I don't know how to get control of my emotions. I pray constantly, read my Bible, and listen to Christian music. What is wrong with me? Oh, Lord. I need You.

I pray that God will surprise us and heal her. What a celebration that would be. His name would be praised and all the credit would be His. I constantly pray for Ron, Regan, and Carson to be comforted and strengthened. Knowing how much I love her, I can't imagine what they must feel.

I'm thankful for the business that my company has right now. Having to work brings me some relief from thinking about Deborah.

* * *

I flew back to Fort Worth to see Deborah in the middle of May, but I was not prepared for her condition. She was suffering with horrible pain from the latest surgery, making sleep impossible. One thing that helped her was for me to massage the terrible muscle spasms that rose up across both hips like knots in a rope. God blessed me with strong hands, so I massaged her for hours. After two days, I finally just moved into the room where Ron and Deborah were sleeping and stayed there. Ron and I took turns staying up with her, so while I was up, Ron slept; when Ron was up with her, I tried to sleep. Rather than sleeping on the floor, Ron said for me to sleep with them. We would laugh as the three of us climbed into their big bed together. I didn't want to leave Deborah's side for a minute.

I discovered that if I ran a hot bath for her and then sat on the floor beside her, she felt less pain or at least was distracted from it. We found things to laugh about and things to cry over during the first two nights we spent together.

On the third morning after I arrived, she reached out with her hand to take mine and said, "Let's walk. I think it helps."

"Do you need anything before we go outside?" I was a bit worried to go too far, but she insisted. We made our way slowly through the house and out the back door. The garden path was shaded, and there was a bench at the far end of the wildflower patch. That first day we made it our goal. The place was beautiful.

The house they had been renting was sold and their new home was not yet completed, so she and Ron had moved in with their dear friends, Alan and Mary Ellen Davenport. Mary Ellen and Deborah have been best friends for years. They had a large home and welcomed me with open arms when I arrived.

The house was located on a very quiet street with nice large yards. Mary Ellen had worked hard in her garden and everything looked beautiful. The backyard was welcoming and gave Deborah and me a nice, quiet place to rest in the afternoons.

"Daphene, you know that 'the Lord is my light and my salvation—whom shall I fear? The Lord is the stronghold of my life—of whom shall I be afraid?' That's Psalm 27:1. Isn't it beautiful?" She spoke it like she walked—slowly, clearly, and with confidence. I thought it was the most beautiful thing I had ever heard. She was still holding my hand.

"Tell me another, would you?" I whispered.

"'And we know that in all things God works for the good of those who love him, who have been called according to his purpose.' That's Romans 8:28. I love that Word."

"Oh, I love it, too," I said. We were getting closer to the bench at the edge of the wall of flowers.

We finally reached another place where we could sit down to let her catch her breath. We sat quietly for a little while and could hear water trickling. There must have been a pond nearby.

"'The Lord Himself goes before you and will be with you; He will never leave you nor forsake you. Do not be afraid; do not be discouraged.' That's another Word I am treasuring, Daphene. You should hide it in your heart—for when you need it. What I do is turn the Word into prayer. Like this one: 'Thank You, Lord, that You Yourself go before me and will be with me; You will never leave me nor forsake me. I will not be afraid or discouraged.' Do you hear what I did?"

Deborah had spent years memorizing Scriptures and had them deeply imprinted into her heart. "I could listen to you quote Scripture all day long. Can I get a tape recorder for our next walk?"

"Absolutely not. For heaven's sake, Daphene. That would be ridiculous," she scolded. I think she didn't want to consider why I would ask such a thing. "God is in the healing business and I expect to be around to quote Scripture to you whenever I want to." I didn't mention it again.

I was cherishing every moment being with Deborah, and for the first time in our lives she was letting me care for her. I was filled with the sweetest peace about it and felt that the love we shared had never been stronger. After our walks each morning, she would rest in bed and we would talk some more. I finally got brave enough to tell her a secret I had been keeping from her for quite a while.

"Guess what?" I asked her one afternoon.

"What? How can I guess when I have no idea what you are thinking?"

"I have something terrible to confess, but I'm afraid what you will think of me." I watched her face as I spoke. I had her attention.

She reached for a glass of water on the nightstand by her bed and took a sip. "What have you done this time?"

I began to wish I had left the whole subject alone. "Now I don't know if I really want to tell you."

"You're not on drugs, are you, Daphene? Or married again? Because if you—" She sat the glass back down hard on the table and took a deep breath in. Her eyes were flashing.

"No, no. But I do have a story to tell you, and I'm not sure how you are going to feel about it."

"Well, just tell me. And then you won't have to wonder, for heaven's sake." She gave the covers on her bed a little shake and smoothed them down over her legs. Then she looked at me and waited.

"Okay." I shifted in my chair and straightened my posture as if I was delivering an important talk to some clients. "When I turned fifty, my dear friend Sue Langston, from

Austin—I don't think you ever met her, did you?—anyway, we were together to celebrate my birthday. After dinner and a couple of glasses of wine, we decided to . . . get a tattoo." I inhaled deeply and waited for her response. It didn't take a split second to get one.

"Oh, good grief, Daphene. Will you ever grow up?" I was surprised at the tenderness in her voice. The Pharisee in her was diminishing more and more, and the Savior, oh, the Savior was so evident. I let out the big breath I had held and said, "Just wait 'til you hear the story, Deborah. So, Sue suggested we get it on our big toe so no one would see it. At the time it seemed like a great thing to do." My pulse had begun to subside and I had such love for her that I could hardly contain it.

"You know how I feel about tattoos, Daphene. Only prostitutes have them." A momentary harshness had sprung up and I winced at her bluntness. She continued, "I mean, well, that people who get tattoos have usually had hard lives—a lot of the people at the mission have tattoos—but I didn't expect this of you."

"Well. I hid it from you for five years by always having a Band-Aid to cover it."

"You're kidding, right? Oh, good grief." Lightness had returned to her countenance.

I slipped off my shoe, lifted up my foot for her to see, and pulled off the bandage. She burst out laughing.

"I hardly think that a little tattoo of a flower on your big toe is worth getting upset over—not with what we are facing." I was relieved and laughed a nervous kind of laugh with her. Then she shouted, "Ron. You have got to see this. Come in here—get Carson and Regan and come here."

Ron and the kids made a big deal about it. They were experts at teasing me by this time, but I tried not to act as embarrassed as I really was. Most of all, I was relieved that I didn't have to hide it anymore.

The two weeks I was there went by way too fast. There had been a constant stream of their friends in and out of the Davenports' home—either coming to visit or bringing in meals for everyone who happened to be there. Her dear friend Cindy Hawkins had headed up the project to make sure Mary Ellen didn't have to prepare meals for all of us. I was struck at the level of love and commitment they all shared. I had never seen anything like it anywhere.

When it came time to say good-bye to Deborah, I felt sick to my stomach. As I hugged her as gently as I could so as not to hurt her, I reminded her about the conversation we had the night before. "I really do want to move back to Texas, because right now all I care about is being with you." She hugged me back and said, "Good."

Tuesday, June 15, 1999
4:15 p.m. (at home, in my prayer chair)

Good news to report on Deborah. She has settled into a kind of routine with her treatments: she has one on Wednesday and Thursday, usually by Friday afternoon she gets extremely tired, and by Saturday and Sunday she can't do much of anything but rest. She said it is impossible to even describe the drop in energy. By Monday she always feels better. It seems like this is a normal routine, and we are so thankful that no other side effects have shown up.

She sees the oncologist again on Thursday. Right now we have no idea just how much of the cancer is being destroyed by the treatment she is receiving. At least most of her pain has subsided, and she has reduced the pain medication she is on. She and Regan have even seen two movies; they go to afternoon matinees because she has to be careful of exposure to any kind of illness. It's wonderful that she is able to get out some and that Regan is close by to spend some time with her. When I was there last, she was either in bed or walking to help with the pain. Thank You, Lord, for this progress. She is now getting the chemo from the port that was put in her chest right after I left. I hated seeing those three cuts they made in her neck for the ports before, but she was so thin that they couldn't do anything else at the time. She said those places are healed up now.

If this phase doesn't do what the doctors want it to, they will hospitalize her for five days to put the chemo directly into an artery that will go to her liver. I just pray she doesn't have to have the liver re-sectioning. Oh, God, heal her completely. She has so many things to live for—and so many things to do.

Deborah and I are planning, if God provides the money through my company, to build an apartment complex for the homeless in Fort Worth. It has been her dream for a long time and now I share it with her. Together we want to see revival on Lancaster Street where the mission is right now. Deborah and Ron have fallen in love with the people suffering in Fort Worth's inner city and that love has given new meaning and direction to their lives. When she talks about the beauty of the flowers she sees in her vision of the inner city gardens, I can see it, too.

Lord, she wants to grow old with Ron and she wants grandchildren. I pray that these things will happen for her.

Thursday, June 17, 1999
8:45 a.m.

Deborah will stop her treatments for two weeks beginning July 4, so Ron is planning a vacation for them. This is certainly a reason to praise God. We have a God that is in the business of healing. Please God, heal her completely—she is just too special to so many people to not have her with us a long time. In 2 Kings 20:5-6, God heard Hezekiah's prayers, saw his tears, and healed him, adding fifteen years to his life. I believe that is what everyone should be praying for Deborah. I cry as I write this because she is doing so much better. God is good, all the time.

John Kevin called me yesterday and said he has officially become a dentist. He was so excited and had a whole list of people to call. I had a million questions for him, but I will wait until he has more time to talk. My son has worked so hard for this day and I am so proud of him.

Saturday, July 3 1999
9:30 a.m. (at home, in my prayer chair)

Deborah had her last chemo treatment Thursday. Her body will rest until July 19, at which time they will do a CT scan to see what the treatments have done so far to kill the cancer in her liver. Of course my prayer is that the cancer will be completely gone. She has had a hard time with different things—she hasn't lost her hair and gotten mouth sores, but there have been many other side effects. She has had a constant urinary tract infection that has been very painful, and either the chemo or the medicine she's on makes her sick to her stomach. She hasn't vomited but feels very nauseous. At times, different parts of her body swell.

She said that the hardest thing is that she feels completely drained. Regan told me that she never complains, but I know how hard it must be for her, not being able to do the normal things that she was able to do before April 1. She no longer can just pick up and go to the grocery store; she's too weak to drive, and she doesn't have the stamina to make the trip to the ranch very often, either. I know her personality is to be brave and not complain . . . but Lord, make these next two weeks good ones for her as the chemo leaves her body. She and Ron were hoping to go on a vacation but had to cancel it because right now she is just too sick.

Oh, God, heal her of cancer so she can have her life back. Ron and Deborah are so committed to the homeless and to serving at the Union Gospel Mission in Fort Worth. Ron is even

attending church there now. Deborah said they asked him to
preach, but he said he's not quite ready. All the people at the
mission love them so much. Being at the mission together has
been a blessing for the people that they minister to, and it has
strengthened their marriage.

Right now the most critical thing I pray for is the CT scan on
July 19. Deborah had Regan write this out and send it to me so
that I could agree with all of them in prayer:
Because you, Deborah, have made the Lord your refuge,
the Most High your dwelling place,
no evil shall befall you,
and no cancer come near your home.
When you, Deborah, call to me,
I will answer you.
I will be with you in trouble;
I will rescue you and honor you.
With long life I will satisfy you and show you my salvation
(adapted from Psalm 91:9, 15-16).

I say "Amen" to that and will bring this before the Lord daily.

Wednesday, July 14, 1999
6:45 a.m. (in Fort Worth, at the Davenports' home)

It's our birthday today. What will I do if she doesn't live? How
can I ever celebrate another birthday without her? Growing up,
Mother always made us each a little star cake and invited our
friends over to celebrate with us. I spent many of those parties

> *wishing I could have my own party—just for me. Now I can't*
> *bear the thought. And I just couldn't let this one pass without*
> *being with her. I'm so thankful to be here with her in Fort Worth.*
>
> *I couldn't be making all these trips without the help of Jennifer*
> *and Kay. I am seeing the hand of God in bringing the kind of*
> *people I need, just when I need them. It is amazing to me how*
> *quickly they have stepped in and kept the work going and the*
> *company running. I believe that, without their dedication to*
> *our clients, I would have lost the company. As God cares for*
> *Deborah, He is also caring for me and the company He gave me.*

At 2:00 p.m. Ron drove Deborah and me over to John and
Jeanie Ott's home to celebrate our birthday. Cindy Hawkins
and Mary Ellen Davenport also had July birthdays, so all
four of us were honored. Each birthday girl was seated in
a special place, and one of the ladies washed our feet and
prayed over us. Of course, I washed Deborah's feet and
prayed over her, and she did the same for me. I will never
forget seeing her kneel at my feet and hearing her voice in
my heart.

There were so many tears that day—so many unspoken fears
that day—but celebrating with Deborah and her wonderful
Christian friends was an amazing experience for me. Before
we left, I just had to share with them what was on my heart:

"I have friends in Snyder, and in Atlanta, and in Manhattan.
But now I have another group of friends here in Fort Worth.
When I met some of you women in Anaheim nine years
ago, never did I, in my wildest dreams, think that I would
one day become one of you all. Amazing love, how can

it be. I just want to thank you—for what you are doing for Deborah, and for me."

Friday, July 16, 1999
10:20 p.m. (back home in Manhattan)

God is so good. I just got off the phone with Deborah and she said that her CT scan showed that all of the cancer is gone from her pelvic area and fifty percent of the cancer is gone from her liver. This is nothing but the grace of God. Even the doctors are surprised. But we aren't. Thank You, Lord.

She hadn't been to the mission with Ron since she found out she had cancer in April, so they went tonight. She called me when they got home and said that everyone was crying and thanking God for the news. They love her there like we all do.

She told me about a dream she had about a black man. Then she saw him at the mission one day and was shocked. She said that while he puts up a real hard front—acting almost dangerous—God has let her see into his heart. I look forward to one day meeting this new "friend" of hers. She didn't tell me his name, but she couldn't stop talking about him.

Then she told me that they had gotten some new information. Since the cancer was only in her liver, now she could be a candidate for an experimental treatment that is being done in San Antonio. It is a nonsurgical outpatient procedure—needles would be put right into the tumors—much like burning off a wart. Only more serious. They report a tremendous success rate with this approach. If the cancer had been in any other part of her body, she couldn't have even been considered a candidate. Please Lord, let the doctors in San Antonio accept her and the treatment remove all the cancer from her liver. The past three and a half months have been such a difficult time for Deborah, Ron, and the kids. She sounded wonderful on the phone, though . . . through her tears.

Chapter *9*

Standing Still

Be still, and know that I am God . . .
(Psalm 46:10)

I so wanted to stand still and know. But the nightmare that was now my life wouldn't let me. Every day brought news that kept me on a rollercoaster: I was either riding high with hope that the cancer in my sister's body was being destroyed by some new treatment or procedure, or I was sliding deeper into a pit of despair over news of spreading cells and increasing pain.

I continued to visit her as often as I could. When I wasn't with her I was miserable. Work helped, but it could not erase from my mind what she was going through. Some of my time with her was actually almost glorious, especially when we could get out of the house and do normal things that other sisters do . . . like eating Mexican food at her favorite restaurant or seeing a movie. On some days she looked so good that I pretended that all was well and we both would live forever. When she looked good, so did Ron. They hugged and kissed like newlyweds until I would have to leave the room.

Other times, though, we sat in her room and stared at the telephone—willing it to ring and bring good news. Waiting is not an easy thing for me to do anyway, but waiting and then being told that the treatments didn't work or that the medication wasn't approved yet for use in America was almost more than I could bear.

I hadn't seen Deborah since July, so when I arrived in Fort Worth for another visit, I was amazed that Deborah was doing so well and counted my blessings. Other than looking tired, she seemed great. I knew that it was her faith that was keeping her smiling. And, believe me, when she smiled, everyone smiled. Especially me.

When we were alone the next morning and just talking to catch up, she told me about the first time she went in for her chemo treatments.

"Daphene, I hate to admit this, but I was scared to death. I thought I would be okay until I got to the door of the treatment room. I stopped because—" She paused. "I felt like I was going to faint." She hesitated again, visibly uncomfortable. "It was such a strange feeling."

"Oh, I wish I could have been there for you."

"You should have seen Ron. He wrapped his sweet arms around me and just held me there until I could get myself together. He didn't say a word . . . he just held me. I could feel his heart beating against mine until I recovered enough to step inside the door."

"How did it go, that first time?"

"Oh, the treatment wasn't that bad. As I sat there waiting for my turn, I began to look around the room and see the other people—how scared and sad they were. I heard the Lord whisper to me 'Let the weak say I am strong . . . .'"

I sat in silence, watching her face as she shared this story. I could just see her going from station to station, touching the arm or face of the patients, speaking life to them until it was her turn to get hooked up.

She is truly an inspiration for all of us, Lord. I know she is giving many people hope . . . because that's who You made her to be, and that's what she does. And that's what she has done for me. God, You are good, all the time. Thank You for helping each of us see that we can trust You to take care of our precious Deborah and for helping us release her completely into Your care—You seem to be doing a great job.

I left on Sunday evening feeling reassured that everything was going to be okay. She seemed almost her old self and weighed about what she normally did, before she'd been sick. I had hope.

* * *

Friday, October 29, 1999
7:20 p.m. (at home in Manhattan)

I can't believe what is happening. How do I help my sweet children get through what is ahead? Oh, I need to talk with Deborah. But is she well enough? Will this be harmful to her—if I call and share what is happening? I have to call her!

"Deborah, how are you doing? Tell me the truth, because I need to talk to you but don't want to burden you if you are not up for it. The truth, now, please." I was talking on my cell phone and pacing the full length of my apartment as I talked.

"What's going on? You sound terrible. I'm fine. Just tell me what's going on." Her voice sounded strong.

"I don't know where to begin, and I can't stop crying."

"Well, just blurt it out and we'll sort through it later."

"Okay. John Kevin just called me. He got a call from the Florida State Police looking for relatives of John Weaver."

"Oh, no. What happened?"

"He's on life support in a Jacksonville hospital. Oh, Deborah. They don't think John Weaver will live."

"Daphene, I am so sorry. What happened?"

"And his wife is in bad shape, too—critical condition, Denise said. She called me, too."

I could hear Ron's voice in the background asking questions. "What happened, Daphene? Do you know details?" Obviously Deborah looked concerned and her persistent questions had attracted his attention.

"The kids asked me to fly out tonight, if possible, to be with them. I'm going to call and get a reservation as soon as I get off the phone with you. In fact, I probably should go and get that done and then I'll call you back tomorrow when I know more. Is that okay?"

When I called her back the next morning, she didn't answer, so I left her a voice message: "Deborah, I'm at the hospital with the kids. Call me back on my cell when you can talk.

Hope you are doing okay this morning. Love you." It wasn't long before my cell phone rang.

"Thanks for calling me back," I said. "How are you doing? Any word on your tests?"

"Nothing new," Deborah snapped back. "I want to know how Denise and John Kevin are doing."

"Wait just a minute. I want to walk outside to talk." I waved to Denise and mouthed that it was Aunt Debbie. She nodded but remained sitting in the ICU family room where we had spent the night. "Well, I finally got the whole picture of what happened. Do you have time to hear it?" I walked to the elevator and then decided to just take the stairs. I heard Deborah yell at someone in their house and then she returned to our conversation.

"Sure. I have some friends coming over in a bit, but go ahead and fill me in," Deborah said hurriedly.

"You knew that John Kevin and Missy were moving into their new home in St. Simons Island, right?"

"Yeah."

"Well, John Weaver and his wife had stopped by to help them with the move on their way to a motorcycle rally in Jacksonville. It was a Harley Davidson rally of some kind."

"Oh, wow. Didn't know that they rode Harleys."

"The four of them had breakfast together at their favorite place and then they said their good-byes. Amazing, isn't it, that you can say good-bye to someone and you never know if you will ever see them again alive?" I had reached the door to the outside and brushed past a couple just coming in. I needed some fresh air badly.

"Yes. Amazing."

"The Highway Patrol gave Denise a copy of the accident report and she told me that it looks like they were hit by a truck as they turned to cross the highway into a truck stop for gas. John Weaver was thrown off the bike but she was dragged quite a ways—"

"What day was that?" Deborah interrupted.

"They were in the hospital a couple of days before John Kevin got that call." I had found a bench where employees gathered to smoke and sat down. Luckily no one was around because I needed some space and decided I could tolerate the cigarette smoke to be free to talk.

"How are the kids taking all of this?" Her voice was suddenly so tender it brought tears to my eyes.

"Oh, Deborah. It is so sad to see them. They dearly love their dad, and they both love his wife. She has been good to them, you know. She's pretty bad, too—still in critical condition with one side of her body crushed and her back broken."

"Oh, no. They *all* need prayer, for sure." She gave a slow, compassionate sigh. "Are there other family members coming?"

"Deborah, the doctors are talking to the kids about taking John Weaver off life support." I had started pacing again, from the bench to the row of trees and back. It was a cool morning, still and quiet.

"How are they handling that?"

"It's terrible. Really. I can't even tell you the pain we all feel."

"I need to go. My friends just got here. But, Daphene, call me this afternoon and keep me in the loop. I love you all. Tell the kids I'm praying for all of you. Love you."

I disconnected from the call and looked around. The visitor parking lot was filling up and people were talking quietly to each other as some entered and others left the hospital. *Lord, it doesn't look like John Weaver will be among the ones leaving. Can it really end like this for him?*

Wednesday, November 3, 1999
8:00 p.m. (in the hotel room in Jacksonville, FL)

I need to write this in my journal, but it is so painful. We gathered this morning in John Weaver's room to say our good-byes before the doctors removed his life support. It had been a unanimous decision among the family. His wife's family had traveled from Louisiana to be with her and help her through this terrible ordeal, and she had improved enough to know what needed to be done. It seemed so unreal. I was thankful to be included in the lineup for last visits . . . but it was not an easy thing to do.

Denise went in first, and my heart broke for her. She was trying to be strong, but I could see the complete devastation in her eyes.

John Kevin and Missy went in together and stayed quite a while with him. I could hear his sobbing from where I was in the hallway outside the hospital room. It was so painful to hear. I couldn't help but wonder what Deborah would do if she were here. She is so good with people in need.

I was the last one to go in and was thankful that John's wife was with me. She had been in several times before—as often as the nurses would push her hospital bed into his room. It was obvious that she didn't want to leave his side even though she was severely injured. I moved around to the other side of John Weaver's bed so that I could see as much of his face as was visible with the life support machines. The whirring and pumping were almost hypnotic, and I had to shake myself to focus.

His face was swollen and bruised and his eyes were closed. Tape covered his mouth to hold the tube inside it. His hands were outside the covers, so I reached over and touched the one closest to me. I tried to see the John Weaver from our high school days in that body lying there so still and helpless, but I couldn't.

I whispered to him that I was blessed to have known him, that he had been a wonderful father to our children, that I was sorry for the pain I had caused him but thankful that he had forgiven me. I told him that I had always loved him and always would—in all the ways people can love each other. I thanked him for bringing his new wife into our lives and for the help she had been to our kids. And then I said good-bye to him. I was relieved when the nurse came in to help his wife say good-bye to the husband she was losing. When we were all out of his room, the doctor went in and removed the equipment. And it was over.

> *I need to call Deborah and tell her that it is over. Tomorrow I*
> *will go back home to Manhattan and to my life . . . a life that*
> *will include only memories of John Weaver. How can this be?*

* * *

Deborah and I cooked for twenty-one people who had been invited to Rocky Top Ranch outside of Fort Worth for Thanksgiving dinner. She had not needed chemo the week of Thanksgiving, so it was a real blessing to see her in the kitchen doing "her thing." We were alone for several hours before everyone arrived, which was wonderful. It brought back memories of the two of us in the kitchen at home in Snyder, and we reminisced about that for a while.

"I love these times when it is just the two of us, don't you?" I asked. She was standing at the sink, both hands in dishwater when she answered. She had on cute jeans and the black turtleneck sweater she loved so much. Her dark hair was shiny, and her green eyes were clear. If you didn't already know it, you would not have thought she was sick. She smiled back at me.

"Yes, I love them too. But they go by way too fast, don't they?

Some of the guests had already arrived but were with Ron on a tour of the scenic spots outside. Soon the house was full of family and friends, and the chatter among them was loud and disjointed. We served dinner and then went outside to walk some of it off before the next round. Ron had started a campfire and people were talking and laughing all around it. It was a beautiful scene.

Oh, Lord, forgive me for being selfish, but . . . what I really want is to have Deborah all to myself. I know her friends and family love her, but they have her all the time. I'm only here once in a while and—

"Daphene, come over here and tell us about your time in Manhattan. How's it going?" Ron's big smile accompanied his invitation. My thoughts were interrupted, but I welcomed the chance to share with some of Deborah's dear friends. *I am sorry, Lord, for my selfishness.*

December 2, 1999
3:15 p.m. (at home, in my prayer chair)

Today Deborah saw a doctor in the Dallas/Fort Worth area that does the experimental treatment called Thermal Ablation. The process is similar to burning a wart. There are reasons to be scared, but a door has been opened. Her oncologist will be contacted tomorrow to see if the surgery can be done before she completes this round of chemo. She is hoping to have it before Christmas, and our prayer is that the cancer will be contained inside her liver, and that he will get it all.

After graduating from TCU in December of 1999, Ron and Deborah's son, Carson, decided to relocate to work with one of his dad's friends who had a gallery in Manhattan. He hated leaving his mom during this difficult time, but Ron assured him that it was the right thing to do. This friend and Ron did a lot of business together and Manhattan would be a great place for Carson to learn the business firsthand. I was thrilled to have Deborah's son move into my apartment building—just one floor beneath mine. After getting settled, he agreed to go with me to Times Square Church one Sunday morning. We took a cab and arrived early.

"Just follow me and I'll find my friend. She always saves a few seats for me and whomever I bring with me." Over the course of the past two years, I had connected with several people there, but my favorite was an older woman who was personal friends of the senior pastor's mother. The senior pastor at Times Square Church traveled so much that he had brought in several other pastors to share the pulpit with him, so you never knew who would be delivering the message—and it didn't really matter. The first service started at 10 a.m., the second at 3 p.m., and the last one at 6 p.m. The presence of the Lord was so strong in that place that many people who came to the early service stayed throughout the day, not wanting to leave.

"Yes, I liked it a lot, Daphene," Carson said between bites of French toast. We had found a great breakfast place not far from the church and had stopped to eat before walking back home. "It's a lot like Mother and Daddy described it. Except you can't really put into words what you feel, can you?" His soft voice matched his sweet smile; his small frame housed a generous heart.

"Oh, have you talked with either of them recently—like this morning? Or last night?" I couldn't pass up an opportunity to get the very latest update on how my sister was doing.

"No. You?" I hadn't, so I went back to our original conversation. "I'm glad you liked it. We can do it every weekend that you're around. That would be nice." Seeing Carson Hall singing and praising the Lord warmed my heart so much. Ron and Deborah had done a great job raising their children—they were both precious.

"Want to watch a movie at my place tonight? I'll cook," I offered as he paid the bill for our breakfast.

"Sounds like a deal." We walked home talking comfortably about all he was doing and my latest clients.

Over the next few months we became "a couple" as my circle of friends welcomed him with open arms. When Carson wasn't going home on the weekends to be with his folks, we would eat out at our favorite restaurants, shop, and go to movies. The Lord had created a family for us there, at least for a time—which comforted us when we were not able to be in Fort Worth with Deborah.

* * *

Friday, March 10, 2000
7:45 p.m. (at home)

The Thermal Ablation procedure that Deborah had December 21 was extremely painful, and it took her a long time to recover. After the surgery, the doctor indicated that she was free of cancer but would be monitored for formation of any new tumors.

Our hopes are high. Carson and I rejoiced together at this news.

Carson told me that at the end of March, he and Ron plan to go on an annual trail ride that Deborah insists they don't miss. Then at the beginning of April, Deborah and Ron will go see Regan in Colorado. She has taken a job as a cook at Crooked Creek Young Life Camp and loves everything about it. Her time in the art world left her longing for something more hands-on, more Proverbs 31 woman-ish. I know her dad was a little disappointed that she didn't take to the art world, but her mother was thrilled for her. I sure miss her, but I know that these will be treasured memories for both of her kids, who need to see their mom and dad.

I love having Carson living in my apartment building. It is good that we have each other, and how blessed I am to have this special time with him as I did with Regan. We love attending Times Square Church together on Sundays. We are able to visit each other in our jommies because we take the stairs rather than the elevator, and it is such fun to spend nearly every evening together.

Tuesday, March 14, 2000
11:10 a.m.

I just received a call from Deborah and Ron as they were leaving the doctor's office. The news is much better than anyone expected: she only has two small surface tumors on her liver that caused the tumor count to go up. There is no cancer anywhere else. She will be able to go back to the doctor who did the original Thermal Ablation to have them "zapped," as Deborah says. The procedure will be much less painful this time. We are rejoicing, but we're having to wait patiently again. And waiting patiently is difficult for me.

> *I just need to know that God is in control of all things, and He loves Deborah more than any of us do.*
>
> **Saturday, April 8, 2000**
> *(at home)*
>
> *It has been one year since Ron called from the hospital to tell us the horrible news. The report at that time was quite grim. All along Deborah has said that they would follow God's report and not the doctor's. To see how well she is doing now is nothing short of seeing the hand of God, and her faith continues to give all of us hope. In fact, just being with her strengthens my faith. I am truly blessed to be her sister and can't wait to see her again when Gretchen and I visit her. It has been a very long time since the three of us have been together.*

Gretchen and I flew in on a Thursday and stayed through Monday. We planned the trip because Ron and Carson were being cowboys on their trail ride together, so we would have Deborah all to ourselves. It was amazing to see Deborah doing so well. On Friday, we spent most of the day working in her flower and vegetable garden, and I really thought she did more work than I did. Gretchen sat in a lawn chair close enough to the garden to visit with us as we worked, and our conversation often drifted back to our Snyder days.

On the second afternoon of working outside, Deborah spoke what we both were thinking. "Gretch, I think you should take off your wig and relax here. It would be much cooler, too."

She looked shocked and started to protest, but I backed Deborah up. "Yes, Gretchen, you really would look much better with your natural hair." I wanted to be kind with my words and my tone. "You can just be yourself here. We love you."

"Maybe later," was all she said then, but before dinner she went to her room and returned without her wig. Her hair was thin and full of electricity but didn't look as bad as we had pictured. It hadn't been colored in years and was a mousey brownish-grey.

"Would you let me style it for you, Gretchen?" Deborah asked.

"I'll get the scissors," I offered. We sat her down at the kitchen table, wrapped a towel around her shoulders, and got to work. Because the ranch was not fully equipped with beauty shop supplies, we ended up using a pair of fingernail scissors to cut her hair. The three of us talked and laughed and made memories together that evening that I will forever treasure. Three sisters . . . three friends.

* * *

Thursday, April 13, 2000
5:20 a.m. (at home in Manhattan)

Deborah has been fighting this battle with cancer for a year now and has overcome obstacles the doctors said weren't possible. God is in control, and we trust Him for her recovery. She was doing so well for a while, but then they found more tumors. She was in surgery nearly four hours yesterday. Instead of two tumors, the doctor found three. One tumor was sitting on her gall bladder, so instead of ablating it, they just removed it. A biopsy was done on the eleven tumors that were ablated last time and all are now benign. She is in a lot of pain, since there are many drugs she can't tolerate. I'm not sure how long she will stay in the hospital, but I'm sure it won't be very long. She is known for not staying long in the hospital.

After talking with Ron yesterday, I think they will go to Honduras before thinking about the next round of chemotherapy. Right now she just can't face the side effects, and the work being done in Honduras and the clinic in Cleveland looks promising.

Wednesday, April 26, 2000
9:30 p.m. (at home, in my prayer chair)

It has been two weeks since her surgery. Deborah had another colonoscopy and there were no signs of cancer there—the report was completely clean. She started taking the experimental medicine that she was going to get from Honduras, although instead of Honduras they are getting it from Ireland. Ron is giving her a shot every morning and then the same medicine is given under her tongue at night. The shots are very painful for several hours after she gets them, but she said it is certainly better than chemotherapy. As always, she never complains and is always looking on the bright side of life. She will do this round of treatments for three months and then will have another CT scan. God, please let this be the end.

She is still very sore from the surgery she had to ablate the two tumors from her liver. The doctor was surprised that her liver was already regenerating. What fantastic news. Ron will be coming to Manhattan next week for business, and Deborah will come, too. It will be wonderful having them here.

Thursday, June 1, 2000
10:20 a.m. (at home, in my prayer chair)

I talked with Deborah last night and this morning. Things aren't looking very good. She won't say much, but if I understood her correctly her tumor count has skyrocketed. I'm going to call a friend of theirs whose husband is a doctor to see what that means for her. She has seen four doctors since she and Ron were here, and three think she may have more cancer because of a bad pain in her abdomen. One of the doctors thinks it's lesions from the last colonoscopy she had. My heart breaks as I think how fearful she and Ron must be. She tries to stay as positive as possible, but I know it is hard.

Saturday, June 10, 2000
12:30 p.m.

When Deborah and Ron visited, it was difficult because she was experiencing pain in her abdomen. Since she just recently had a colonoscopy, she was worried and called her oncologist, who said she shouldn't worry and he would see her when she returned. After they returned to Fort Worth, several of her doctors made a decision to do another scan to see if the cancer had spread. Not knowing has been hard on both Deborah and

Ron. *The reality of the possibility of more cancer is frightening, as she has done so well since last April. They are spending the weekend at the ranch on the Brazos River—their place of refuge. It has become to them what the river's original name, Brazos de Dios, means: the Arms of God. We are trying hard to have faith in her healing. My heart breaks every day when we talk. They are both growing very weary.*

Tuesday, June 13, 2000
9:30 p.m.

The cancer has shown up in her liver and pelvic area, and the pain she has been experiencing is a tumor in her abdomen. I talked with Deborah tonight and they will see the oncologist as quickly as possible. This is not what we wanted to hear. Regan and Carson will leave by Thursday so they can be with Deborah and Ron when they talk with the doctor. I want to be there, but I just haven't decided what to do. My heart is breaking for my twin sister. She is such a fighter and won't give up anytime soon. I'm trying hard not to let myself think too much.

Wednesday, June 21, 2000
4:45 p.m.

Deborah went to the oncologist today expecting to have surgery this week to remove the tumors in her abdomen. He told her he didn't want her to go through any more surgery at this time, and she is being referred to the cancer center at University of

Texas Medical Center. This is much more hopeful than what she thought was going to happen. As long as hope isn't taken from her, she will put up a big fight.

Friday, June 30, 2000
5:10 a.m.

After talking with Deborah last night, I don't really know or understand much of what she told me. Yesterday was their appointment at the University of Texas Medical Center in San Antonio. The doctor was sure that the pain in her abdomen is from cancer tumors that have spread. It probably happened when she had the last liver ablation. There is an approved chemotherapy that she might be given in Fort Worth, but the side effects will also be terrible. There will be several more doctors to talk with, both at Sloan Kettering and at a research clinic in this area.

We are all getting the picture loud and clear. There is no cure for her and it will take divine healing for her to beat this horrible disease. This has been such a difficult year, and it is getting ready to be so much harder, not just for her, but also for Ron, Regan, and Carson. They are an unbelievable family and their love radiates. She will not give up this battle.

God says He will never leave us or forsake us. He says we need to trust Him for all things. Maybe one day I will understand why she has to suffer. I want to believe in prayer, but I don't think God is hearing me anymore.

Friday, July 14, 2000
(Our birthday—in Fort Worth)

Praise God that Deborah and I can celebrate another birthday. She told me she made it very clear to her friends that this year's party needed to be different from last year's—no sorrowing (even though she is much worse now than she was then). She wants it to be filled with laughter.

Her friend, Mary Ellen, hosted a wonderful party this afternoon. We all loved seeing Deborah laugh at the great skits that these women performed. She adored the white pajamas that I gave her—they were a fine cotton and very plain, just the way she likes them. Deborah and I love our "jommies" and always laugh and say that "jommie time" is our favorite time of the day. She gave me a beautiful cross necklace that I treasure.

When I left the party, I called my granddaughter, who is now ten years old. It is her birthday, too. Millicent Marie Jones was a gift to me from God. I'm still amazed by the miracle of her birthday.

Sunday, August 6, 2000
1:15 p.m. (at home in Manhattan)

Deborah, Ron, and Carson have been in Colorado visiting Regan at the Young Life camp where she works. They drove instead of flying so they could take Regan the yellow lab they bought her for her birthday. Carson went along to help Ron with the driving.

The first night after they arrived at the camp, Ron had to take Deborah to the emergency room because she couldn't breathe. She has trouble in high altitudes anyway and had to be put on oxygen. The first day I talked with her she sounded very weak, but she was doing better once they went to a lower altitude. They start the trip back to Fort Worth today. I know this trip meant so much to all of them even though she was so sick.

She has her next chemo treatment Tuesday. I leave here Tuesday morning, and I will stay with them for a week. We are praying that this treatment will be easier than the last one. As always, she is very positive. We were together on our fifty-fifth birthday, which was such a blessing. I try not to think about not having Deborah to celebrate with.

I hate having to think about losing her. The cross necklace that she gave me will one day be given to Millicent, the other birthday girl. Deborah would want it that way.

Deborah continues to amaze me. She is such a testimony of what it means to walk in faith, but as hers gets stronger, mine grows weaker.

* * *

Deborah had her second chemo treatment on August 8, so I went to help out since she got so sick the first time.

"How are you doing, Deborah?" I asked when she got home. I was already there waiting for her. Ron helped her into the house, and I helped her into bed. She didn't say much until she got settled and rested a bit.

"It feels very different this time." She was taking big cleansing breaths between sentences. "And I'm still in a lot of pain." Every once in a while a small tremor or shudder went through her body as I watched.

"You know when soldiers go into battle they always have R & R to get ready for the next one? Well, I've been in this battle since April of last year–" She took another breath. "–without enough time to get my rest and relaxation in order to prepare for the next thing." I understood perfectly how she felt. Even though I was not the one fighting cancer, I still felt like a soldier, a soldier needing a break from the fighting. But we both kept at it.

When she was having chemotherapy, our time was tortuous. She dreaded going in; we dreaded her coming out sick. She would go from weak to weaker, and we would watch in helplessness and fatigue. Most of the time, it was either like a merry-go-round or a rollercoaster. Some days I didn't know which one I was on or how to compensate for the rapid change. Some days it felt like they had invented a new ride and I was on both at the same time. The ride just kept going on and on.

One morning, I went in to get her for a walk and found her on the floor. "Good grief, Deborah. Are you okay?" I knelt down beside her on the floor. "You need to get back into bed this minute. Should I call Ron?" My heart was beating fast and I was having a hard time catching my breath.

She turned her head to look me in the eye. "Listen, Sister Dear." Her voice was soft from weakness but firm with resolve. "As long as I can put one foot in front of the other, I plan to walk. You can go with me or not–that's entirely up to you. But I'm going. It makes me feel alive." I helped her up but we sat for a few minutes collecting ourselves before we went out.

"I'll stay as long as I can, you know. I want to be with you." I had planned to stay a week, but after I saw how sick she was, I stayed two. Taking care of her brought me so much joy, even in the midst of the pain.

Wednesday, August 23, 2000
(Back home in Manhattan)

I watched Ron care for her day after day while I was there. He is such a wonderful husband and gives her so much love and support. She has her next treatment on August 28, and Gretchen will go to help out this time. If the chemo isn't working after this treatment, they will probably stop. She is very weak but determined to fight. She and Ron get up early every morning before it gets hot and walk together. Before I left, she was up to three miles.

The kids are planning to go back home to Fort Worth to be with their parents for ten days or so the first week of September because Ron and Deborah are both worn out. Their friends are wonderful support to them–both in love and prayer–but there is nothing like having your children close by.

When I talked with her yesterday, she told me that she is not ready to give up hope and is still trusting God for a miracle. "We have got to learn to live in the day we are in," she said. I told her I would try.

Wednesday, August 30, 2000
10:30 p.m. (in my prayer chair)

I've cried so much for the past two days that my eyes are nearly swollen shut. Tuesday, Deborah went in for another CT scan and they discovered that the cancer had spread. When she called me she was not doing well at all. I talked with Ron briefly last night, and I told him I knew what the report was, and he didn't need to say anything.

When she called me that night, we both finally just broke down and cried together. After a while she said, "I want to live, Daphene." She had stopped crying and spoke calmly.

"I want you to live, Deborah." Tears flowed but I held back my sobs.

"Please just keep asking God to heal me."

"You know I will."

"And I want to see Regan and Carson married. I want to be there when they have babies. I want to be a grandmother." She was breathing hard and her voice was breaking on and off throughout her speaking.

"We have some time, Deborah. The main thing . . . right now . . . is that your new medication is helping you with the pain. I can hardly bear to see you in pain."

There was a long pause. Then she asked, "You want to hear something funny?"

I could not imagine anything being funny at this point, but said, "Sure."

"I think the new medicine has marijuana in it. I feel a little bit like a Volkswagen Beetle with a peace sign painted on. You know, we completely missed the hippie era–it just didn't make it to Snyder, Texas." She laughed out loud when she said this, and I loved to hear it. She had lost a lot of things during this illness, but she certainly had not lost her sense of humor. I tried to laugh, too, but it came out like a squawk of some kind. She went on talking.

"You know, it feels a lot like a big wave hits me," she said, paused to take a deep breath, and then continued, "and as soon as I stand up, another one knocks me down again."

"I kind of feel the same way, really." I got up from my chair and began my habit of pacing back and forth in my apartment. "I think I am doing fine–trusting the Lord for you–and then I just fall apart. I don't know . . . I think I am losing my faith." I was sorry I said it the minute the words were out of my mouth because her faith and strength were nothing short of a miracle.

"Regan is moving home from Colorado," she said, as if she hadn't even heard me. "I told her she didn't have to do that but she is insisting. But, really, Daphene, I will love having her help."

I gladly let her change the subject. "I'm leaving Friday morning for a church family camp in North Carolina for the Labor Day weekend. We decided this was the year to go as a family." I knew that I was truly blessed to be loved so much by both my children and grandchildren, and I felt guilty that I already had what she longed for.

"I'm glad you are going, Daphene."

"I want to be respectful of your need to process all of this as a family, so I won't come right away." I paused, pressing a hand to my forehead. "But I will come, Deborah."

When I got off of the phone, I grabbed my journal and quickly wrote down random Scriptures I had darting through my mind because I was desperate for His promises and needed to hold onto them for dear life:

God is able and faithful to deliver what He promises

Peace that surpasses all understanding

All things are possible

God is good . . . all the time

His ways are not our ways

* * *

I went to Fort Worth at the end of September to be with Deborah and the family. There was a lot of discussion and activity around treatments and doctors and medications that I found confusing and frustrating. They continued doing tests and scans and biopsies and trying new drugs. After I left, she tried to keep me up to date, but it all just overwhelmed me. I knew the battle was intense and they were all fighting hard. At times I wondered if it was worth the fight, but until you walked in someone's shoes, it was probably impossible to know. I didn't think she could fight much longer. Seeing her this time broke my heart–in one month she had deteriorated so much.

I desperately needed to get back to work so I wouldn't lose what I had struggled so hard to build, but it was difficult to leave her. I really couldn't imagine how God was going to comfort me if I didn't get to see her alive again. Her tumor count was going up fast, and they were spreading all over her abdomen and liver. I knew that she was fully aware that she was dying. I prayed that God would prepare all of us for what was ahead.

I tried to thank Him for the fifty-five years that we had together as twins. I also was thankful for the last few months that I had with her and the opportunities to tell her how much I loved her and to thank her for all the things she had done for me. What was the most difficult for me, though, was our inability to talk together about her dying; there was no closure for me. At times I felt like I was about to implode.

I thought we would grow old together.

Later that week, Deborah was taken to the emergency room and then admitted to the hospital. After tests, they found she had a complete blockage in her colon, which was something they had feared would happen. Ron called, and he said I needed to get back to Fort Worth as quickly as possible. I had lost all sense of time and place and was moving in a kind of fog.

I went immediately. Several days passed before the doctors finally told us to take her home so she could die there. With much sorrow, we did it. After a few days, her sweet friend Patricia Chambers arrived at the house to see Deborah one last time. She had purchased a beautiful Lalique vase containing a single white rose for her. The vase looked to me like it had been hewn from crystal jasper–the building materials of the New Jerusalem–heavy, solid, and pure.

She knew how much Deborah loved white roses, and instead of participating in the delivery of food, she chose something she knew Deborah would love. She placed it on the nightstand beside her bed and sat down to say her good-byes. She stayed quite a while and left in tears.

After she left, I read the card that accompanied the gift and wept. The Lord said that the world would know His people by the way they love each other. The world was receiving a message—a powerful display of love among the people in Ron and Deborah's lives.

Even though Ron had arranged for twenty-four-hour nursing and hospice care, her friends and family kept vigil at her side twenty-four hours a day. We were all so thankful that the doctors had finally found medication that helped control the pain. None of us could bear to see her suffer.

After a week of being home, she had Ron invite her closest friends over so she could share with them what was on her heart. I sat next to her on her bed as she called each by name and spoke words of love and thankfulness. Then she presented each with one of her cherished perfume bottles along with a handwritten note attached. She told them what their friendship had meant to her. When she was almost done with her friends, I prepared myself, thinking I was next. I didn't want to cry. I waited expectantly for what she would say to me. My heart was pounding and the room went completely silent. I couldn't look at her, but I glanced at the gold box she had retrieved the perfume bottles from . . . and it was empty. Then I looked up at her and her eyes were closed. The little gathering was over.

I got up from where I was sitting and walked out with the other women. I needed to be alone—my heart was breaking—

and I tried to understand how she could do that to me. I wished I knew why not getting a perfume bottle meant so much. Maybe her friends were able to minister to her in a way I couldn't.

It was an almost unbearable pain for me to know that she was dying, and I felt so helpless. The closer to death she got, the less I felt a part of the little life she had left.

Ron suggested that I summon my daughter and son so that they could say good-bye to their Aunt Debbie. Both flew in the next day and had a short time with her. After Denise and John Kevin came out, I went into her room.

* * *

"Deborah," I began. There were so many things I wanted to say to her, but I didn't know where to start.

"Daphene," she interrupted. Her eyes were closed; her voice was weak but stern. "Please don't make a fool of yourself at my funeral. Don't cry." She opened her eyes and turned her head toward me. "Just tell some of the funny stories about when we were little girls." She closed her eyes again and turned away.

I felt like I was the one dying, right then and there. I stood there stunned and immobile. My heart was breaking, but I knew she didn't have the strength to hear what I longed to say. I left the room dry-eyed and breathless, my heart pounding wildly, numb from head to foot.

When I came out, Ron, Regan, and Carson went in and closed the door.

I knew I should go and find my kids and try to comfort them, but I went to my room and closed my door, too. I picked up my journal and then threw it across the room. I couldn't write any more words . . . I couldn't. I just couldn't.

* * *

Ron called me several weeks after I got back to Manhattan and said she had gone into a coma. He recommended that I get on the next flight to Fort Worth so I could see her before she died. Of course, I went immediately, again. Even though hospice care was there around the clock, one of us was always with her, lying in bed beside her, because we had to make sure she didn't go into convulsions. The pain medication was no longer effective.

During one of my times in bed with her, I moved closer to her and drew her into my arms, almost like a mother would a young child. I needed to tell her how much I loved her and how thankful I was for all she had done for me. *How can I live without you? You taught me how to walk with God and live a life that would honor Him. You have brought me so much joy in allowing me to care for you.*

As I talked to her, her stiff body began to relax in my arms. I imagined that was what it must have been like when we were curled up in our mother's womb together. I remained with her in my arms until Carson came in for his turn.

"Daphene. You're smothering her, for heaven's sake," Carson half whispered as he rushed to the other side of the bed. He took her from me and laid her back down on the pillows in the middle of the bed. I was dumbfounded and horrified. *You have no idea what was happening here, Carson. No idea, whatsoever.*

I was deeply hurt by Carson's accusation that I was smothering her, but I just tried to move past it and go on.

Everyone in the house was exhausted and overwhelmed at what was unfolding. I will forever believe in my heart that although Deborah was in a deep sleep, she knew I was there and wanted me to know that she had heard me. That was the last time I felt like she knew I was with her.

It was a little after 10 p.m. on Friday night, November 3 that I told Ron to go and get some rest for a while and I would stay with her. When he left the room, I pulled my chair closer to the edge of the bed and leaned over her to take in as much as I could. The room was completely silent, and her breathing was so shallow that the movement of the sheet over her was barely visible. I took deep cleansing breaths, trying to breathe for her, wanting to impart life into her dying body.

As I sat there I watched her slowly breathe in and out, in and out, in and out . . . and then . . . nothing. I held my breath. One . . . two . . . three . . . four. Still nothing. My heart was pounding and my mouth went completely dry. I knew that Ron had wanted to be with her when this time came, and I opened my mouth to call him but could make nothing come out. I stood, trying to collect myself enough to move.

She is gone. Oh, Lord, she's gone.

Chapter 10

Letting Go

❄

When you pass through the waters, I will be with you; and when you pass through the rivers, they will not sweep over you. When you walk through the fire, you will not be burned; the flames will not set you ablaze.

(Isaiah 43:2)

Mary Ellen, Deborah's best friend and a nurse, went to the funeral home to help get her ready to be buried at the ranch. When she returned, she told me that Deborah had saved the beautiful white "jommies" I bought for her on our last birthday and had instructed Ron to make sure she was wearing them on this special day. I wept as she told me.

Right before the service started, Denise leaned over and whispered in my ear. "Mother, Aunt Deborah died exactly one year after Daddy did. Isn't that . . ." She didn't finish her sentence. I hadn't realized it before that minute. November 3–one year apart–sorrow upon sorrow. So much loss. I blew my nose and patted my cheeks in hopes that I didn't look absolutely terrible. I had to speak in a few minutes.

She was buried at Rocky Top Ranch on November 6, 2000, at 2:00 in the afternoon. There were many dear friends, along with immediate family and our aunts, uncles, and cousins, all gathered to honor her. It had rained earlier in the day, but a warm breeze had swept across the ranch and dried up most of the puddles that had formed. The pine casket that Deborah requested was draped with a blanket of white roses—her favorite. Her two dogs found a dry place on the red dirt mound by the grave to lie down on. Ron asked one of the ranch employees to hold the reins to Deborah's paint horse not far from where we were gathered—saddled and without its rider. Chairs were arranged in a semi-circle around the casket, which had been placed near the edge of the cliff where Ron and a friend had built the beginning of a little cemetery. Beyond the cliff you could see the Brazos River. The gentle rustlings from the horse's movements, the occasional cawing of a bird in a nearby mesquite tree, and the whispers of the guests as they assembled and found places to sit all joined together into a kind of soft cushion that muffled the sound of breaking hearts.

I asked later and was told that Patricia Chambers, along with the Wednesday Watchmen ladies, had arranged for the blanket of white roses that covered her casket. What dear friends she had. I loved Patricia, Mary Ellen, Cindy, Jeanie, and all those other women for loving Deborah so much.

I was one of those asked to speak at this private burial service for her family and friends and had prepared ahead of time because I didn't think I could do it any other way. Besides, Deborah had instructed me not to cry and make a scene. I didn't want to disappoint her, so I just read. I took a deep breath, looked around quickly, and jumped in.

"Where do I even begin to share with you the deep love I have for my precious Deborah? I'll never forget the first day she called to ask me to pray for her because the doctor was sending her to have a test run after her yearly checkup. We all know the rest. That call changed my life forever." I paused a moment to stifle a sob that I felt surfacing. "What I began to realize is that over the past ten years, my love for Deborah deepened so much that it overshadowed the love I should have for my Heavenly Father. She became my 'everything.' I made no decisions without checking with her first. Once she was sick, I knew I had to learn to take care of myself. She had raised the standards so high for me I was afraid I couldn't go it alone." Tears were running down my cheek but I wiped them away quickly with a tissue I had wadded in my hand and continued.

"God in His mercy has been pouring out His love for me to show me He is my 'everything.' My faith has deepened, my company is doing well, and maybe someday my heart will be happy again." I looked up, trying to smile and pretend that this could really one day happen. I could not imagine it.

"The most wonderful gift I have been given is the honor of giving back to her these many months for a lifetime of her caring for me. Even though it was also painful for us, she allowed me to do many wonderful things, for her. I stayed several weeks with her at the Davenports after her first surgery. For the first time, she let me serve her in ways she never had before. One night, after she had a very difficult day, she looked at me and said, 'I didn't know you loved me this much.' 'You've never let me love you like this,' I told her.

"There were other times when I had opportunities to be with her that continued to bless me. God gave me strong hands that could massage her body for hours without ever getting tired. That would bring me so much joy.

"When I arrived on October 24, I had no idea what the next days would be like. She had not been expected to live but a few more days." My voice broke and I had to stop again to collect myself. I didn't look up, but I heard several people in the group blowing their noses. "Until she took her last breath on November third," I gulped for air and tried to continue, "she was still ministering to all of us. She left us with memories we will have in our hearts forever." When I said that, I was flooded with a peace that settled my rapidly beating heart and evened out my labored breathing. I took another deep breath and continued.

"Once the grief of no longer seeing her beautiful face lessens, I know God will make her presence even stronger in my heart. I praise God that for the last ten days of her life I was privileged to be with her. She glorified God in her life, and He is now being glorified in her death. Heaven is rejoicing.

"God spoke to me clearly on October 30, through the daily devotional book by L.B. Cowman, *Stream in the Desert:*

'Many of us could tearlessly deal with our grief if only we were allowed to do so in private. Yet what is so difficult is that most of us are called to exercise our patience not in bed but in the open street, for all to see. We are called upon to bury our sorrows not in restful inactivity but in active service—in our workplace, while shopping, and during social events—contributing to other people's joy. No other way of burying our sorrow is as difficult as this, for it is truly what running with patience means' (from Hebrews 12:1).

"I understood from this that what I was to do is give to others, and I did experience such joy in giving to Deborah. But I feel like today—well, I have nothing left to give. Who would want all this sorrow?" As I was reading this part, I glanced up from my notes, and my eyes caught a glimpse of Ron's face. It was ashen and blank with grief. He was staring at Deborah's coffin as if waiting for it to open and her to step out, like Sleeping Beauty in the movie. There had been quiet talk of resurrection, and Lazarus, and miracles, and the ministry that could come of it . . . but the coffin remained closed, and I finished reading. Every once in a while Deborah's horse whinnied, a painful reminder that she was no longer with us.

The service continued with Deborah's friend Patricia speaking after me, but I remember only bits and pieces: "more than conquerors," "working all things together for good," "nothing can separate," "knowing Deborah is with Him now." And then Ron read a poem he had written to her. He wept and sobbed, trying hard to get all the words out, and finally came to the end. I was relieved for him—it was agonizing to watch. I hardly remember getting through the rest of the day.

The next afternoon at 3:00, a memorial service was held for her at McKinney Memorial Bible Church in Fort Worth where they attended. Deborah had ordered that it be a celebration, and John and Jeanie Ott carried out her plans exactly as she would have wanted. The service opened with "I Can Only Imagine," a new song that Deborah loved the moment she first heard it. There were hundreds of people there to honor her that day—many sharing stories about what Ron called "a life well lived."

I remember one, specifically, though. It was her "friend" from the Mission. He introduced himself to the crowd as Denver. I was surprised how nice he looked in his dark pinstripe suit and tie—not like a homeless man at all. His voice was arresting, and his message touched my heart as he spoke of Deborah's strong courage and great love. He never looked at notes since he couldn't read, and the longer he spoke, the louder he got. I heard echoes of my own story through my quiet sobbing: *She never gave up . . . she loved me anyway . . . that kind of love changes things.* It began to feel like I was at Times Square Church. When he finished speaking, people stood and applauded him. I stood and wept as the applause continued on and on.

When it was my turn to speak, I collected myself and read from another set of prepared notes. As I made my way to the podium on the platform, I adjusted the jacket of my black skirt-suit and centered the cross necklace I had around my neck. It was the one Deborah had given me on our birthday.

"I was fortunate, as some of you were, to say good-bye to Deborah. Many of us have experienced her 'pointed finger' that would always guide us in the direction she wanted us to go. How much we'll miss that finger.

"She told me if I wanted to say something at her service I could, but she had some specific guidelines for me to follow. She instructed me both with words and with that finger of hers, pointed straight at me: 'Don't cry a bunch and embarrass yourself, Daphene. Tell funny stories about us growing up and don't talk too long.'

"To honor her, I've chosen some of our favorite stories to share with you."

I shared story after story of our early childhood escapades, and the people at the memorial service had a good laugh or two. The crowd was bigger and the setting less intimate, so the laughter was appropriate and appreciated. I talked about the fire club she started, the piano recital that we performed, and the bridge game we messed up with flying frogs. Deborah would have been proud of me. Then I jumped ahead to junior high school.

"When we were in junior high, living in Snyder, we were both cheerleaders. We never understood a thing about football but we loved our pom-poms, megaphones, and certain cheers. One of our very favorites was 'push 'em back, push 'em back . . . wayyyyyy back!'" I yelled it out like we used to, waving the imaginary pom-poms in the air, and the audience erupted into laughter. I continued: "It didn't matter who had the ball–we just loved to do it over and over again. That might have been the reason we never got to be high school cheerleaders." I took a few seconds to catch my breath and let the crowd quiet back down.

"When I started my company on January 1, 1991, I didn't have two nickels to rub together. God had given me a vision, and I knew I needed to follow Him. My first big client was Estée Lauder in New York, and Deborah had me come to Dallas so she could show me how to dress. She assured me that no one would do business with me if I looked poor. She took me to Neiman Marcus to a department I'd never set foot in. I'm sure the woman helping us thought I wasn't able to speak, because Deborah would say, 'Oh, she loves that; no, that won't work; she won't look good in that.' When she finally decided what I'd take and we went to pay for the clothes, the lady looked to Deborah for payment. Quickly she said, 'Oh, *she'll* take care of it.'" I laughed out loud, myself, as I recalled the whole scene. "Some of y'all know exactly what I'm talking about, too!" I ad-libbed to the audience. There were chuckles around the auditorium. She was the "boss" of many of us.

"I wasn't going to share this part of our life because I was afraid I'd cry, and Deborah asked me not to. But my dear friend, John Ott, asked me if I would." Then I told them about my time with Deborah and her friends at the Anaheim Conference in 1990 and how God had promised to send a southern breeze to blow over the hearts in our family. "I was so overwhelmed at the time with what God was doing inside of me that I did not have the capacity in my heart to even imagine the ripple effect upon others. But as I look back on all that has happened in our lives during the past decade, I now see that many of us will never be the same. For the past ten years, our God has been completely true to His Word.

"We all have our wonderful memories of Deborah. I consider myself blessed that God ordained that we be twins. I'm sure He knew I'd need a bunch of help. Her love, encouragement, and deep faith have made me the woman I am today. I've grieved at the thought of never celebrating another birthday with her." I had to stop and collect myself again. "But God has been gracious to give me a new birthday partner—my granddaughter, Millicent Marie Jones. She was born at 1:30 a.m. on July fourteenth, 1990. What an awesome God we have.

"I consider myself blessed to have been able to serve my dear sister Deborah over these past nineteen months; after all, she took care of me for fifty-five years. I will continue to try to be the person she knew God wanted me to be."

It seemed for a few moments that time stood still. I looked at Ron and Regan and Carson sitting together in the front row and my heart broke all over again. Memories of Ron and Deborah's wedding flashed upon my mind like a PowerPoint presentation from the past; then the babies when they were brought home after the adoption signings; then our wonderful Thanksgivings at Rocky Top Ranch.

Denise and John Kevin were sitting in the front row, too, and the pain on their faces brought back memories of the hospital . . . and saying good-bye to their dad and my first love.

Next to them was Denver Moore–silent, strong, broken– and the cluster of close friends filling the rows all around the family. I was again overwhelmed with such conflict from my love for them, sorrow for all of us, and such emptiness because she was not there. She was not with us anymore. The emptiness of that fact left me hollow and breathless, almost in panic. But I had to finish my talk. I snapped back to reality and whispered the words into the microphone, "I will leave you with Revelation 21:4: 'He will wipe every tear from their eyes. There will be no more death or mourning or crying or pain, for the old order of things has passed away.'"

A new and strange strength rose up in me as I said the last line of my prepared talk. "I will miss you so much, my sweet Debbie." I stretched up straight and tall, looked up at the crowd one last time, gathered up my notes, and left the podium trusting that I could hold on until God did that for me–wipe away my tears, take away my mourning and pain, and make me into the woman He intended me to be from the beginning . . . without letting bitterness and anger spring up in my heart.

Chapter 11

Reaching Out

❧

So do not fear, for I am with you; do not be dismayed, for I am
your God. I will strengthen you and help you; I will uphold you
with my righteous right hand.

(Isaiah 41:10)

I returned to Manhattan with a completely broken heart
and a sense of being alone in a way that staggered me. Losing
a sibling is one thing; losing a twin is another. Although
Deborah and I had gone our separate ways for a stretch of
our early years, I always knew that she was there for me.
Now she was gone. The emptiness that this reality brought
to the pit of my stomach was so physically painful that I
considered seeking medical help for it. What would I tell the
doctor? My twin sister is dead and I feel her loss right here,
then point to my gut? My soul ached and I felt adrift.

I forced myself to return to work, determined to be strong
and go on to make Deborah proud of me. But when I
returned home each day, the first thing I did was sit down
in my prayer chair, prop my feet up, push the play button

on my message machine, lean my head back, and close my eyes. Her voice was all I had left. I had recorded many of our last conversations and clutched at them like a starving person would at food. I listened to them over and over again until one day I pushed the wrong button and erased them all. I sat staring at the machine in horror. *Oh, now even her voice is gone from me.* And I wept far into the night.

I had only slept a few hours when I woke up with a start. I was sweating and crying and so thirsty that I left my bed and was down the hall to the kitchen in what seemed like a giant step. As I filled a glass of water, my dream came into view. It was Deborah, in her white jommies, talking to me. But I couldn't hear what she was saying, and I so wanted to hear her. She kept talking and I kept straining to hear her. It was terrible. Just terrible. I finished drinking the water and then went into the living room and collapsed into my chair, where it was dark and quiet. *I need you, Lord. I need you more than I think I have ever needed You before. I love You, I know I do, but I don't feel the way I used to. Help me, Lord. Please, help me.*

Day after day I returned to my prayer chair with my Bible and my journal. I read but the words hit a barrier somewhere between the page and my heart; I wrote the date in my journal each time, but ended up doodling a bit around the edges of the page because I had no thoughts that were worth remembering. I tried reading other Christian books, but my mind would not stay focused long enough to get the gist of what they were saying. I prayed and waited. And then prayed some more. And waited some more, too. It had been nine months since Deborah died and I just kept waiting to . . . to start living again.

* * *

In September of 2001, I was still in Manhattan, waiting and praying, while working with Pfizer. Pfizer is located on 42nd Street and 2nd Avenue. It was a beautiful morning and I had chosen to walk the thirty blocks to work from 72nd Street, something I did more and more after Deborah died. It seemed to help me somehow.

I was in the main building working with a new client when we were suddenly interrupted by an intercom announcement. That never happens at Pfizer, so I knew immediately that something was very wrong. Our section of the floor was directed into the conference room down the hall, where there was a television playing loudly. I could hear it before I got to the door. When I went in, I could feel the hush that was hanging in the air—a very tense hush. I looked up at the screen and saw fire and smoke coming from one of the towers of the World Trade Center. The client I was working with came up behind me and whispered, "They are saying a plane hit it." We both stood there with our mouths open, trying to breathe.

Then we saw the second plane hit the second tower. The woman let out a moan and started crying. "My best friend works in that building," she wailed. I wrapped my arms around her and stepped out into the hall so I could pray for her. "Lord, we don't know what's going on, but You do and we need You to put a hedge of protection around all those people to protect them from the fire." While we were praying, security guards came by and requested that we quickly leave the building via the stairs because the United Nations was only one block away, and the possibility of another plane was clearly the unspoken message.

Both of us were frozen in fear for a second or two, and then we moved quickly out the door and into the hallway. All around us people were pouring out of offices and cubicles, arms loaded with as many of their personal belongings as they had time to grab; they looked like newly caused tributaries full of debris and rushing into the main stream after a storm. Heads were unnaturally bent as people tried holding their cell phones between their shoulders and ears while they jostled both their belongings and their colleagues rushing to get out of the building. We joined in the push for the stairway exit and entered the flow.

The crowd was moving fast down one flight of stairs after another. I tried not to think too far ahead and just kept my feet moving. At each landing, a security guard instructed us to be quiet and move quickly. They were not allowing anyone to take the elevator because no one knew what might happen next.

When I finally got out of the building, I headed straight back to my condo. Smoke was filling the air, and ambulances and police cars were racing past all of us who were fleeing the area. Those thirty blocks seemed like thirty miles that day. I was walking fast and breathing hard. My feet hurt and my lungs were burning, my heart was pounding, and my mind was jumping in all directions. I could not think straight. As I looked at others—some rushing past me on their way to safety and others racing back to the buildings—I was struck by the looks on their faces: terror, shock, determination. The farther away I got from the Towers, the easier it was to breathe. But the sirens, millions of them, it seemed, were in full blare mode. It was deafening.

I expected Kay, my employee from Minneapolis, to be waiting for me at home. She had been staying with me since she had been working at Pfizer and was scheduled to leave the next day. I knew her departure would be delayed now and was thankful because I didn't want to be alone.

I was so thankful to reach my front door and find Kay standing there. She was dressed for her flight home but looked like she had been in a tussle with someone. "I can't go home, Daphene. I can't get out of the city. Oh, Daphene. I am so scared." She started to cry and so did I.

We both changed our clothes and then stayed glued to the television for the rest of the day. I knew that my kids were frantically trying to locate me, but I could do nothing to relieve their fears. Most of the phones were dead, and cell phone service was disrupted. The news reporters announced several times that all flights had been grounded indefinitely, so we knew Kay would be staying the rest of the week. I was thankful for the company, and she was thankful to have a place to stay. We had done it before and could do it again.

After we had heard the news at least a hundred times—and seen those horrendous images of both towers collapsing—we finally peeled ourselves away from the television to find something constructive to do. Thankfully, I had just done major grocery shopping, so I suggested that we make sandwiches for those brave people stationed downtown who were trying to help people locate their loved ones. We also decided to take some of the extra Bibles I had. After we loaded up our supplies, and after walking several blocks, we came face to face with National Guard troops toting machine guns and stationed on almost every corner. Manhattan looked like a war zone. It was shocking to see, and I felt like I was on a movie set.

We weren't the only ones who wanted to help. Food was piling up at designated places, where people by the hundreds had gathered with pictures looking for their loved ones. We hoped that what we brought would be eaten, but eating seemed to have become a forgotten luxury amid the chaos. Not one person refused a Bible when we offered it, to our amazement. Kay and I hugged every single person we encountered and told them that we were praying for them, which, many times, brought instant tears. After we had delivered everything we had, we returned to my apartment completely exhausted but strangely rejuvenated. We spent the rest of the week watching television and shaking our heads in disbelief along with the rest of the country.

* * *

Once Kay left, I tried to think of what else I could do to be helpful because Pfizer was my main client and they were not allowing anyone to return to work yet. I poured myself a cup of coffee, sat down in my prayer chair, and leaned my head back. My first thoughts drifted to Deborah. I could see her in that furniture store a couple of years back "modeling" for me how I would look. It had been almost a year since she died, but my heart still felt broken. Then my thoughts jumped to Times Square Church—and a firehouse that I passed each time I went there. I needed to go and see what I could do to help those firemen. After all, they were my neighbors now. And I wanted to be their Samaritan.

I found Engine 8, Ladder 2, Battalion 8, just where I thought it was. I had to pass through piles of flowers that had been placed along their south driveway as I made my way. Just to the right of their front door, a huge poster had been hung that listed the names of all the firefighters lost on that horrible day, along with photographs. I stopped and looked at each one and whispered his name. These men had all died on 9/11, and their families were grieving. Oh, how I could relate to their sorrow. Mine was still so very fresh.

Before going inside, I turned slowly around and felt the great sadness that hung in the air over that neighborhood. The firehouse was a brick two-story building with huge doors for the fire engines. An American flag flew at half staff in front of the building. This fire station, just like so many others, had lost many of their own and had to have other firefighters brought in from faraway places to fill the void. *The void.* What a word. I didn't even need to ask what I could do. I would just try to find a way to fill a small portion of that void I knew so well.

* * *

I finally returned to work at Pfizer and kept busy there, but over the next few months I found time to befriend many of those firefighters and to make food for them several times a week. They were working hard and bearing their grief, along with all the rest of New York City's finest, like well-trained soldiers on a battlefield. It was good for me to think of them. I learned their names and their favorite dishes. Homemade biscuits became the biggest hit, so I made them almost every weekend. My kitchen was small, which made cooking for so many men a challenge, but I loved doing it so much that I just went ahead. My biggest struggle was to make it to the station with the food still hot. I loved sitting with them at their long, wooden table and hearing them talk to each other—mostly about the men who hadn't returned when the towers fell. The food I brought seemed to ease their pain . . . and mine, although none of them knew about mine. When I wasn't with them, I took time to write cards of encouragement to each one. It was a sad time for all of us, but I was blessed to share their sorrow.

With Christmas just around the corner, and so many children of firefighters without one or both of their parents, I got the idea to raise some money to buy Gap gift cards for each child who was affected by a loss from that firehouse. I met with the manager of a Gap store to let him know what I was doing, and he offered to match whatever I raised. I was thrilled. I also sent emails to all of my Manhattan, Georgia, and Texas friends asking for money.

When the firefighters got word that money was pouring in for that fund, they officially invited me to their Christmas party. It was wonderful, and the gift cards were a real hit. That family of firemen extended their love to me and considered me a new member of their tight-knit family. I was so honored, so humbled. *Deborah would be so proud of me. I can hear her say this to me again now, just like she did in the hospital when she forced me to go and pray for the patient next door:* "You just need to step out of your comfort zone and trust the Lord to use you, Daphene, and He will."

During one of my visits to check on "my guys," the bell rang and the men rushed around to get ready to go out of the station. Because they knew it wasn't a fire, just an exercise, they offered to take me home—in the big red fire truck. I was thrilled. It brought back in a flash my childhood memory of Deborah's fire club. Wouldn't she have loved to see this scene in my life. When I climbed on board, the driver handed me one of their fire hats. Knowing that everyone in my apartment building would see me arrive home in a fire truck, I got pretty excited. I sat next to the door so I could see out and held on to my red fire hat so it didn't fall off. It was way too big, but I didn't care. The seat was big enough for three of us, and we laughed and talked all the way to my front door. But when we pulled up in front of my building, there was not a soul around. Not one person saw me!

Not long after that, I got a call from one of my friends at the station. He didn't say much except that they wanted me to come to the station the next Saturday afternoon at 2:00. Since I had been invited several times before for dinner, I wasn't too surprised by the call. I knew it wasn't dinner this time, but I really didn't care why I was invited. I was just happy to be wanted.

When I got there, I discovered that I was the reason for the gathering. After a few words of introduction, they presented me with an official Engine 8 t-shirt signed by each member of Ladder 2, Battalion 8. I clutched it to my heart, my smile wide. I looked around at all those men and thanked the Lord for them. *You have answered my prayers. My waiting is over—I am living again. I can feel it. Oh, thank you, Lord, so much!*

"It's our way of saying 'thank you' for all that you have done for us since 9/11. Your presence here, Daphene, has cheered our hearts and fed our souls . . . and our stomachs." Then they introduced me to some of the "big wigs" that had been invited. It was exciting yet humbling to me as I tried to explain to them how much they had done for me. They couldn't really understand, but I will cherish the t-shirt, the memories, and those men forever.

After several more months of stopping by to say hi to the guys, I began to realize that many of my friends were being sent back to their home stations and new firefighters were now taking their places. I felt in my heart that the season for me there was over and another season was about to begin. I said my good-byes and moved on.

* * *

After 9/11, America changed forever. And I felt it and decided to make a move. In June 2002, I found a condo a few blocks from my apartment and prepared for another move—still within Manhattan. I was feeling more and more like the city girl that Deborah had told me I could be.

The move from my old apartment to the newly-purchased condo did not go smoothly. I was glad when it was almost over, but as I walked out of the door for the last time, I was hit by a wave of sadness as I remembered the wonderful times that I had there with Deborah. We had shared in this place, unpacking boxes and arranging furniture. This was also the place where I fell in love with Regan and Carson and crammed my apartment with my family for our New Year's visits.

That first night in my new place I cried myself to sleep just wishing she could have been with me to see my beautiful new home. I longed to hear her laughter as I relived those crazy days of moving and getting settled in that first place. But I woke up the next morning with an expectation . . . a subtle joy . . . of taking the next step in my life.

I had a three-day weekend planned—Monday was Presidents Day and I didn't have to work. But when I woke up, it was snowing and continued snowing all day. I had to change my plans and just spend the day inside, getting things more settled in my new place. From time to time, though, I stood at my front window and watched the snow falling. I had never seen so much snow in my whole life. The whole world seemed painted over with whitewash.

Early Tuesday morning I braved the weather and trudged through the snow to the subway in order to get to work.

I was excited that I had a chance to wear the winter boots I had recently purchased. As I stepped carefully from rut to rut in the street outside my condo, I slipped and fell facedown in a huge snowbank, and although I wasn't hurt, I sure felt stupid. The people behind me must have had a good laugh and a story to tell about this woman they saw, who one minute looked like a businessperson and the next, like a big snowman. Oh, the joys of snow. How humbling. How cold!

By the third day, the snow was finally beginning to melt, but deep snowbanks were still everywhere. On Thursday, I decided to take the bus home instead of the subway after working with a client at Pfizer; but because of the snow, I had to stand in the street rather than on the sidewalk to wait for the bus to come. As I waited, another bus roared past me, drenching me in filthy slush from head to foot.

I gasped in surprise and then loudly burst out laughing. The man standing next to me, who hadn't gotten splashed quite as badly as I had, said, "Why in the world are you laughing, lady?"

"It's better than crying," was my quick response. I was weary of tears. After all, I had come to know what life events were worth crying over. And this wasn't one of them.

Hearing myself laugh, I felt a great sense of relief. Something was happening inside—like I had learned a huge life lesson or had passed an important test. I stood there as revelation flashed all through me like lightning: *The Lord my God is in the midst of me, a Mighty One, a Savior—Who saves!—He is rejoicing over me with joy; He is resting in silent satisfaction and in His love He will be silent and make no mention of my past sins, or even recall them; He is exulting over me with singing!* I looked around, thinking that I must have been transported to heaven . . . but I was still standing there drenched, while a stranger stared at me like I was a crazy woman, with the Amplified version of Zephaniah 3:17 playing like a symphony in my head.

"He's a Mighty One, a Savior–Who saves!" I told him, smiling from ear to ear. He just kept staring at me in disbelief.

Someday maybe I will understand why Deborah had to suffer the way she did. I wanted her to live so badly. But God had bigger plans for her, and He has big plans for me, too. So I took a firm hold of Psalm 30:11 later that day as I sat in my prayer chair reading and journaling. I wrote this:

You turned my wailing into dancing; you removed my sackcloth and clothed me with joy, that my heart may sing your praises and not be silent.

Epilogue

The Blowing Breeze

Awake, north wind, and come, south wind!
Blow on my garden . . .

(Song of Solomon 4:16)

When God promised to send a southern breeze over Deborah and me at Anaheim, California in February of 1990, I never thought so many people would feel the same breeze and be forever changed. So much happened during the decade that followed Anaheim, and I have shared most of it with you already. But the breeze has continued to blow into the new decade and on into the new century.

By September 2002, living single had become a happy and healthy way of life for me. I had finally discovered this truth partly because I was fulfilled and busy with my company, partly because I was blessed with so many wonderful friends in my life, and partly because dating was no longer a necessity for this Texan-turned-New Yorker. I was using my time alone to let the Lord heal my heart from the many wounds that I had tucked away there over the years. Some of them were stuffed pretty deep.

I had been in my new condo for a couple of months when I got a call from Debbie Kirtland in Atlanta. She was still working with me–God had indeed come through when we trusted Him, such that now I couldn't imagine working without her–so we spoke often about business issues. But we had become friends over the years, too, and I valued our relationship very much. When she suggested that I get on eHarmony, a new website for matching single individuals based on compatibility, I laughed her off. I was fine and didn't feel the need to complicate my life. *Or did I?* I replayed our conversation over and over again in my mind and then decided to check out the website for myself. I called Debbie a few days later to tell her that I was "sticking my toe in the water" and she laughed. "You go, girl."

I explored the eHarmony website for over a week before I signed up and then completed a very lengthy questionnaire. Early one morning not long after, I got an email that said I had a match. The match was with a man named John Angelo Pisiona from North Bergen, New Jersey.

After going through the initial "getting to know you" questions and looking at each other's Personality Profiles, John and I started corresponding on November 2, 2002. Then we spent hours emailing back and forth, getting to know each other better. I learned in the course of those emails that John was very involved at his church and had been on staff for many years. And I shared about my life. He wrote back: "I don't know what to say about your past. I cannot begin to imagine how it must feel to go through what you did. The important thing is that God has made you whole."

At noon on November 12, my phone rang and we heard each other's voices for the first time: he heard my southern twang and I heard his strong New Jersey accent. Our first date was incredible—a Broadway show, dinner, and dancing at a beautiful restaurant, and then to Times Square Church to hear the music. Over time we fell deeply in love with each other.

When it came time for us to get engaged, I was in Florida at a beach house on a weekend vacation with my kids and some of their friends. Denise had met John Angelo but John Kevin hadn't yet; even so, they managed to plan an enormous surprise for me.

He called to let me know that he had received the ring we had ordered. I couldn't wait to get it, so I asked him if he would send it Federal Express to me in Florida. He agreed to and then called me several times wanting to know if I had gotten it yet. I was a nervous wreck, and when the doorbell finally rang I ran to answer it.

I opened the door and was so focused on the envelope that I didn't even look up. When I did, I burst into tears, because standing before me was John Angelo. He had flown into Panama City, rented a car, and dressed up like a delivery man. It was his way of delivering my engagement ring. I was overwhelmed with love and awe for this wonderful man who was soon to become my husband. My kids and their friends had helped him plan the whole thing, and they all thought that he was just about the most romantic man any of them had ever met.

We spent the next year getting to know each other's grown children. John Angelo had been single for thirty-three years so it was going to be quite an adjustment for Lance, Parris, and Tracy. But I loved them immediately and they welcomed me into their family with open arms.

We were married on Saturday, October 11, 2003, at the Bible Baptist Church in Hasbrouck Heights, New Jersey. I wanted to run off and make it easy for everyone, but John Angelo not only wanted a big wedding, he also wanted to take me to Paris, France for our honeymoon. I continued to be completely overwhelmed by his love for me.

But the morning of the wedding I woke up with a dark foreboding, and I felt unworthy of walking down the aisle adorned like a pure bride after being married twice before. A gripping sadness settled in and nothing my friends said proved helpful. This should have been the happiest day of my life.

I arrived at the church and walked to the door of the sanctuary, trembling and tearful. When it opened, the sun behind me shone so brightly all around me that all anyone could see from inside the church was my silhouette. My fear was hidden.

The minute I looked up and saw my future husband standing at the front of the church crying, my whole heart changed. What the sun was doing on the outside, God was doing on the inside of me. I became aware that I was completely forgiven, cleansed, and free to walk down the aisle to become Mrs. John Pisiona. *I am entering into a new life altogether. This is what Ron and Deborah had—the kind of love that lasts forever.*

The winds of change blowing that day sure felt good. Our love story is precious and amazing . . . and could be the subject of my next book.

My daughter, Denise Jones, still feels it, too. Denise and Greg have chosen to raise their two daughters God's way in a wonderful and stable Christian home. Once in a while I will say something to Denise about how sorry I am that I wasn't able to be the kind of mom to her that she needed, but she refuses to "go there." Once she forgave me it was as if it had been forgotten. *Is that what God meant when He said He had removed my sin from me as far as the East is from the West?* That is a miracle. Denise and I have a wonderful friendship and the laughter we share comes so easily. Once John Angelo and I moved back to Atlanta in June of 2005, we began to make up for the time I had spent in Manhattan. The life I have with Denise is more than I could ever have hoped for. Sometimes I wonder why God blesses me as He does. And Greg's hunger for God led him into youth ministry in addition to running the clock business he's had for many years.

My son, John Kevin, and I missed out on so much during his early years. He grew up without his mom; that is a fact I will always grieve over. John Weaver's wife did a wonderful job in my place, but I should have been there to raise my own son. He went on, though, to a very successful time at the University of Georgia where he made the Dean's List, graduated near the top of his class, and met his future wife, Melissa Rose. She eventually became a veterinarian, and he became a very successful orthodontist. On one occasion he was asked who his hero was. He later told me he responded that his hero was his mother. I was not prepared to hear that at all, and I asked him, why me? He told me it was because he was proud of me for what I had done with my life.

I had tried over the years to share with him that it was because of Jesus that my life had been changed, but he couldn't hear it then. But when his Aunt Debbie was dying, she told him it was time for him to seek after a relationship with Jesus. When he and Missy left the beautiful memorial service for Deborah, he told Missy that he wanted what his Aunt Debbie had. That began a journey that would change his life forever. They started attending a church, and he met regularly with the pastor. One day the pastor said, "John, it's time . . . you're either in or out." He called me that night and told me he had something important to tell me. Because he and Missy had been trying to get pregnant, I assumed that he was calling with good news about that. He said, "Mom, I prayed that prayer. I gave my heart to Jesus." Those are the most precious words a parent can hear. The prayers Deborah and I had prayed for so long had been answered. On August 18, 2002, John Kevin was baptized.

And then the babies started coming. From January 3, 2003 to June 5, 2009, they gave me five beautiful grandsons: Bo, David, Mitch, Sam, and Thomas. We now refer to their place as "the man farm."

John Kevin was asked to speak at the memorial service for his dad, John Weaver, which had been postponed until his wife was recovered enough to attend. They held it in February of 2002. He chose to read a letter he had written to his dad but never mailed:

Dear Daddy,

I'll have to say that this letter is way past due, but I figured now was a better time than ever to write it. Basically, I want to say "Thanks." I'm sure you are thinking to yourself, "What in the world is he thanking me for?" Well, the list is long, but most of all I want to say thanks for being such an awesome father to me. Awesome may sound a bit juvenile, but to me, it's perfect. You have showed me how to dig for fool's gold; how to be an Indian guide; how to compete in a pinewood derby; how to react quickly in stressful situations (when the acid exploded in the kitchen all over Wayne and me); you've taught me to not start a sentence off with "me"(e.g., "Me an' Missy are coming home for Christmas"); how to make a potato gun; how to refinish furniture (Mama Lee and Dad's old furniture) . . . . And the list went on and on until there was not a dry eye in the service.

The letter John Kevin wrote to his father still brings tears to my eyes. During such a difficult time I realized what amazing children I have and how blessed I am. His dad never received that letter, but it certainly made people stop and think about letting the ones we love know it.

As I got older and my life got better, I came to know how much Gretchen loved and needed me and I tried to love her back. I was faithful about calling her but didn't take the time to go see her in Texas. Because of her health issues, she had to retire early from her job and her financial picture was not good. I made the decision to help her by sending money. It eased my conscience to do it.

It was my sweet husband, John Angelo, who pointed out to me that I had not taken the right position with my older sister. A very poignant email he sent changed things completely for Gretchen and me. The minute I read it I sat down and wept for how I had treated Gretchen. Deborah and I had rejected, excluded, and dismissed her as unimportant in so many ways. I asked God to deliver me from the deep resentment I felt toward her over the years and to forgive me for treating her so badly. I really wanted to love her like God loved me, even when I was at my worst. God helped me to see that *He does not treat us as we deserve.* The day I received that email from John, I sat down and wrote Gretchen a letter. I'm so thankful that I actually wrote it out and mailed it to her because it became a spiritual marker in both her life and mine.

Gretchen came one week before our wedding on October 11, 2003, to be with me. I had not seen her since Deborah died three years before on Nov 3, 2000. Because of the daily phone calls and deep love we were developing for each other, when she arrived she was a completely different person. She was confident, happy, and felt truly loved by John Angelo and me. What Gretchen had needed all along was unconditional love—the kind of love that melts icebergs. I wish that Deborah and I had taken her to Anaheim with us; I wish that I had realized sooner that she longed to be a part of our lives. I will be forever grateful for the courage my husband showed in telling me how wrong I had been and what I needed to do to make things right between us. He had eyes to see when I didn't, and he had a heart of compassion toward her that I needed. Because of him, the week before the wedding was the sweetest week we had ever spent together. The southern breeze was blowing over all of us.

Then on December 5, I was sitting in our living room alone on a snowy day in New Jersey when the phone rang. John Angelo was away at a men's retreat. When I answered, a woman asked if my name was Daphene and if I had a sister named Gretchen. I said yes. She responded by saying, "I'm sorry to have to tell you this, but I am at your sister's apartment and she is dead."

She was buried in Luling, Texas where our daddy grew up and our parents were buried. John and I took care of the details: we shopped for "jommies" like Deborah's, we selected "Shout to the Lord" and "I Can Only Imagine" for the music, and John did the service. Gretchen's kids,

Dee Dee and Kyle, along with their children, were there to say good-bye to their mom and grandmother, along with our aunts and uncles, cousins, and several close friends.

A month after she died, I had a dream about her. She said, "I came back to leave you my voice." After erasing the tape with Deborah's voice on my answering machine years before, I thanked God for giving me such a sweet gift.

Deborah always dreamed of Regan and Carson marrying their soul mates and of becoming a grandmother. And her dream finally came true. Carson married Megan Christenson on August 23, 2003. Deborah would have been so happy because Megan was the young woman she had picked out for Carson. Kendall Deborah was born November 27, 2007, and Whitney Campbell born August 11, 2011. So far, Ron has four little cowgirls to keep up with when they all go to the ranch.

Regan married Matt Donnell on May 1, 2004, at Rocky Top Ranch. I had found a wedding folder of ideas for Regan's wedding that Deborah had been keeping for years in her files. I was not able to be there but wept at the pictures of the ceremony. She was a beautiful bride . . . Deborah would have been so happy. Regan and Matt have been blessed with two beautiful daughters, Griffin Elizabeth Donnell, born December 28, 2005, and Sadi Jane, born May 25, 2007. They are wonderful parents and raising beautiful little girls. Ron and Deborah often talked of the times they would have at Rocky Top Ranch with their little cowgirls and cowboys. Now those little children visit their grandmother's gravesite there and feel the gentle wind.

Deborah's legacy continues to grow. The Deborah Hall Memorial Chapel groundbreaking was held on September

12, 2001, and the dedication ceremony followed after the building was completed. After her death, more than half a million dollars was given to the Fort Worth Union Gospel Mission for the homeless in her name. With the publication of Ron Hall and Denver Moore's *New York Times* best seller, *Same Kind of Different As Me*, along with speaking opportunities for both of them, over $70 million dollars has been raised to help the homeless around the country. One of Deborah's friends shared with Ron that she saw Deborah as a kernel of wheat from John 12:24: *Very truly I tell you, unless a kernel of wheat falls to the ground and dies, it remains only a single seed. But if it dies, it produces many seeds.*

I want to be one of those seeds. When Deborah was in the hospital the first time, she sent me to the patient in the next room because she felt led to pray for the family but couldn't go. I remember what she said: "You just need to step out of your comfort zone and trust the Lord to use you, Daphene, and He will." When I did for the first time, I think she was proud of me. Then, after 9/11, I got brave and reached out to the people on the street and then to the firefighters at the station not far from my home in Manhattan. I think she would have been proud of me, again. And now, with this book, I am stepping out once more. I want it to be used to touch the hearts of people who need the Lord. *You instructed us to ask You, Lord, to send out workers into Your harvest field. Well, here I am—Your servant-seed—on my knees before You. Send me.*

Awake, north wind, and come, south wind!
Blow on my garden
that its fragrance may spread abroad.

(Song of Solomon 4:16)

Acknowledgments

I want to thank the following people for the parts they have played in my life—as family, as business friends, as Deborah's friends, as personal friends, as writing friends, and as church friends. My story would have been very different without each of you in my life. My prayer is that I will leave a legacy for my children, my grandchildren, and beyond. How blessed I am to be a child of God, forgiven and free. "Thank you" is so inadequate.

My sisters – Gretchen (Short) Molmen and Deborah (Short) Hall, who have gone on ahead.

My husband – John Angelo Pisiona, for his steadfast love, devotion, encouragement, wisdom, and the amazingly unconditional love that comes from above. He calls me his Princess and refers to me as his Beloved! Our story is worthy of a book in itself.

My children – Denise (Weaver) Jones and John Kevin Weaver, for their undeserved forgiveness, respect, and love.

My children's spouses – Missy Weaver and Greg Jones, who have made wonderful homes for my children and have given me seven incredible grandchildren.

"Our" children – Lance, Parris, and Tracy Pisiona, for accepting me into their family and sharing their dad with me.

My grandchildren – Millicent and Madi (Greg and Denise's daughters); Bo, David, Mitch, Sam, and Thomas

(John Kevin and Missy's boys). We refer to their home as the "Man Farm."

"Our" grandchildren – Michael, Lillian, Francine, Parris John (PJ), Angelo, Aaron, John Ronald

My sister's husband – Ron Hall, for loving Deborah in such a way that lives around both of them were changed. His labor of love in writing their story has done so much to keep Deborah's dream for the homeless alive, not only in the Dallas/Fort Worth area, but also around the country. She always referred to the homeless as "God's people"–the forgotten group in our society. Because of her they are not so forgotten anymore.

Denver Moore – Thank you for loving our Debbie and being willing to keep her dream alive for "God's people." She loved you even before she met you at the mission.

Deborah and Ron's children – Regan (Hall) Donnell and Carson Hall, who became like my own children when God gave us time together in Manhattan. We had no way of knowing that God was creating a special relationship that we would desperately need as we walked together during those hard days while their much-loved mom and my precious sister suffered and then died of cancer. They gave Ron the four beautiful granddaughters that Deborah dreamed about having.

Gretchen's children – Dee Dee and Kyle who have said goodbye to their mother and daddy. Gretchen loved her three grandchildren dearly.

My special business relationships – Janet Reese, Marilyn Draper, Linda (Davis) Friedman, Jennifer (Schwieters) Eibensteiner and Kay Duffney, Diane Coleman, Larry Blair, Melissa Rice, and Caroline Munroe

Deborah's friends – Cindy and Pat Hawkins, John and Jeanie Ott, Alan and Mary Ellen Davenport, Patricia Chambers, and The Fort Worth Wednesday Watchmen

My personal friends – Milton and Barbara Holloway and family, Karen Finley and her family, and Ron and Lois Jane Wallace, Jane Lowett, Caryl Avery and Les Zuke

My writing friends – Ann Platz, Charlotte Hale, and Ann Gooding

My church friends – Terri and Jim Hicks, Alan and Jeri Dunaway, Barry and Kim Ward, Sugar Hill United Methodist Church, Sonrise Sunday school class, and Wednesday Night Life Group

Special Acknowledgments

Debbie Kirtland – She has been my business partner and dear friend for the past twelve years–the person who shared in the vision that God gave to me for my business. Her constant encouragement and hard work enabled me to continue on toward the dream of writing my story. She literally "ran the company" much of the time that I worked on the manuscript. I especially appreciate her willingness to read and reread every word of my story.

The *two* of us have made a perfect "one." The story of how God brought my business into being and kept it going is another story, too. I have it on my list to write. Debbie Kirtland will be a major character in that one.

Sue Langston – My friendship with Sue began in Houston, Texas in 1975, when we worked together at Southwestern Bell, and that friendship has continued to grow over the years. Although we have shared many struggles, we never judge each other. I will always treasure that about Sue.

After Anaheim, I prayed that she and her husband, Ken, would come to experience the wonderful peace that comes with knowing Christ personally. When I received an email about this in October of 2007, I was completely overjoyed! She and Ken had stepped over the line of faith and had entered into the life of the Lord–together. This is what she said: *I have been told that Christ does his best work through other people, and you, Daphene, are that other person for me. I love you so much and have always admired you. Thank you for helping us find God.*

I was always open with her about my faith and never gave up on their need for a relationship with Jesus Christ because I knew that God had something in mind for them. I am honored to call Sue my best friend, and I'm so thankful for all that she did to help me launch my book. What a blessing it is to see the southern breeze blowing over her life.

Gail Walker – Thank you for being my dear friend from the time that we moved to Atlanta in 1979. Your parents, kids, and Pierce have been like family to me. You always believed in me when I didn't believe in myself.

Philip Elston – Without your Word from God at the Anaheim conference, Deborah and I would not have understood all that God was doing and going to do in our lives and in the lives of those around us. Without you, there would be no story. May the Lord richly bless you for your obedience to share that day what was on your heart.

Andrea Taylor, Ph.D. – Our meeting was nothing less than the providential hand of God–and we both knew it. I had a story to tell and you had the passion in your heart to make my story come alive. It is truly amazing how many ways my life parallels yours: Texas roots, dysfunctional parents, influential grandparents, an oil-field working daddy, two sisters, troubled marriages, meeting Jesus, and so many more. It was as if you had taken hold of my hand and actually walked with me through my life. I have been astounded at what you "knew" about my story.

Thank you for spending a year helping me write my story while yours sat on the shelf and waited patiently; for bringing my journal and early drafts to life; for believing that God had something in mind for my book; for encouraging me when I let fear come in . . . and letting me encourage you when you let fear come in.

Thank you for pursuing excellence and not perfection for His sake and for agreeing to publish my book at *Third Chapter Press*—even before I had money to do it. Working with your consulting editor, Tim Boswell, and your graphic designer, Michelle Kenny, was such a blessing. What professionals.

Financial Supporters – I can never thank each of you sufficiently for believing in me enough to help finance the publication of *Our Southern Breeze* with no guarantee of repayment. I have sensed from the beginning of this journey that it is God's story about Deborah and me, not my story about Him, and that He has a purpose for it. My prayer is that many lives will be touched for the Kingdom and that all of you will be blessed for your part in bringing *Our Southern Breeze* into being. My heartfelt gratitude goes out to: **Patricia Chambers, Travis and Helen Hatter, Pat and Cindy Hawkins, Alan and Mary Ellen Davenport, Kirk and Sue Blackmon, and Roy Gene and Pamela Evans.**

About the Author

For over nineteen years Daphene "DJ" Jones has run DJ Consultants, Inc., a company that focuses on helping overwhelmed clients utilize technology to manage their time and information. Working with Fortune 500 companies, she has gained a reputation for providing simple solutions to improve efficiency and productivity in the workplace.

When *Same Kind of Different As Me* was released, many people asked her why she didn't write a book about growing up with "Miss Debbie." She reviewed the journals she had kept since her life changed when she and Deborah were in Anaheim, California in February 1990. She began to see how much Deborah's life had influenced hers. Mustering up the courage to embark on a new journey, she started the first draft. Her story is about her fight with depression, fear, and attempted suicide, and the amazing way that God gives second chances to His children. This story of learning to live without her beloved twin and of experiencing the amazing restoration of their relationship, along with many others in her family, is sure to inspire. She and her husband, married since 2003, live in Suwanee, Georgia with their precious border collie, Hanna. Daphene enjoys painting, going to the gym, swimming, and spending time with her children and seven grandchildren.

Daphene "DJ" Jones
daphene@oursouthernbreeze.com
(404) 542-3586

Virginia Annette Bulow in her early 20s–
Poplar Bluff, Missouri
My beautiful mother

Daphene (left) and Deborah Short
in Beaumont, Texas

Celebrating their second birthday with little star cakes

Deborah (left), Gretchen (center), and Daphene (right)
in Beaumont, Texas

The Short sisters

Daphene (left), Deborah, Susie Free and Helen Hatter
in Snyder, Texas

Best friends in high school

Inside Rocky Top Ranch in Fort Worth, Texas
The discussion about me moving to Manhattan
took place around that table.

Daphene (left) and Deborah (standing) in Manhattan Apartment

Who needs a $50 per hour repair man?

Regan Hall (left) with her mother, Deborah
Daphene's new apartment in Manhattan on the second day!

Deborah Hall
Rocky Top Ranch

She was doing what
she loved to do—
cooking for a crowd at
Thanksgiving.

This was our last
Thanksgiving
together.

Gretchen (left) Daphene (center) and Deborah
at John Kevin and Missy's wedding in Athens, GA
After all those years, we finally felt like sisters and friends.

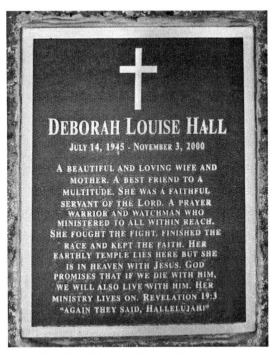

Resting Place at Rocky Top Ranch

"Her ministry lives on."

Daphene (seated center) in Manhattan

The "thank you" I received from "my guys"
at Engine 8, Ladder 2, Battalion 8

John Kevin Weaver's baptism at St. Simon's Georgia
The southern breeze blew across my son's life
after his Aunt Debbie died.

Daphene and John Angelo Pisiona
at Sea Side, Florida
Our engagement became official!

Daphene and John Angelo with Gretchen
in New Jersey
At our wedding and the last time I saw Gretchen alive

Ken and Sue Langston being baptized in Austin, Texas
The southern breeze blew across the lives of my
best friend and her husband.

Denise (left), Madi, Millicent, and Greg Jones
at Sea Side, Florida

My beautiful daughter and her family
What a treasure they are to me.

Missy with son Thomas (left) Mitch behind Bo (center) and John
Kevin with David and Sam
at Sea Side, Florida
What a blessing they all are to me!

We call their home "The Man Farm."

Sadi–05/07 (left), Griffin–12/05 (middle), Kendall–11/07 (right) Whitney-08/11 (not shown) placing flowers on their grandmothers grave on our birthday

These are the little granddaughters that Ron and Deborah prayed for long before they came into the world.

Daphene and Deborah

This was our last birthday together, at the home of Alan and Mary Ellen Davenport in Fort Worth, Texas.

I still miss her so much.